Democracy and Bureaucracy

Democracy and Bureaucracy: Tensions in Public Schooling

Edited by
Judith D. Chapman and Jeffrey F. Dunstan

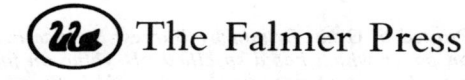

The Falmer Press
(A member of the Taylor & Francis Group)
London · New York · Philadelphia

UK	The Falmer Press, Rankine Road, Basingstoke, Hampshire, RG24 0PR
USA	The Falmer Press, Taylor & Francis Inc., 1900 Frost Road, Suite 101, Bristol, PA 19007

© Selection and editorial material copyright J. D. Chapman and J. F. Dunstan 1990

All rights reserved. No part of this publication may be reproduced, stored in a retrieval system, or transmitted in any form or by any means, electronic, mechanical, photocopying, recording or otherwise, without permission in writing from the Publisher.

First published 1990

British Library Cataloguing in Publication Data
Democracy and bureaucracy: tensions in public schooling
  1. Australia. Education. Management.
  I. Chapman, Judith D. II. Dunstan, Jeffrey.
379.1540994
ISBN 1-85000-790-X
ISBN 1-85000-791-8 pbk

Library of Congress Cataloging-in-Publication Data
Democracy and bureaucracy: tensions in public schooling/
  Editors, Judith D. Chapman and Jeffrey Dunstan.
    p. cm.
  Includes index.
  ISBN 1-85000-790-X — ISBN 1-85000-791-8 (pbk.)
    1. School management and organization—Australia. 2. Public schools—Australia—Administration. 3. Democracy. 4. Bureaucracy—Australia. I. Chapman, Judith D. II. Dunstan, Jeffrey (Jeffrey F.).
LB2979.D45 1990
371.2′0094—dc20   90-44426
                                                         CIP

Jacket design by Benedict Evans

Typeset in 10.5/13 pt Bembo by
Graphicraft Typesetters Ltd, Hong Kong

Printed in Great Britain by Burgess Science Press, Basingstoke on paper which has a specified pH value on final paper manufacture of not less than 7.5 and is therefore 'acid free'.

Contents

Foreword		vii
Introduction Judith Chapman and Jeffrey Dunstan		1
Chapter 1	Democracy and Bureaucracy in the Organization of School Systems in Australia: A Synoptic View Hedley Beare	9
Chapter 2	Balancing Competing Values in School Reform: International Efforts in Restructuring Education Systems William Lowe Boyd	25
Chapter 3	From Charity School to Community School: The Unfinished Australian Experience Brian V. Hill	41
Chapter 4	Democracy, Bureaucracy and the Politics of Education Grant Harman	57
Chapter 5	Governing Australia's Public Schools: Community Participation, Bureaucracy and Devolution Lyndsay G. Connors and James F. McMorrow	75
Chapter 6	Exploring Trails in School Management David McRae	99
Chapter 7	Democracy, Bureaucracy and the Classroom Garth Boomer	115

Contents

Chapter 8	Democracy and Bureaucracy: Curriculum Issues *Christine Deer*	131
Chapter 9	Accountability in Changing School Systems *Clive Dimmock and John Hattie*	155
Chapter 10	Financial Issues in the Tension between Democracy and Bureaucracy *Ross Harrold*	175
Chapter 11	Tensions in System-wide Management *George Berkeley*	193
Chapter 12	Reforming Bureaucracy: An Attempt to Develop Responsive Educational Governance *Fazal Rizvi and Lawrence Angus*	215

Notes on Contributors   239

Index   245

Foreword

I commend this book to all those who are committed to the idea of high quality public education. Public education is by its nature controversial. It is controversial because it seeks to express what is best in a culture, to find a worthwhile and workable balance between continuity and change.

In many countries over recent years this has grown more difficult. The nature of our societies, with their recognition of cultural distinctions and their unwillingness to grant undisputed authority, means that there is a more difficult task in obtaining agreement on purposes, on the processes for their achievement and on the validation of that achievement. Where we once had an unspoken consensus, it now needs to be hammered out in a series of processes that can be long and difficult. That is the price we pay for democracy. That price is worth paying.

The edited collection which follows arises from a project sponsored by the Research Committee of the Australian College of Education. That Committee was conscious of the enormous tensions which had been developing in the organization of public education in Australia. They felt that consideration of the issues associated with these tensions could only be handled through an amalgam of personal experience and theoretical insight. That amalgamation has been achieved to a remarkable degree in this book.

The Australian College of Education is fortunate to have had Dr Judith Chapman and Dr Jeffrey Dunstan as the organizing force behind this book. They represent that productive interchange between research and experience which is helping to illuminate some of Australia's educational dilemmas. They have assembled a distinguished and appropriate group for this important task.

On behalf of the Australian College of Education I welcome and

Foreword

commend this incisive and important collection of contributions focused on the issue of democracy and bureaucracy.

Phillip Hughes
President, Australian College of Education

Introduction

Judith D. Chapman and Jeffrey F. Dunstan

Theme

In recent years and in many countries there have been major changes in the organization of public education. In association with these changes there have been substantial revisions to the principles governing the organization and operation of schools and a reshaping of relations between the centre, regions and schools within the education system. In most countries shifts in the locus of educational decision-making have been accompanied by tensions and difficulties. This book examines the tensions and difficulties associated with the reorganization of public education in Australia. Contributors explore these tensions through a variety of related antinomies: bureaucracy and democracy, control and autonomy, centralism and devolution.

In the late nineteenth and early twentieth centuries public schools in each of the Australian states were organized in large bureaucratic systems, characterized by a high degree of centralized control, a clearly defined hierarchy of authority, an extensive set of regulations designed to ensure fair, equitable and uniform treatment of members of the teaching service and an efficient, equitable distribution of resources to schools. The operation of this system was rarely questioned. School principals and staff exercised few degrees of freedom. Structures were in place to enforce compliance in curriculum, personnel, finance and facilities administration.

Recently, however, there has been considerable divergence from this pattern as school systems, in response to a broad range of social, political, economic and management pressures, have attempted to decentralize administrative arrangements and devolve responsibility to regions and schools. In so doing it has been necessary for policy-makers, system level administrators and representatives of teachers' and parents' associations to address the considerable tension between bureaucratic concerns for hierar-

Introduction

chy, impersonality, consistency, economy and maximum efficiency, which characterized traditional practices, and the concern for participatory decision-making and increased localized autonomy in the pluralist society of Australia in the late twentieth century.

This book is devoted to an account and critical analysis of these changes. It contains contributions from many who were major actors in this period of change. Their accounts and interpretations, based on insights gained from practical experience, are complemented by the analyses and critiques of leading academics who draw on a range of disciplinary perspectives that are used to inform their commentaries and judgments.

Despite the momentum towards democratic structures reflected in the efforts to move towards decentralization and devolution, bureaucratic structures are still in place in Australia, and in the view of most contributors to this book they are an indispensable requirement in any successful system of administration of public education. The tension emerges in decisions about how much control central authorities should retain and how much autonomy should be granted to regions and schools.

While contributors are generally agreed that schools and regional administrations are increasingly introducing democratic decision-making involving teachers, parents, students and administrators, they also acknowledge that such decision-making is constrained. It is exercised only within the boundaries of government policies and guidelines, although the nature of these guidelines is consistently under review. Differing understandings and interpretations of 'the boundary line' contribute to the difficulties.

Problems also emerge from suspicions about 'motive'. Is the intention in relocating decision-making to the local level supposed to increase democratic approaches, or to contain expenditures and to allocate resources more effectively and with less opposition? To what extent is local decision-making a bona fide endeavour to acknowledge the professionalism of teachers, to make more meaningful decisions about the educational needs of students, and better to match school programs with the wishes and circumstances of school communities? Or is it to be regarded as an abdication of responsibility by government and central administrators?

In any examination of the changing relationships and governance patterns a recurring issue is the question of dual responsibility and accountability. This issue manifests itself in a number of ways, but it is particularly acute for teachers as they attempt to address the tensions that sometimes emerge in responding to the expectations of those with whom they are in vertical relationship (bureaucratic line authority) and those

Introduction

with whom they are in horizontal relationship (democratic local accountability to principal, school council and school community).

Several contributors argue that the 'democracy–bureaucracy' antinomy is a false dichotomy. Democratic structures apply throughout many modern educational bureaucracies, including state boards of education, regional boards, school councils and a vast array of participative committees. It is structures such as these that are introduced to achieve the goal of 'responsive bureaucracy'. Are these 'less bureaucratized structures' to be located somewhere along the bureaucracy–democracy continuum? Is it appropriate to consider the notion of a continuum? Or are the notions mutually exclusive?

The thesis generally propounded in this book is that democratic structures, participation and school-based decision-making are all elements of school improvement which enable a bureaucracy to be more responsive, less authoritarian and in control only over the macro issues of policy, thereby leaving to schools the maximum degree of freedom possible for their own determination of principles, policies and practices.

School communities should thus be given increasing decision-making opportunities within clearly stated government policies, together with the necessary support and resources to make such participation successful. Although democratic processes are a necessary part of a participatory system, their mere existence is not sufficient to ensure widespread adoption of a participatory approach to learning and management. An extensive program of professional development, action research and dissemination of ideas and practices is required to support the change process at each level of a system to ensure that both democracy and bureaucracy contribute in their necessary ways to the education of children and the effective outcomes of schooling.

Contents

The collection begins with an historical account of major developments in the organization of public education in Australia. In Chapter 1 the author, Hedley Beare, documents the shift from the highly centralized and bureaucratic administrative systems that organized the provision of public education in Australia in the past. He shows the extent to which moves in the direction of more decentralized structures and democratic practices were accompanied by turbulence and influenced by the increasing professionalization of teaching, the dismantling of large central offices, citizen participation in policy-making, parental choice in schooling, the

Introduction

appearance of councils and boards and the movement towards self-managing schools. The day of single, centralized control of education exercised through a large bureaucracy and located in a state capital city has gone forever, he concludes.

The relationship between the centre and the periphery becomes all the more complex in a decentralized and democratic public education system, argues William Lowe Boyd in Chapter 2. The tensions in Australian education today are similar to those in many developed industrial nations, he suggests. World-wide social, economic and technical trends have generated needs that few existing school systems can meet. Needed reforms are difficult to achieve partly because we often want to operationalize and maximize competing values, such as equity, excellence, efficiency, liberty and choice. Even though Australia and other education systems, such as those in North America, differ radically in the origin and evolution of their school systems, Boyd shows how both face the same need to achieve a balance between competing values.

Issues of values and assumptions underlying education are explored and developed by Brian Hill in Chapter 3. Educational administration is not a value-neutral technology, he claims. Bringing perspectives from philosophy to his analysis of long-term developments in education, Hill argues that centralized bureaucracies have attempted to move towards a professed value-neutrality which disguised the substitution of administrative objectives for goals expressive of the common good. Hill concludes that the myths of technocratic neutrality and ideological neutrality, which had been associated with bureaucratic systems, must be exploded and forceful attempts launched to embed schools more securely in their local communities through the development, at the local level, of negotiated charters of democratic values from which administrative protocols can be devised.

This proposal highlights the need to consider issues associated with the relationship between democracy and bureaucracy from a political dimension. Thus in Chapter 4 Grant Harman examines the political conflicts in Australian education over the last two decades from the perspective of the tension between bureaucratic concerns of consistency, economy and efficiency and democratic ideals of participation and local autonomy. Harman concludes that to a significant extent the conflicts of educational politics in Australia have concerned different value positions regarding democracy and bureaucracy, but they have also been about other value positions related to such matters as the purposes of schooling, morals, the role of the family and individual liberty. In addition, he argues that educational politics in Australia, as elsewhere, to a major extent have been about the competition for scarce resources and the efforts of interest groups and political actors to win more power and position for themselves.

The participation in public schooling of one such interest group is discussed in Chapter 5. Lyndsay Connors and James McMorrow document demands for greater community and parent participation in the governance of Australian public schools that emerged during the 1960s and 1970s, when a growing body of educated and articulate parents and teachers, themselves the product of post-war expansion in secondary schooling, began to challenge the legitimacy of the highly centralized bureaucracies which had run public schools for over a century. In the context of the 1980s Connors and McMorrow indicate the ways in which the emphasis on economic reform, and the concepts and rhetoric of community participation, developed from collectivist political and social ideologies in the 1960s and 1970s, began to be accommodated in the notion of individualized choice among diverse forms of schooling and to be identified with forms of devolution of decision-making to local school communities designed to place responsibility for managing schools with the consumers rather than the producers of public education. The identification of community participation with devolution of powers to self-governing schools, they argue, has profound educational and political implications for Australian schooling in the 1990s and embodies a direct challenge to the egalitarian ideology which had hitherto underpinned the development of Australian public education.

In Chapter 6 David McCrae also highlights some of the dilemmas facing those responsible for educational management. 'Democracy' as it has commonly been implemented in schools misunderstands the nature of both 'role' and 'accountability' in school settings, the nature and significance of school leadership, how schools operate and the absolute requirement for both speed and efficiency in decision-making, McCrae argues. He suggests that the mechanisms used to introduce it have been often clumsy, bland and badly focused, and have ignored the necessity for variety and responsiveness to individual situations.

In Chapter 7 Garth Boomer offers an educational perspective on the tensions between democracy and bureaucracy, beginning with a micro-analysis of democracy and the classroom and an analysis of power relationships between teachers and students. 'Democracy' is seen as a problematic term and democratic practices as inevitably contaminated by non-democratic influences. Nevertheless, features of an ideal 'democratic' classroom are postulated and discussed. An examination of bureaucratic structures and practices then follows in relation to the question: 'What kind of bureaucracy would best serve the kind of democratic classroom described?' 'Bureaucracy' is set in the context of political and individual

Introduction

influences and portrayed as 'contested'. The myth of a group of like-minded public servants implacably serving the system is questioned. There follows a depiction of the type of bureaucracy which would be congruent with the democratic classroom previously described. Features elicited include explicitness, negotiation, questioning and reflection. In tension with the postulated ideal, the realities of 'containing and conservatizing rules and structures' are then examined. The chapter concludes with a consideration of the barriers and impulses to reform and action which might improve bureaucracies and promote democratic classrooms.

The educational perspective is expanded in Chapter 8 where Christine Deer examines the tension between centralized curriculum development and school-based curriculum development. She points to the changing patterns of control over the curriculum from the highly centralized state control that existed in the first hundred years of provision of public education in Australia, to the move towards local school-based development in the 1970s and 1980s and, finally, to the emergence of national influence in the production of a set of 'common and agreed goals for schooling' by the Australian Education Council in 1989. In the attempt to achieve a balance between central control and local autonomy on curriculum matters, Deer posits that there are still two fundamental questions to be addressed: 'What knowledge is of most worth for the individual student and for society as a whole?' and 'How can this knowledge be brought alive for students?'

The reader may well wish to keep these questions in mind when considering the issues raised in Chapter 9. Clive Dimmock and John Hattie argue that the forces and pressures for greater accountability in the provision of public education reflect more general societal trends demanding efficiency and effectiveness of performance in the public sector. The authors predict that Australian school systems will spend much of the 1990s fashioning and determining the forms of accountability they regard as feasible and desirable. Emergent patterns and schemes will be a reflection of tensions already existing between the bureaucratic form of accountability associated with centralized ministry control and influence and the democratic model of accountability inspired by participatory decision-making at school and community levels. They suggest that in our attempt at arriving at a satisfactory and workable form of accountability one way forward would be to try to achieve a balance between bureaucratic and democratic elements. Provided these elements are managed in coherent and sensitive ways, the authors contend that it is possible for them to be complementary and to provide a positive and pluralistic pattern of checks and balances.

Proposals for resolving some of the tensions between democracy and

Introduction

bureaucracy are also put forward in Chapter 10, in which Ross Harrold addresses some of the financial issues involved in the implementation of educational policy. Harrold argues that the instruments used to implement school policy can be either 'hard' or 'soft', depending on the discretion allowed the responding schools. 'Hard' instruments, which include rules, regulations and directives, have been the preferred option of bureaucracies in the past, because they have been easier to devise, cheaper to implement and their compliance easier to monitor. However, they tend to be insensitive to local needs, they suppress local initiatives and they reduce professional responsibility. 'Softer' policy instruments use financial inducements and sanctions to 'steer' voluntary responses consistent with policy goals and give more opportunities for staff and community involvement in adapting policy responses to local situations. Harrold indicates ways in which the use of 'softer' instruments could resolve some of the tensions between democracy and bureaucracy in public education systems. He supports this argument by considering the likely educational impact of educational funding being channelled through families rather than through systems.

The management of systems is considered in the final two chapters. George Berkeley hypothesizes that changes in management reflect change and reform in the wider public sector, and the nature of much of the change is not peculiar to the administration of education. He illustrates this by reference to the movement from centralized, monolithic, bureaucratic structures to much more diversified and responsive organizations attempting to adjust to their changing public and to the need for more accountable and responsive administration.

While Berkeley offers his analysis from the perspective of one who has been Director-General of one such system, Fazal Rizvi and Lawrence Angus offer a more theoretical perspective in the last chapter. They begin by restating the central problem of bureaucracy, which was so clearly recognized by Weber: 'How to bring democracy under effective democratic control?' They argue that the only way of resolving the tension between democracy and bureaucracy lies in the constant search for ways of reforming organizations to retain some of the virtues of democracy — predictability, precision, impartiality, efficiency — while at the same time enabling them to acquire a character that makes them more responsive not only to the demands of innovation and change but also to the democratically expressed wishes of the community.

Chapter 1

Democracy and Bureaucracy in the Organization of School Systems in Australia: A Synoptic View

Hedley Beare

Terminology

In a strictly literal sense, bureaucracy and democracy cannot exist together because they are mutually exclusive terms. Both words contain the suffix (*cracy*) meaning 'rule' or 'governance'. Bureaucracy is a technical term meaning government by departments (*bureaux*), by dividing the task into several components and then by allowing specialist units each to control the component allocated to it. Democracy, on the other hand, is government by the people (*demos*). In the case of bureaucracy, the government structure is hierarchical with the person at the top of the pyramid finally responsible for the whole function and for the organization which carries it out. Bureaucracy is literally feudal in its design. It is none the worse for being so, but the format should be used only in those circumstances or with those tasks where centralized, top–down control is appropriate.

Democracy, on the other hand, is egalitarian, not feudal. In its most elemental form, it is government through a kind of town meeting or an assembly of all those citizens who make up the city-state. Because decision-making this way is usually unwieldy and quite impractical, democracy most frequently works through representative government. The city-state forms itself into electorates and they each elect someone to represent their views on the governing body of the *polis*. Democracy therefore tends to operate in a committee or parliamentary mode. It is the exact opposite to autocracy (rule by one person), whereas bureaucracy is not. Bureaucracy implies top–down management, whereas democracy implies round-the-table discussion and collective decision-making.

Because both terms deal with control, with governance, the critical question behind both words is, 'Who has control; who is in charge; who has the power and must therefore accept the final responsibility?' On that issue there has been considerable contestation over recent decades, not the least in education. Among other things, it has fuelled the transfer of children between the government and non-government school sectors.

It would be hard to argue the case that democracy had replaced bureaucracy in the public school systems of Australia, although there have been changes in the governance patterns particularly in the last two decades. The governance issue can be considered from a variety of perspectives, but to understand the nuances in the arguments it is necessary to have some knowledge about the major developments in Australian school systems. In this chapter we take the broad-brush approach and try to identify those megatrends (to use John Naisbitt's term) which have been impacting on Australian education, and which have helped to raise the issues of bureaucracy and democracy.

Transitions in the Economy

It was understandable that bureaucracy became associated with the state school systems from their earliest days. In the decades after the 1870s, when the Australian states — still sovereign and separate — were enacting and implementing their 'free, compulsory and secular' education provisions, the industrial economy was in the process of supplanting the pre-industrial. Australia as a nation moved from a heavy dependence on rural commodities (wheat, wool and mining) during the Victorian era into factory production and into diversified manufacturing industries in the years following the First World War. The organizational form which was almost universal in the industrial state, and which seemed to guarantee its success, was bureaucracy, being preached by writers like F.W. Taylor, Fayol, the Gilbreths and Max Weber.

It is hardly surprising that school systems adopted the model which was at the time considered so effective elsewhere in business and industry, the more so because the model delivered the very qualities which Australian education needed at that point in its development. To ensure an even quality in all schools scattered across a vast land, an education bureaucracy imposed control from the centre, particularly over the supply of resources — the chief of which were teachers. At a time when those same teachers were variable in their qualifications and their competence, the centre assumed the role of prescribing the nature and content of the curriculum, and of policing its implementation. When local communities consisted of people with little knowledge or experience of education, the centre provided coordination, quality controls, planning and the setting of priorities. The critical quality check at the key points in the educational continuum — at the passage from elementary to secondary, at the school 'leaving' level and at the transition from secondary to tertiary study — were centrally set external examinations which seemed to certify uniformity in educational attainments. In short, bureaucracy seemed to serve the systems well at a time when paternalism, the 'father knows best' approach, was probably appropriate.

After the turn of the century the same decisive action from the centre was required if the Australian states were to capitalize on the 'new education' movement and the extension of public education beyond elementary schooling. In the first two decades of the century each state moved to introduce a secondary school system which could run parallel with the independent schools which until then had monopolized the post-school sector, and had thereby controlled who did or did not proceed into the universities. It was the states also which established teachers' colleges and introduced teacher training during these decades.

Especially in the period following the First World War technical education became a priority. If the Australian economy were to shift into technically sophisticated factory production, it was an expanding technical education area, including apprenticeship training, which would make possible the re-gearing. The public utterances of the Directors of Education of this time contain many references to the German system for training technicians, always with the implication that Australia should copy that system. Without central planning and financing, it is doubtful whether the nation could ever have effected the transition.

Centralization in Australian education was therefore understandable throughout those years from the 1870s until the Second World War. In comparative studies Australia often features as the archetype of central control, but observers understood why it had to be like this. In 1938, for example, the year before the Second World War began, the international scholar I.L. Kandel (1938: 48) could observe that the high degree of central control had 'resulted from the recognition that voluntary initiative and local autonomy had failed ... to attain a moderate standard even of elementary education.' By 1955, however, another visitor, Freeman Butts (1955: Ch. 2), could question whether such tight centralism was any longer appropriate in Australia.

In retrospect, because it was identified so closely with the industrial economy, it was almost inevitable that bureaucracy should go out of favour in educational organizations with the onset of the post-industrial economy, and especially after the 1960s. The wartime Prime Minister John Curtin had signalled a new national orientation when, at the height of the Pacific campaign and with Australia facing the prospect of invasion from the north, he turned without regret to the United States as an ally more to be relied upon than Great Britain. By the time the Whitlam government was elected in 1972, Australia had developed a stance independent of Britain in key areas like foreign affairs (the recognition of China, involvement in Vietnam, new diplomatic relationships with Indonesia, sponsorship of nationhood for Papua New Guinea, an alliance with USA) and trade (less reliance on European markets, new trading relationships with Japan, China, Taiwan and Korea). To compete in a sector of the globe where some of the most vigorous new economies were developing, Australia could survive only by making a rapid accommodation to the new international economic order.

Put bluntly, a business which operates on bureaucratic lines cannot compete in a post-industrial economy which guarantees survival only to those firms which are flexible, which can make quick, strategic decisions, which encourage innovation and entrepreneurship, which value creativity rather than conformity, which give their members the power to take local decisions and to exercise initiative, and which regard the people in the organization more as partners than as property.

These qualities abound even in those post-industrial organizations which appear to be huge, international and multifaceted. They have discovered that there are better models of organization available than bureaucracy. The centre does not necessarily know best. While there are some frameworks, probably centrally devised, which all will honour, and while there is a set of priorities (some of them literally global) which all members of the firm must observe, it would be presumptuous, if not arrogant, of those at headquarters to think they should or even could impose controls on all the day-to-day operations of the firm, or monitor all the activities of its several parts, or make all the strategic decisions for all the company's members. In short, the post-industrial business world also appears to be a post-bureaucratic one.

The post-industrial economy depends heavily upon the information and the services sectors; education is centrally placed in both. By and large, the public education systems responded, as they always seem to do, by borrowing their modes of operation from business. The way they did so in the period between the wars has been well documented in Callahan's *Education and the Cult of Efficiency* (1962). So in a spate of 'restructuring' through the late 1970s and 1980s, virtually all Australian school systems were remodelled in terms of 'corporate management' ideas, together with all the accompanying vocabulary.

Democracy and Bureaucracy in the Organization of School Systems

Transitions in Teaching

The movement away from strictly imposed bureaucratic procedures and centralist controls was also fed from the 1950s onwards by the campaign to win full professional status for teaching. The reforms around this period were extensive. The short courses of teacher training were abolished; the admission point to pre-service education rose to matriculation level; teacher education programs increased in length and complexity; the training institutions were distanced from the employing authorities, and were upgraded into diploma-granting and then degree-granting colleges; people without a teacher education qualification (even if they were graduates) were not permitted to practise as teachers; in-service education programs burgeoned, and almost all teachers participated in them; higher degree courses became prevalent, and an increasing number of teachers acquired the Master of Education degree; and teachers became so well regarded (in spite of the popular rhetoric of the newspapers and politicians) that literally thousands of them quit schools to take good positions in businesses, the public services and in their own companies. It was a remarkable achievement that teaching should have become virtually a graduate profession in the short space of about twenty-five years.

The status was hard-won. A turbulent period in the 1960s and early 1970s saw teacher militancy in all states, and some bitter and protracted strikes largely fought on the basis of securing working conditions more in keeping with the new sophistication among teachers, better remuneration for professional work, protection of children from unqualified instructors, and a wider recognition of the responsibilities which teachers were being asked to shoulder. The militancy has left a legacy of public cynicism, but the gains from collective teacher actions are in retrospect historic.

The consequence was that teachers began to tolerate much less domination from the centre. Professionalism invested them with the confidence to demand greater autonomy in the way they worked and were organized. They were well enough educated now to know what needed to be done in particular schools and with individual students. Guidelines are acceptable in a profession, but prescriptive rules are not. Most important of all, the bureaucratic framework puts the client at the very base of the hierarchical pyramid, in the most powerless position where centralized control takes precedent over individual need, a situation intolerable in professional terms where responsiveness to one's client subsumes all other considerations.

It was not that the persons in authority positions wanted the service to be like this; they usually did not, because they were professional

13

educators too. It was the model which was inappropriate. From about the mid-1950s, therefore, it became clear that school systems could be organized in ways more sympathetic with the professional service being given. A variety of developments occurred through the 1960s and 1970s. The position of School Inspector — for decades, indeed since the previous century, a powerful authority figure — all but disappeared, replaced by curriculum consultants (collegial rather than status positions), new school-based reviews, peer or panel assessments for promotion purposes, and increasing responsibility on the principal to be a professional counsellor to staff. School-based decision-making (SBDM) implied the devolution of power and initiative to individual schools. A plethora of consultative bodies came into existence, ranging from project teams and task forces to high level committees like the New South Wales Education Commission, the Victorian State Board of Education and, of course, the national Schools Commission.

An Educated Parent Population

When the 'free, compulsory and secular' Education Acts were being passed in the Australian states during the last decades of the nineteenth century, the view abroad was that to bureaucratize education was in part to save schools from the limited vision of the pupils' parents. In the Victorian Parliament, for example, J.W. Stephen, who introduced the 1872 Education Bill, stated that 'one of the paramount principles of the Bill' was to ensure that 'the whole management and control of the education system should be vested in the Minister' and that 'the less parents, and particularly uneducated parents, had to do with the management of the schools, the better' (quoted in Badcock, 1988: 230). The compulsory attendance clauses were inserted in the Acts to ensure that parents could not withhold education from their children, who could otherwise be put to work, often as cheap labour in their father's business. Teachers welcomed the centralization of staffing arrangements, removing them from the vagaries of appointment by local citizens; the move also guaranteed that over time there would be some uniformity of teaching standards across the country, including in those remoter areas which, on their own, could have been badly disadvantaged. The system was deliberately paternalistic.

A hundred years later, the situation had changed fundamentally. A 'secondary education for all' was now practice, put in place after 1945. Commonwealth and State Scholarships had widened the access to tertiary education. The general level of education in the Australian community was high, and rising. So it was inevitable that both parents and the public would demand more access to the decision-making apparatus of schools. In a sense, education became the victim of its own success. An educated person tends to be more critical and inquiring than someone who is uneducated, more demanding over customer rights, more articulate and informed on issues, more capable of understanding and contributing to policy formation, more politically aware, less inclined to take things for granted or to leave matters to those occupying power positions. An educated population tends to be a 'noisy' population. Generally speaking, it tends to demand if not democracy, then at least the right to participate and to be heard. Bureaucracy and top–down management, especially when they are seen as control from afar, find it hard to survive in this kind of climate.

Was there a point in time when the new organizational patterns (like participation and democracy) supplanted the older ones (like bureaucracy), at least in education? Probably not, but throughout the 1960s and the 1970s there developed a public opinion that education, particularly the work of schools, should not be left to bureaucrats, and that there were several legitimate partners with an equal right to be involved in setting the policy and assessing the outcomes of schools. Teachers constituted one set of partners; as they became better qualified and more accepted as a profession, they expected to be party to the decisions being made about the areas of their professional practice. Parents were a second set; they are para-teachers anyway, inextricably involved in how and what their children learn — a realization which became widespread after the publication of the Coleman Report in the USA in 1966. Once they are of an age where their ideas can be articulated, children, as clients of the schools, can no longer be treated as though they are passive recipients of whatever the school chooses to wheel up to them. Finally, the patrons of schooling, the public who supply its operating finances and resources, can legitimately call the school and its operators to give an account of themselves.

In short, Australia (along with the rest of the Western world) had acquired an educated and therefore an articulate population which demanded participation in the management and policy-setting activities of schools. The most obvious manifestation was the appearance of school boards.

The Advent of School Boards

By the time the Whitlam government formalized the Commonwealth presence in primary and secondary education by setting up the Australian

Schools Commission in 1973, there was a widespread view that the way schools were governed and administered needed to change. Several of the states — notably Victoria and South Australia — were well advanced in creating governing boards for each school. In the two mainland Commonwealth territories, the federal government took action from 1970 onwards to disengage the schools from the states (South Australia and New South Wales) and to create free-standing school systems; both of them incorporated a degree of local control for each school. A NSW initiative to set up school boards foundered with union opposition.

The 'ideas whose time had come' were crystallized in the second chapter of the Karmel Report (Interim Committee for the Australian Schools Commission, 1973), the report of the interim committee set up to be the forerunner of the Schools Commission. For more than ten years thereafter the Karmel Report was the base-line document guiding the thinking and planning concerning Australian education. 'Devolution of responsibility' headed the list of principles. The report argued for 'less rather than more centralised control over the operation of schools', basing their case on the premise that 'responsibility will be most effectively discharged where the people entrusted with making decisions are the people responsible for carrying them out' (*ibid.*: 10).

The matter of school-based governance was addressed in the Keeves Reports (Committee of Enquiry into Education, 1981, 1982) in South Australia, the Hughes Report (Assessment Panel, 1982) in Tasmania, and the Beazley Report (Committee of Inquiry into Education in Western Australia, 1984) in Western Australia. By 1983 the Victorian Minister could assert in his *Ministerial Paper No. 1* (an evidence of the priority accorded the point) a firm commitment to 'genuine devolution ... to the school community', to 'collaborative decision-making processes' and to 'a responsive bureaucracy, the main function of which is to service and assist schools' (Fordham, 1983a).

What occurred in Australia was simply part of a world-wide movement. In Great Britain the Taylor Report (Committee of Enquiry into the Management and Government of Schools, 1977) followed hard upon the reconstruction of local authorities and advocated a 'new partnership' for schools through a revision of the powers and membership of the Boards of Governors and Managers. The report led during the 1980s to the Education Reform Acts under the Thatcher administration. At the same time there was a new balance developing in the United States following the tax revolt of the late 1970s which saw a shift in the relative powers of the federal government, the states, the school boards and local schools.

The movement for 'formalized parent participation' was so strong in Europe that Nicholas Beattie chose to make a comparative study of it. In his article, published significantly in 1978, he pointed out that there was 'remarkable unanimity' about the need for 'participatory democracy' resulting from an 'underlying crisis of confidence in democratic institutions' which surfaced earlier on the continent — in West Germany, France and Italy, for example — than it did in Great Britain (Beattie, 1978: 42). Beattie argued that when people have lost faith in the current institutional frameworks, they are unwilling to leave the important decisions and policies to be worked out between officials and elected representatives. As more people become involved, however, there is an inevitable 'leakage of information from the bureaucracy' which demonstrates to the new participants that decision-making is 'pragmatic and piecemeal, and not determined in any simple way by large principles' (*ibid.*: 44), a realization which confirms the determination of the participants and leads to increasing politicization.

The movement towards creating self-determining schools in the public sector was also strengthened by the popularity in the 1980s of conservative or right-of-centre political views and of economic rationalism. Both views favour a situation in which individual schools should be relatively independent and should be made to compete in the market place; their survival should be consequent upon their satisfying what their clients want and on their demonstrating their own proficiency.

During the 1980s, therefore, there was a consistent trend throughout Australia to give more powers to the individual school, and for governments to negotiate, either formally or metaphorically, a performance contract whereby the school showed cause why it justified continuing funding. Program budgets, such as were introduced in Victoria, were a means of ensuring that the school planned and then delivered according to predetermined priorities. The period also saw a number of documents, like the *Better Schools* paper in Western Australia (Western Australian Ministry of Education, 1986), which aimed to make schools more autonomous. The trend was accompanied by a reconsideration of the role of Regional Offices, leading to their consolidation (as happened in South Australia and Victoria) or to their virtual replacement (as happened in Western Australia). In short, the 1980s saw localization in a form that would not have been considered possible two or three decades earlier.

Federal Intervention in Australian Education

A powerful factor which came into play from the 1960s onwards was the intervention of the federal government in education in a way never envisaged when the Australian constitution was first drawn up. When the

Australian states federated in 1901, the responsibility for education was one of the powers left with the states. The federal parliament could allocate funds to the states as grants tied to specific projects, and it also had the power to grant scholarships to individual students, but it was the clear expectation that schooling and higher education were state matters outside the jurisdiction of the national government. It was an interesting acknowledgment even at this stage in Australia's history that schools belong with local communities, not with national parliaments; none of the states was very populous at the turn of the century, of course.

Until the end of the Second World War in 1945, Commonwealth intervention in education at any level was piecemeal and unsystematic, limited to actions like setting up the National Fitness Council, giving some grants for research and becoming involved with apprentice training. Post-war reconstruction, however, began to embroil the federal government unavoidably in education. The Commonwealth Reconstruction Training Scheme (CRTS) injected thousands of returning armed service personnel into colleges and universities to rehabilitate them for civilian life; in the process post-school education became no longer a preserve of late adolescence.

Simultaneously, Commonwealth Scholarship schemes democratized entry to the universities. The Commonwealth's immigration scheme began to change radically the mix in the Australian community, and forced a federally funded Migrant Education Program. Industrial development, which capitalized on the new technologies which the war had spawned, required increased capacity in technical education. There was an explosion of population with the post-war baby boom which began to put huge pressure on the schooling facilities (including the supply of teachers) in all states and territories.

But the states were now not in a position to raise sufficient funds to cope with their own responsibilities and those added as the result of federal policies. This situation had arisen because of an extraordinary action taken at a critical stage in the war when the Japanese had advanced as far south as Papua New Guinea. To raise sufficient money to finance the war effort, the Commonwealth Parliament annexed the income taxing powers from the states. When the war ended, these powers were not returned, as had been expected. A High Court challenge in 1945 failed, and since then the federal government has retained control of the most significant growth tax, thereby becoming the nation's principal financier. As a consequence, each year the Premiers must sit down with the Federal Treasurer to determine how much revenue will be allocated back to the states.

Progressively too, in every Western country, national governments felt impelled to impose their own priorities on education, even where they had neither historical precedent nor constitutional power to do so. Sometimes the national intervention was for defence purposes. Usually, however, it was as the result of economic imperatives. If the country were to compete within the new international economic order, within a context which rewards market competitiveness, where employment openings occur in the services sector rather than in factory production and manufacturing, and where a highly educated workforce is a necessary condition for success, then educational provisions would become the means of national regeneration and a legitimate concern of national government.

The impact on education was dramatic. Because it is relatively self-contained as a case, let us consider the post-school sector where the strength of the Commonwealth influence became first apparent. With the state finances so severely straitened, it is obvious in retrospect that the most costly part of the educational spectrum would evidence the shock first and most dramatically.

A decade after the end of the war the universities had run down to such a point that the federal government was forced to intervene, because the nation's performance in several key dimensions was at stake. It set up an inquiry which led to the Murray Report of 1957 (Committee on Australian Universities, 1957) and acceptance of the recommendation that the Commonwealth should subsidize the states' efforts by means of an Australian Universities Commission (modelled on Britain's University Grants Committee). About seven years later another federal inquiry produced the Martin Report (Committee on the Future of Tertiary Education in Australia, 1964), which led to the creation of the non-university sector of higher education, the invention of Colleges of Advanced Education, the merger of the state teachers' colleges into that sector, the extension of the same subsidy arrangements as applied to the universities, and the entrenchment of the Commonwealth as a powerful instrumentality in the post-school sector. The coup was completed by the Whitlam government which, on its election to office in 1972, abolished university fees (the ultimate in their scholarship scheme, we must say!) and took over the entire funding of tertiary education around Australia.

By the mid-1970s the Technical and Further Education (TAFE) area had been absorbed into the post-secondary sector, and there existed national councils administering the Commonwealth's endeavours in the university, advanced education and TAFE sectors. It was a natural step in 1977 to bring them all under one body, the Commonwealth Tertiary Education Commission (CTEC), which remained in existence until the Dawkins reforms of 1987 abolished the Commission, replaced it with a

19

Higher Education Board, and made it a subsidiary of a jumbo body called the National Board for Employment, Education and Training (NBEET).

All of these actions could hardly be labelled a transition from bureaucracy to democracy. Even so, there was a strong common thread of participation and consultation running through the changes wrought by the Commonwealth. Indeed, until NBEET came into existence with its powers only advisory and not executive (as were those of CTEC), the higher education sector was insulated by representative or 'buffer' committees from direct control by politicians.

The case of the post-school sector gives some indication of the complexities which invaded the administration of education, from the relatively simple period prior to 1945, when each institution had its own charter and governing council legislated by the state parliaments and when the teachers' colleges were controlled by the Education Departments, much like a school. The diversity, expansion and institutional autonomy which developed after 1964, the Martin Report and the act of the Whitlam government to bring tertiary education under the Commonwealth's jurisdiction were construed at the time as enlightened, and as liberating the tertiary colleges from state parochialism. But the development had overtones of centralization, which was forestalled by the states themselves when each set up its own tertiary education coordinating body.

The case is parallel to what occurred in the pre-school, primary and secondary areas and about which a great amount has been written. Before the Australian Schools Commission was created in 1973, the Commonwealth involvement had been minimal until the post-war years. The federal programs for science laboratories and school libraries, the states' lobbying which culminated in the Australian Education Council's document, *A Statement of Needs in Australian Education* (1970), the financial problems in Catholic education through the 1960s, the creation of the federal Department for Education and Science in 1967, and the pressure to create Commonwealth-sponsored school systems for the two mainland territories (the Currie Report appeared in 1967) were harbingers for the massive Commonwealth intervention which followed the election of the Whitlam government in 1972, and which precipitated or fostered so much of the change which has characterized the 1980s.

The Changing Nature of the Australian Population

Thus it is evident that from 1970 onwards extensive changes — not the least in attitudes — have overtaken public education in Australia and that the 1990s are shaping as a period of important transitions which will have local, regional, state and national implications.

The movement to involve parents, students and the public in the governance of schools and of school systems must be seen against the social background which developed through the 1970s. Society and the schools were affected fundamentally by several long-term trends.

1 Post-war reconstruction had made Australia much less dependent on England, and much less influenced by European frames of thinking. Australia began to develop independent policies across a range of areas, including trade and foreign affairs, the structure of industry and its modes of organization.

2 The baby boom and post-war immigration had substantially changed the population mix in this country. Apart from new Mediterranean and southern European cultural influences, the Asian perspective became strong with Australians realizing that they were in competition with the newly developing nations like Singapore, Taiwan, China, Japan and Korea.

3 In particular, English values, and especially those of institutions like the Church of England, no longer had a position of privilege. There were profound changes in the Catholic Church too; it was no longer dominated by Irish-Catholic traditions, and became subject to Catholic traditions from southern and eastern Europe, and from Asia. University and school traditions from North America were as influential as those of Great Britain.

4 The 1960s and early 1970s was a period of social revolution with the emergence of issues like civil rights, civil liberties, the sexual revolution, sexism, the women's movement, racism, age-ism, social justice, zero population growth and conservation. It was a time when authoritarianism of any kind was challenged, when higher education was not regarded as an élite preserve, when professional privileges came under assault. Pertinently for our purposes, established institutions, especially large and powerful ones, were challenged — including the church, the school, multi-nationals, public service organizations and entrenched power élites. People broke out of what they perceived as inherited cages, and bureaucracy became a target wherever it was identified. They claimed the right to a piece of the action; they demanded participation.

What appears to have occurred is a transformation in attitudes — which was not universally applauded — and with the change came an unwillingness to take at face value the actions and policies of those in positions of authority. A profound consequence was that a generation of people grew up in Australia in the 1970s and 1980s who were suspicious of established power, and who chose not to follow the conventions their parents had known in the 1950s. They rejected some of the influences which had shaped the views of the adults before them.

It is important to note, however, that it was the *parents* of those born in the 1960s and 1970s who were largely responsible for replacing representative democracy with participatory democracy, and for transforming the typical public service bureaucracies into something less heavy-handed and more appropriate for post-industrial conditions. Their *grandchildren* are now in school, a second generation of Australians raised with post-bureaucratic expectations. The way the non-government sector has grown at the expense of the government sector is one manifestation of the new approaches they and their parents have brought with them into schooling.

The issues of parental choice, the autonomy of schools (especially public schools), regionalization and local control, government funding procedures (for both public and independent schools), ministerial responsibility, measuring schooling outcomes and school governance are likely to be on the policy agenda for some time to come because no system has yet discovered final answers to them. But on one matter there does seem to be consensus: the days of centralized, single control by means of a large bureaucracy headquartered in a capital city are gone, presumably for ever.

References

ASSESSMENT PANEL ON THE ACT EDUCATION AUTHORITY (1973) *A Design for the Governance and Organization of Education in the Australian Capital Territory* (Hughes Report). (Chairman: P.W. Hughes). Canberra: Australian Government Publishing Service.
AUSTRALIAN EDUCATION COUNCIL (1970) *A Statement of Needs in Australian Education*. Adelaide: Australian Education Council.
BADCOCK, A.M. (1988) *Devolution at a Price: A Review of the Quality and Equality of Controls Relinquished by the Restructured Education Department of Victoria*. Mt Waverley, Victoria: A.M. Badcock.
BEARE, H. (1979) 'Lay Participation in Education'. In T. LOVEGROVE and K. TRONC (Eds), *Open Education and Secondary School: A Book of Readings*. Adelaide: Education Department of South Australia.
BEARE, H. (1983) 'The Structural Reform Movement in Australian Education and Its Effects on Schools'. *Journal of Educational Administration*, 14, 2.
BEARE, H. (1984a) 'Education and the Post-Industrial State'. *Unicorn*, 10, 2.

BEARE, H. (1984b) 'Community/Parent Involvement and Participation in Education'. *The Educational Magazine*, 42, 3.
BEATTIE, N. (1978) 'Formalized Parental Participation in Education: A Comparative Perspective (France, German Federal Republic, England and Wales)'. *Comparative Education*, 14, 1.
BEATTIE, N. (1985) *Professional Parents*. Basingstoke, Hants: Falmer Press.
BERINGER, I., CHOMIAK, G. and RUSSELL, H. (1986) *Corporate Management: The Australian Public Sector*. Sydney: Hale and Ironmonger.
BIRCH, I.K.F. and SMART, D. (Eds) (1977) *The Commonwealth Government and Education 1964–1976*. Melbourne: Drummond.
BOYD, W.L. and SMART, D. (Eds) (1987) *Educational Policy in Australia and America: Comparative Perspectives*. New York: Falmer Press.
BUTTS, F. (1955) *Assumptions Underlying Australian Education*. Melbourne: ACER.
CALLAHAN, R. (1962) *Education and the Cult of Efficiency*. Chicago, Ill.: University of Chicago Press.
COLEMAN, J., et al. (1966) *Equality of Educational Opportunity*. Washington, D.C.: US Government Printing Office.
COMMITTEE ON AUSTRALIAN UNIVERSITIES (1957) *Report* (Murray Report). (Chairman: Sir Keith Murray). Canberra: Government Printer.
COMMITTEE OF ENQUIRY INTO EDUCATION (1981) *Education and Change in South Australia*. First Report of the Committee of Enquiry into Education (Keeves Report). (Chairman: Dr J.P. KEEVES). Adelaide: SA Government Printer.
COMMITTEE OF ENQUIRY INTO EDUCATION (1982) *Education and Change in South Australia*. Second Report of the Committee of Enquiry into Education (Keeves Report). (Chairman: Dr J.P. KEEVES), Adelaide: SA Government Printer.
COMMITTEE OF ENQUIRY INTO THE MANAGEMENT AND GOVERNMENT OF SCHOOLS (1977) *A New Partnership for Schools* (Taylor Report). (Chairman: Councillor T. Taylor). London: HMSO.
COMMITTEE ON THE FUTURE OF TERTIARY EDUCATION IN AUSTRALIA (1964) *Tertiary Education: Report to the Australian Universities Commission* (Martin Report). (Chairman: Sir Leslie Martin). Melbourne: Victorian Government Printer.
COMMITTEE OF INQUIRY INTO EDUCATION IN WESTERN AUSTRALIA (1984) *Education in Western Australia* (Beazley Report). (Chairman: Kim E. Beazley). Perth: WA Education Department.
FORDHAM, R. (1983a) *Decision Making in Victorian Education*. Ministerial Paper No. 1. Melbourne: Victorian Minister of Education.
FORDHAM, R. (1983b) *School Councils*. Ministerial Paper No. 4. Melbourne: Victorian Minister of Education.
HANS, N. (1951) *Comparative Education*. London: Routledge and Kegan Paul.
HARMAN, G. and SMART, D. (Eds) (1982) *Federal Intervention in Australian Education*. Melbourne: Georgian House.
HUGHES, P.W. (1982) *Review of Efficiency and Effectiveness in the Education Department*. A report presented to the Tasmanian Public Service Board. Hobart: Government of Tasmania.
INTERIM COMMITTEE FOR THE AUSTRALIAN SCHOOLS COMMISSION (1973) *Schools in Australia* (Karmel Report). (Chairman: Prof. P.H. Karmel). Canberra: Australian Government Publishing Service.
KANDEL, I.L. (1938) *Types of Administration, with Particular Reference to the Educa-*

tional Systems of New Zealand and Australia. Melbourne: Melbourne University Press.

NAISBITT, J. (1982) *Megatrends: Ten New Directions Transforming Our Lives.* New York: Warner Books.

NEW ZEALAND DEPARTMENT OF EDUCATION (1988) *Tomorrow's Schools.* Wellington: NZ Department of Education.

REPORT OF A WORKING PARTY (1967) *An Independent Education Authority for the Australian Capital Territory* (Currie Report). (Chairman: Sir George Currie). Canberra: Department of Adult Education, Australian National University.

TASKFORCE TO REVIEW EDUCATIONAL ADMINISTRATION (1988) *Administration for Excellence: Effective Administration in Education* (Picot Report). Wellington: NZ Government Printer.

WESTERN AUSTRALIAN MINISTRY OF EDUCATION (n.d., c.1986) *Better Schools in Western Australia: A Programme for Improvement.* Perth: WA Ministry of Education.

WORKING PARTY FOR THE ESTABLISHMENT OF AN EDUCATION COMMISSION (1977) *Second Interim Report* (Hagan Report). (Chairman: Prof. J.S. Hagan). Sydney: NSW Government Printer.

Chapter 2

Balancing Competing Values in School Reform: International Efforts in Restructuring Education Systems

William Lowe Boyd

The tensions in Australian education today are similar to those in many developed industrial nations. World-wide social, economic and technological trends have generated needs that few existing school systems can meet (Coombs, 1985; Plank and Adams, 1989). At the least these developments require major reform efforts. In reality they seem to require a fundamental restructuring of education systems. Unfortunately, even modest reforms are hard to achieve (Plank, 1988). Still more so is the ambitious idea, now spreading across national boundaries, of restructuring educational systems. This is so partly because we often want simultaneously to maximize competing values, such as equity, excellence, efficiency and liberty or choice (Boyd, 1984; Garms, Guthrie and Pierce, 1978).

The chapters in this book highlight the tension between the values underlying democracy and bureaucracy. After a hundred years of a highly centralized approach to governing education, it is not surprising that Australians now want far more opportunity for democratic participation at the school site level.[1] Yet at the same time policy-makers are understandably concerned that some centralized control must be maintained in the interest of educational standards, equity and accountability.

American reformers are facing the same need to strike a balance between competing values, even though we differ radically from Australia in the historical starting point and evolution of our education system. America began with a highly decentralized education system that was high on local participation, but low on central control, standards and equity. Since the 1950s there has been a steady movement to enhance equity, raise standards and reduce fragmentation. But this movement toward more centralized control has come at substantial cost to local control and participation, and it has alternated in a trade-off between an emphasis on excellence and an emphasis on equity.

In designing policies and structures to govern education, our societies can learn much from each other and from other nations' experiences (Boyd and Smart, 1987; Hancock, Kirst and Grossman, 1983). Every society has to pick a particular policy mix or balance among competing values, but no choice is final. Whatever choice is made today favours some values over others, thereby sowing the seeds for tomorrow's reform movements (Kaufman, 1963). In time this leads to what, in the spirit of the Gorbachev era, can be called the politics of 'perestroika', i.e., the manoeuvring to determine whose interests and preferred reform agenda will shape the round of restructuring or reform that is unfolding. Whether radical restructuring or modest reforms are pursued, however, no program, even if fully achieved, will prove a panacea. Instead, the cycle of reform will continue, driven by the need for periodic adjustments in the balance of competing values (Kaufman, 1963).

International Movements to Reform Education Systems

Although the main emphasis in recent Australian restructuring has been on the imperative for decentralization and devolution, concerns for efficiency, effectiveness and higher standards are also very much in evidence. For instance, the *Ministerial Papers* (Minister of Education, 1983) in Victoria stressed devolution to the school site, but at the same time acknowledged the need for state-wide standards and guidelines to protect equity concerns. Similarly, the Scott Management Review of the New South Wales state system emphasizes devolution, but within a performance-oriented approach with system-wide standards (Management Review: NSW Education Portfolio, 1989). More broadly, not only in Australia but also in other nations which have lacked national curriculum standards and guidelines, there is a clear trend in this direction — especially in the United Kingdom, but also in the United States. Paradoxically, policy-makers, not just in Australia but in many nations, seem to be striving simultaneously to increase both the centralization and the decentralization of their education systems (Caldwell, 1989).

This effort to move simultaneously in what appear to be opposite directions has generated much of the tension and ambiguity in the international movement to restructure or reform education systems. I believe that much of the confusion here can be resolved by an analysis based upon

Lortie's (1969) classic discussion of the delicate balance of control and autonomy in elementary schools. Lortie argued that the nature of schools and school teaching requires a balance between the professional autonomy and discretion needed by teachers and the control and coordination required for effective management. In this chapter I will illustrate, through a discussion of international developments, the need for a sensitive balance between control and autonomy in designs for school reform, 'bureaucracy and democracy', 'control and autonomy' being parallel concepts which capture essential facets of the dialectic embedded in contemporary school reform. The American experience with this dialectic resonates with many of the tensions in Australian school restructuring.

The Evolution of American School Reform

Developments in the US education reform movement of the 1980s have been widely characterized in terms of two 'waves' of reform. A great irony of the reform movement has been that the first and second 'waves' were driven by competing impulses. The first wave emphasized control; the second, autonomy. The conflict between the standardization and centralization embodied in the first and the emphasis on teacher autonomy and professionalism embodied in the second has been called the 'San Andreas fault' in the reform movement.

Following the prescriptions of the influential, federally sponsored report, *A Nation at Risk* (National Commission on Excellence in Education, 1983), the first wave of reform efforts centralized control at the state level. It focused on the pursuit of 'excellence' through state mandates intensifying much of what already was being done, e.g., higher graduation requirements, more testing, a more standardized curriculum. When carried to the extreme, this approach has tended to 'deskill' teachers by reducing opportunities for professional discretion (McNeil, 1986).

By contrast the second wave built on the notion of professionalizing teaching and restructuring schools. Epitomized in the Carnegie report, *A Nation Prepared* (Carnegie Forum, 1986), and the National Governors' Association (1986) report, *Time for Results*, the second wave argued that decentralization, flexibility and autonomy are essential, both to foster engagement in teaching and learning and to meet the diverse needs of our increasingly heterogeneous student bodies. Remarkably, 'parental choice' (i.e., autonomy for the consumers — parents and students), a component of the second wave that was dismissed initially by many observers, has been gaining support rather dramatically.

There can be little doubt that the conflicting 'undertow' from the first wave has impeded the progress of the second wave reforms (Hawley, 1988). Now there is talk of the coming of a 'third' wave, but its character is still unclear. One candidate might be even more pronounced 'nationalizing' and centralizing forces. Certainly, the momentum behind the curriculum alignment and state and national level testing movement is growing. Some see the US evolving toward a de facto national curriculum (Doyle, 1988), a development now being pursued de jure in the United Kingdom.

Thus it is significant that at the first annual meeting of the Business Roundtable to be devoted to a single topic, education, 'a recurring theme in both [President] Bush's speech and the panel discussion was the need for an overarching national strategy for reform' (Walker, 1989: 1, 17).[2] Corporate leaders at the meeting agreed that fundamental reforms and restructuring were needed, not incremental improvements here and there. But Ernest Boyer emphasized the challenge, in developing a national strategy, of balancing 'this need for coordination with the need for more school-based innovations' (Walker, 1989: 17).

Even though we are unsure how to ensure this balance we already have simultaneous efforts in the United States to increase both the centralization (to the state level) and decentralization (to the school level) of governance arrangements in education. In fact, as noted earlier, this is a world-wide phenomenon. The foremost international expert on school-based management, Brian Caldwell, writes that:

> In general, governments in many countries are adopting a more powerful and focused role in terms of setting goals, establishing priorities and building frameworks for accountability — all constituting a centralizing trend in the centralization-decentralization continuum — at the same time as authority and responsibility for key functions are being shifted to the school level — a decentralizing trend. Much uncertainty arises because these trends, almost paradoxically, are occurring simultaneously or in rapid succession. (Caldwell, 1989: 3)

School teachers and administrators may well feel caught in a no-man's land between these diverging thrusts. Must we choose between them or can they co-exist effectively?

Toward a New Balance

When properly understood, I believe that these diverging thrusts reflect not schizophrenic tendencies, but simultaneous imperatives for organizational improvement (see Caldwell and Spinks, 1988; Peters and Waterman, 1982). Unlike freestanding private schools, public schools are not independent islands. They are, and must remain, part of a larger system serving broad social interests. To accomplish their purposes, they need a balanced combination of autonomy and coordinated control. If each school were allowed to go entirely its own way, local whims and biases could undercut educational coherence and equity. Thus, to realize the simultaneous imperatives, an interconnected system of public school governance is needed as much as ever — but in a revised form. Schools, school districts, regional authorities, state departments and state boards of education need one another; none is likely to be complete and adequate without the other.

In this view a key role for district/regional and state level education authorities is the collaborative development of (1) a strategic plan for educational improvement and (2) a broad, overall scheme for encouraging, supporting and assessing the implementation of the goals of this plan. Research shows that schools seldom become and remain effective and innovative on their own. They need impetus and support from higher levels (Coleman, forthcoming). In assessing the American and Canadian experience Leithwood and Jantzi (forthcoming: 16) remark that:

> Research on effective districts suggests considerable involvement of school staffs and 'experts' in district-level decision-making. Such involvement is often delegated within a strong, centrally developed framework which may take the form of a strategic plan. Feedback channels are developed which permit central coordination, monitoring, and long term planning activities. Decision-making in effective schools parallels that of effective districts. Teachers are involved in school-level policy decisions often including, for example, the assignment of students to classes. Effective schools have considerable school-level discretion for determining the means to be used in addressing problems of increasing academic performance. Effective secondary schools are organized and managed to support the purposes of the curriculum and the requirements for instruction implied by the school's philosophy of education.

Further support for the strategic planning responsibility is found in the experience of other nations. Reflecting on the international experience, a recent report of the Organization for Economic Cooperation and Development (OECD) on the quality of schooling concludes that:

However great the autonomy enjoyed by schools, they are still answerable to administrative authorities at local, regional, and national level that have responsibility for:
1 setting quality targets and providing the means of attaining them;
2 monitoring the implementation of appropriate strategies;
3 conducting regular appraisals of performance in association with the schools concerned (OECD, 1987: 89).

In all of this, however, policy-makers and administrators must remember the modern management adage that 'to manage is not to control, but rather to get results.' It is all too easy to become unnecessarily prescriptive and intrusive, even when pursuing a strategic planning approach. After all, as Ellen Goodman (1989) asks, how 'can you manage flexibility? Is that a contradiction in terms? Businesses want plans and controls. The new workers want options and individual treatment.' Can we have both?

The way toward a resolution of this tension is shown by Peters and Waterman's (1982) observation that the excellent companies they studied were characterized by 'simultaneous loose–tight properties'. That is, they were 'both centralized and decentralized' (p. 15) and distinguished by 'the co-existence of firm central direction and maximum individual autonomy' (p. 318). The firm central direction sets the key values and parameters which guide activity, but the sphere of activity has an openness that encourages individual initiative and creativity. Firm guidelines, accountability arrangements and staff socialization processes advance and protect the core values, such as equity considerations. Exemplary practice in school administration already demonstrates the merits of this approach (see, for example, Hill, Wise and Shapiro, 1989: 26; Murphy, 1989).

Restructuring via School-based Management

Although restructuring covers a range of possibilities, much of the recent discussion has focused on school-based management and various schemes to improve and 'empower' the teaching profession.[3] Success in achieving the latter goal depends heavily on effective movement toward school-based management. As with all restructuring arguments, the claim is that fundamental improvement in school and student performance cannot be achieved without significant changes in the traditional structure and operation of public schools. If this claim is valid — and I believe it is — we need to consider carefully the arguments and issues involved.[4]

Why School-based Management Is Needed

The critical ingredients in successful education occur where students, teachers and parents actually come together. Consequently, school-based management is founded on the belief that many key decisions inescapably must be made at the school level. This is where the people closest to the students and their distinctive needs can decide what needs to be done and how general goals and policies set at higher levels can be best implemented.

In the past we perhaps assumed that school principals could accomplish these purposes. However, the traditional view of the school principal, as a kind of 'super-teacher' with all the answers, is giving way to a more realistic view of what principals can and should try to accomplish. Although most principals subscribe to the ideal of providing 'instructional leadership', research documents that few principals have the skills, or can find the time, to execute this phase of their role successfully (Boyd and Hartman, 1988). Indeed, as Sykes and Elmore (1989) argue, the traditional conception of the principal's role creates a nearly impossible job. Consequently, the role needs to be reconceptualized to facilitate and share leadership opportunities with the teaching staff.

Thus school-based management typically involves the creation of a school council, composed of the principal and members representing the teachers and parents, which is responsible for a variety of programmatic and operational decisions as well as the allocation of a small budget. Obviously, this shared decision-making model modifies the role of the school principal. This approach requires some careful negotiation and delineation of the new spheres of responsibility and authority and the ground rules for decision-making, all of which is grist for the politics of perestroika, a point well illustrated in the Victorian experience with school site councils (Chapman and Boyd, 1986).

School-based management is consistent with trends in modern business management that emphasize the advantages of maximum delegation of decision-making to the operational level within a centrally coordinated framework — the 'loose–tight' approach popularized by Peters and Waterman (1982). It also builds on the widely documented finding that effective schools are characterized by active staff involvement in school improvement efforts, involvement that fosters commitment and a sense

Democracy and Bureaucracy

of ownership. By contrast, highly prescriptive, 'top–down' approaches to school governance diminish the professionalism and commitment of educators and may even result in them performing substantially below their capacity (McNeil, 1986).

Implementing School-based Management

Experts agree that it is far easier to recommend school-based management within a 'loose–tight' framework than to implement it. It is by no means a 'quick fix' for what ails the schools. Indeed, this innovation must be approached as a developmental process requiring fundamental changes in roles and relationships that can be achieved only over a period of years, even when there is continuous and strong support from system level leaders (Chapman and Boyd, 1986). For example, in the Edmonton Public School District in Alberta, Canada the process has been underway almost ten years. Begun with a three-year trial of school-based budgeting, it now has reached a stage in which:

> the elected school boards sets priorities each year which must be addressed in all schools. Budget preparation and staff selection are wholly decentralized to schools. Accountability in an educational sense is addressed through a system-wide set of standardized tests in language, mathematics, science and social studies at two points in elementary schooling and at one point in secondary. Target levels of performance are set each year (Caldwell, 1989: 14).

A key reason why a substantial period of time is needed for implementing school-based management is that its implications ultimately may affect so many stakeholders: parents, teachers and school principals; superintendents, central office personnel and local school boards; and state boards and departments. Ideally, collaborative planning and deliberation on the governance issues involved should be carried out in a spirit of cooperation and trust. At the least they must try to move in this direction. Safeguards need to be built into school-based management schemes to protect a variety of equity considerations, such as guaranteed access and equity across neighbourhood boundaries. A collaborative, professional relationship between teachers and school principals must be forged.

If policy-makers and the public believe that meaningful citizen participation in school councils is important, then vigilance will be required to prevent the councils from being dominated by the professional educators

(Malen and Ogawa, 1988). The greater fear in governance circles, generally, is that school councils could become the captives of narrowly-based, external interest groups. School-based decision-making rules and system level accountability requirements must be designed to minimize this danger.

The Politics of Perestroika

Having sketched the objectives and implementation of school-based management as a key step in contemporary restructuring of school systems, we need to consider the politics of perestroika that are likely to ensue despite admonitions to the contrary. To begin with, school administrator associations in the United States have taken a very leery view of the Carnegie Forum (1986) recommendation, in *A Nation Prepared*, for empowering teachers and sharing school decision-making more broadly (Thomson, 1986a, 1986b). Issues of power, turf, authority and labour-management relations abound here. Apart from the power issue, there is no guarantee that the changes, by themselves, will lead to better performance. Hawley (1988: 434) remarks that 'the idea that teachers will change the way they teach because we free them from bureaucratic constraints and provide them with opportunities to shape school policies and practices has a mystical quality to it.' Without doubt, in the absence of positive leadership there is a danger that school-based management ventures could bog down in power grabs and fractious relationships. As noted above, educators fear that if parents and community members are involved, further dangers of politicization will be opened up. What is more likely, as Malen and Ogawa (1988) found, is that citizen involvement in school-based management usually will remain perfunctory and ineffective.

Adding Democracy to Control and Autonomy

Significantly, in a prescient discussion of school-based management a decade ago, Garms, Guthrie and Pierce (1978: 278–94) emphasized that parental choice among public schools may be needed to bolster and make effective parental political voice in school councils. Indeed, discussions of the problem of balancing control and autonomy in teaching and school management, now and in the past, have tended to leave students and parents as the odd men out. As I have argued elsewhere (Boyd, 1989), there are at least three legs on the schoolhouse stool, and meaningful student and parental choice of public schools is needed to counterbalance the strong current thrusts toward managerial control and professional autonomy.

A persistent theme in the study of American educational politics is the power of professional interests to triumph over parental preferences (Boyd, 1976, 1982a; Guthrie and Thomason, 1975; Tucker and Zeigler, 1980; Zeigler and Jennings, 1974). Even when school boards resist the strong tendency toward conversion into 'rubber stamps' for the approval of professional recommendations (Kerr, 1964), they are blunt instruments, at best, for representing and protecting the interests of individual families. Moreover, political 'voice' through the ballot box is of limited value when dealing with public school systems that enjoy near monopoly status and that may still prefer to offer a 'one best system' approach to education (Tyack, 1974). Thus an increasingly diverse set of groups, from left, right and centre, is emerging to demand that far greater choice in public schooling arrangements in the USA be made available to parents and students (Nathan, 1989). Given the inclination of professional educators, many of whom hope that demands for choice will go away, it is not surprising that efforts to promote parent choice of public schools are being played out largely outside professional education circles, mainly in state legislatures.

There is substantial evidence that greater choice for consumers of educational services can go a long way toward reducing the problems, in focus and goal displacement, that plague public schools.[5] Choice not only restores an element of consumer sovereignty in public education, but at the same time increases the effectiveness of political voice (Hirschman, 1970). The power of consumer choice alters the political economy and dynamics of behaviour within bureaucracies (Boyd, 1982b). Perhaps most important of all, choice facilitates movement toward building communities of shared values and educational purpose (Powell, Farrar and Cohen, 1985; Coleman and Hoffer, 1987). However, this goal requires that educators, as well as clients, have greater freedom of choice in devising educational programs or choosing the kind of program with which they wish to affiliate. Indeed, Elmore (1988) shows that demand-side choice for consumers necessitates greater supply-side choice on the part of public providers, if they are to be able to respond successfully to public demands. Moreover, greater choice and hence discretion for teachers are essential for the real professionalism now being sought for the occupation by the 'second wave' of the current reform movement. Clearly, the more that communities of shared educational values and purpose can be created through reciprocal choice, the less will be the need for the kind of compulsion and coercion in teaching and learning that critics of schools have long deplored. The dramatic success story provided by Community School District No. 4, serving a low-income population in Spanish Harlem in New York City, is based upon exactly the dynamics and advantages that such programs of educational choice enable (Fliegel, 1989; US Department of Education, 1987: 60).[6]

In working toward a new balance we have to recognize, as Lortie argued (1969), that the reality of professional work in publicly controlled and funded schools requires a compromise between professional and bureaucratic models of control. Neither the entirely professionalized nor the entirely bureaucratized model is workable or desirable, although it seems clear that we need a new compromise that is more professional and less bureaucratic. Yet, because parents and the public at large can be frozen out, even from a better compromise of these two models, one of our vital concerns has to be for the creation and enhancement of governance models that effectively combine politics and markets (in other words, voice and choice) along with elements of professionalism and bureaucracy. School site management plans, involving parental choice and parental representation alongside teachers and administrators in the governance of schools, offer one promising model for public education in the future.

Conclusion

Whether in the United States or Australia, it will not be easy to achieve a new, more effective balance in the organization of education that includes the consumers as well as the producers of education. Restructuring in Victoria, Australia for example, made a strong move in the direction of democracy and participatory management with extensive devolution to school councils. However, the Victorian system seems caught in a whirlwind of turbulence that impedes consolidation of gains, as changes have been piled on top of other changes in rapid and continuous succession.

School-based management schemes, of course, are not the only alternatives for restructuring. But it is hard to see how school improvement can be widespread without adopting many elements of these schemes, regardless of what one calls them. The benefits that a coordinated approach to school-based management can bring, when properly implemented, justify the time and complications that inevitably are involved in pursuing this form of restructuring. More effective schooling cannot be mandated or legislated. Nor is it fruitful to intensify or continue pursuing a standardized, 'one best system' of education. Instead, a school improvement process that involves both bottom–up and top–down forces must be brought into play. Particularly when coupled with parental choice of public schools, school-based management is an ideal vehicle for increasing the professionalism and creative engagement of teachers and school principals, and for gaining the involvement and commitment of students and parents that are needed for effective education. When school-based management is linked to a well designed strategic plan, to comprehensive and focused efforts to improve instruction, and to the community and commitment that can flow from *reciprocal* choice, the result can be true improvement of teaching and student learning.

It appears that most Americans and Australians favour school-based management schemes that provide for a meaningful voice for parents, as well as for teachers. However, as emphasized earlier, research has repeatedly documented just how difficult it is to realize the democratic intention of school councils, particularly when the voice of parents and teachers is not augmented by choice. Bureaucratic authority and educators' professional interests tend to push parents into the background. Moreover, the lack of a sense of community created by reciprocal choice often leads to an unfocused and diffuse school climate and philosophy.

Public opinion polls show that most Americans today support parental choice of public schools. The Australian experience with private schools shows that Australians place a high value on choice of schools. Perhaps it is time for Australians to be more venturesome with parental choice of public schools as a means of reinvigorating state school systems. Put another way, perhaps it is time to re-examine whether democracy in public education can only be realized by maintaining the fiction that all state schools are the same and equal.

Notes

1 What is surprising, from an American viewpoint, is that this demand did not come sooner.
2 Needless to say, this is a theme that is quite familiar to Australians in the era of restructuring under the Commonwealth Minister for Education, John Dawkins.
3 Advocacy of school-based management in the US and Canada dates back into the 1970s, but the idea was not widely pursued at that time, partly because we already had local school districts and partly because it raises sensitive issues *vis-à-vis* teacher unions and higher levels of management. Even now no American state has pursued school-based management as extensively as Victoria has.
4 The best discussion of school-based management is by Caldwell and Spinks (1988).

5 I want to stress that I am advocating only state support of parental choice among public or state schools, not state-subsidized choice for parents among private as well as public schools. As many Australians recognize, the latter approach has disadvantaged state schools, with serious consequences for Australian education. This is a complicated and controversial topic which I have dealt with in depth elsewhere (Boyd, 1987).
6 Obviously, unrestricted and promiscuous choice could lead to serious problems, including those detailed in *The Shopping Mall High School* (Powell, Farrar and Cohen, 1985). Any system of choice within public education will need provisions to ensure equity, to protect and promote a sound, basic curriculum and to protect client welfare, particularly in light of the growing proportion of the student body that is composed of minority and 'at-risk' students. Note, however, that equity and democracy do not require that all state schools be dull replicas of each other (Nathan, 1989).

References

BOYD, W.L. (1976) 'The Public, the Professionals and Educational Policymaking: Who Governs?' *Teachers College Record*, 77, 539–77.
BOYD, W.L. (1982a) 'Local Influences on Education.' In H. MITZEL, J. BEST and W. RABINOWITZ (Eds), *Encyclopedia of Educational Research*, 5th ed. New York: Macmillan and The Free Press.
BOYD, W.L. (1982b) 'The Political Economy of Public Schools.' *Educational Administration Quarterly*, 18, 3, 111–30.
BOYD, W.L. (1984) 'Competing Values in Educational Policy and Governance: Australian and American Developments.' *Educational Administration Review*, 2, 2, 4–24.
BOYD, W.L. (1987) 'Balancing Public and Private Schools: The Australian Experience and American Implications.' In W. BOYD and D. SMART (Eds) (1987) *Educational Policy in Australia and America: Comparative Perspectives*. Lewes : Falmer Press.
BOYD, W.L. (1989) 'School Reform Policy and Politics: Insights from Willard Waller.' In D. WILLOWER and W. BOYD (Eds), *Willard Waller on Education and the Schools*. Berkeley, Calif.: McCutchan.
BOYD, W.L. and HARTMAN. W. (1988) 'The Politics of Educational Productivity.' In D. MONK and J. UNDERWOOD (Eds), *Micro-level School Finance*. Cambridge, Mass: Ballinger.
BOYD, W.L. and SMART. D. (Eds) (1987) *Educational Policy in Australia and America: Comparative Perspectives*. Lewes: Falmer Press.
CALDWELL, B.J. (1989) 'Paradox and Uncertainty in the Governance of Education.' Paper presented at meeting of the American Educational Research Association, San Francisco, March.
CALDWELL, B.J. and SPINKS, J.M. (1988) *The Self-Managing School*. New York and Lewes: Falmer Press.
CARNEGIE FORUM ON EDUCATION AND THE ECONOMY (1986) *A Nation Prepared: Teachers for the 21st Century*. Report of the Task Force on Teaching as a Profession. New York: Carnegie Forum on Education and the Economy.

CHAPMAN, J. and BOYD, W.L. (1986) 'Decentralization, Devolution, and the School Principal: Australian Lessons on State-wide Educational Reform.' *Educational Administration Quarterly*, 22, 4, 28–58.

COLEMAN, J.S. and HOFFER, T. (1987) *Public and Private High Schools: The Impact of Communities*. New York: Basic Books.

COLEMAN, P. (forthcoming) 'School District or Regional Management and School Improvement.' In Supplement 2 to the *International Encyclopedia of Education*. Oxford: Pergamon Press.

COOMBS, P.H. (1985) *The World Crisis in Education: The View from the Eighties*. New York: Oxford University Press.

DOYLE, D.P. (1988) 'The Excellence Movement, Academic Standards, a Core Curriculum, and Choice: How Do They Connect?' In W.L. BOYD and C.T. KERCHNER (Eds), *The Politics of Excellence and Choice in Education*. New York: Falmer Press.

ELMORE, R.F. (1988) 'Choice in Public Education.' In W.L. BOYD and C.T. KERCHNER (Eds). *The Politics of Excellence and Choice in Education*. New York: Falmer Press.

FLIEGEL, S. (1989) 'Parental Choice in East Harlem Schools.' In J. NATHAN (Ed.), *Public Schools by Choice*. St Paul, Minn.: Institute for Teaching and Learning.

GARMS, W.I., GUTHRIE, J.W. and PIERCE, L.C. (1978) *School Finance: The Economics and Politics of Public Education*. Englewood Cliffs. N.J.: Prentice-Hall.

GOODMAN, E. (1989) 'Mommy Track Poses Risks, Possibilities.' *Centre Daily Times*, 17 March.

GUTHRIE, J.W. and THOMASON, D.K. (1975) 'The Erosion of Lay Control.' In NATIONAL COMMITTEE FOR CITIZENS IN EDUCATION, *Public Testimony on Public Schools*. Berkeley, Calif.: McCutchan.

HANCOCK, G., KIRST, M.W. and GROSSMAN, D.L. (Eds) (1983) *Contemporary Issues in Educational Policy: Perspectives from Australia and USA*. Canberra: ACT Schools Authority and Curriculum Development Centre.

HAWLEY, W.D. (1988) 'Missing Pieces of the Educational Reform Agenda.' *Educational Administration Quarterly*, 24, 4, 416–37.

HILL, P.T., WISE, A.E. and SHAPIRO, L. (1989) 'Educational Progress: Cities Mobilize to Improve Their Schools.' RAND Report R-3711-JSM/CSTP, Santa Monica, Calif.: Rand Corporation, January.

HIRSCHMAN, A.O. (1970) *Exit, Voice, and Loyalty*. Cambridge, Mass: Harvard University Press.

KAUFMAN, H. (1963) *Politics and Policies in State and Local Government*. Englewood Cliffs. N.J.: Prentice-Hall.

KERR, N.D. (1964) 'The School Board as an Agency of Legitimation.' *Sociology of Education*, 38, 34–59.

LEITHWOOD, K.A. and JANTZI, D. (forthcoming) 'Organizational Effects on Student Outcomes.' In Supplement 2 to the *International Encyclopedia of Education*. Oxford: Pergamon Press.

LORTIE, D.C. (1969) 'The Balance of Control and Autonomy in Elementary School Teaching.' In A. ETZIONI (Ed.), *The Semi-Professionals and Their Organizations*. New York: Free Press.

MCNEIL, L.M. (1986) *Contradictions of Control: School Structure and School Knowledge*. New York and London: Routledge and Kegan Paul/Methuen.

MALEN, B. and OGAWA, R.T. (1988) 'Professional-Patron Influence on Site-based Governance Councils.' *Educational Evaluation and Policy Analysis*, 10, 4, 251–70.
MANAGEMENT REVIEW: NSW EDUCATION PORTFOLIO (1989) *Schools Renewal: A Strategy to Revitalize Schools within the New South Wales State Education System* (Scott Report). Milsons Point, NSW: Management Review, NSW Education Portfolio.
MINISTER OF EDUCATION (1983, March), *Ministerial Papers 1–4*. ('Decision Making in Victorian Education'; 'The School Improvement Plan'; 'The State Board of Education'; 'School Councils') Melbourne, Victoria: Minister of Education.
MURPHY, J.T. (1989) 'The Paradox of Decentralizing Schools: Lessons from Business, Government, and the Catholic Church.' *Phi Delta Kappan*, June.
NATHAN, J. (1989) *Public Schools by Choice*. St Paul, Minn.: Institute for Learning and Teaching.
NATIONAL COMMISSION ON EXCELLENCE IN EDUCATION (1983) *A Nation at Risk: The Imperative for Educational Reform*. Washington. D.C.: US Government Printing Office.
NATIONAL GOVERNORS' ASSOCIATION (1986) *Time for Results: The Governors' 1991 Report on Education*. Washington, D.C.: National Governors' Association.
ORGANIZATION FOR ECONOMIC COOPERATION AND DEVELOPMENT (1987) 'Quality of Schooling: A Clarifying Report.' Restricted Secretariat Paper ED(87)13. Paris: OECD.
PETERS, T.J. and WATERMAN, R.H. (1982) *In Search of Excellence: Lessons from America's Best-Run Companies*. New York: Harper and Row.
PLANK, D.N. (1988) 'Why School Reform Doesn't Change Schools: Political and Organizational Perspectives.' In W.L. BOYD and C.T. KERCHNER (Eds), *The Politics of Excellence and Choice in Education*. New York: Falmer Press.
PLANK, D.N. and ADAMS, D. (1989) 'Death, Taxes, and School Reform: Educational Policy Change in Comparative Perspective.' *Administrator's Notebook*, 33, 1, 1–4.
POWELL, A.G., FARRAR, E. and COHEN, D.K. (1985) *The Shopping Mall High School: Winners and Losers in the Educational Marketplace*. Boston, Mass.: Houghton Mifflin.
SYKES, G. and ELMORE, R.F. (1989) 'Making Schools Manageable: Policy and Administration for Tomorrow's Schools.' In J. HANNAWAY and R. CROWSON (Eds), *The Politics of Reforming School Administration*. New York: Falmer Press.
THOMSON, S.D. (1986a) 'School Leaders and the Carnegie Agenda.' *American School Board Journal*, September, p. 32.
THOMSON, S.D. (1986b) 'Strengthen, Don't Diffuse, School Leadership.' *Education Week*. 28 May, p. 28.
TUCKER, H.J. and ZEIGLER, L.H. (1980) *Professionals versus the Public: Attitudes, Communication and Response in School Districts*. New York: Longman.
TYACK, D. (1974) *The One Best System*. Cambridge. Mass.: Harvard University Press.
US DEPARTMENT OF EDUCATION (1987) *Schools That Work: Educating Disadvantaged Children*. Washington. D.C.: US Government Printing Office.

WALKER, R. (1989) 'Bush to Appoint Group to Proffer Education Ideas.' *Education Week*, 14 June, pp. 1, 17.

ZEIGLER, L.H. and JENNINGS, M.K. (1974) *Governing American Schools*. North Scituate, Mass.: Duxbury Press.

Chapter 3

From Charity School to Community School: The Unfinished Australian Experience

Brian V. Hill

In a naive view of the world the term 'administration' identifies those management structures which free the specialist workers in an organization to fulfil the mission of that organization.[1] Administration is not an end in itself; it has no agenda of its own. Similarly, administrators are to be distinguished from those whose direct responsibility is to realize the mission. Hence the nouns 'administration' and 'administrator' acquire shape only when preceded by some such qualifier as 'military', 'business' or 'educational'.

So runs the myth. Two facts of life tell against it. One is that despite some appearances to the contrary, administrators are as human as everybody else, and have the same tendencies to tailor their environment to their own comfort or drive for power. Unless they too clearly understand and support the mission of their organization, they will tend to adopt goals which make administration an end in itself, favouring a 'steady state' (except, of course, for incremental salary creep) in preference to reform and innovation. It is no accident that the English television satire *Yes, Prime Minister* is being seen to have training potential (though whether for civil servants or politicians is not clear).

The second and more profound fact is that in all organizations administrative structures and procedures *do* to some extent set their own agendas. This has special import for *educational* institutions, where the explicit mission of the institution is to promote learning. Students are to be given an understanding of many things: facts, theories, skills, values, relationships and so on. But students do not suspend their learning activities when the siren blares or the teacher considers 'the lesson' completed. They go on absorbing, continuously, the messages which are

41

conveyed by the administrative *structures* of classroom, school and system, and the administrative *styles* of teachers, clerks, principals and others with authority over them. These are part of what is coming to be recognized as 'the hidden curriculum', a variable which sometimes seriously subverts the stated objectives of the explicit curriculum.

To add to the complications, administrative patterns themselves are partly determined by wider cultural assumptions about authority and the common good which transcend the particular missions of specific institutions in the society. Britain administered her colonies through a civil service that faithfully reflected a hierarchically organized society in which people knew their place and deferred unquestioningly to their superiors. The pattern was faithfully reproduced in the education departments formed in each Australian state during the nineteenth century, with classroom teachers at the base of the bureaucratic pyramid. It is no wonder that it even flowed on into teaching strategies which implicitly endorsed such values, down to such mundane details as the teacher operating from a dais at the front of, and above, the students in their fixed rows of desks.

We are, therefore, obliged to recognize at least three interacting variables affecting the values which are eventually transmitted through schooling. Professional teachers develop statements of aims and objectives for the curriculum which reflect *educational* considerations. At the same time other influences affect what is actually learnt, particularly due to the *administrative* apparatus built up around the social project of schooling. And both are affected by wider *cultural* assumptions about social structure and the common good.

At the turn of the century, and again in the era following the Second World War, there were waves of innovative thinking typified by references to the 'New Education'. In each case the mainspring was ostensibly a concern for the development of the individual, carrying with it the idea of a society in which personal achievement and democratic participation were possible. So said the official curriculum, as fashioned by the emerging profession of trained teachers. But if this were not to be subverted by the values of the larger society on the one hand and the administrative agenda on the other, then the endorsement of both was needed. It is a moot point whether those endorsements have been forthcoming. This book proceeds on the assumption that tensions exist today between such variables, and the present chapter seeks to trace some of the shifts in philosophical assumptions which have occurred in the history of schools in Australia.

Authority Unchallenged: The Charity Model

At the beginning of European settlement of Australia the priorities were survival and surveillance. After a few years the increasing number of child waifs led to a demand for schooling, for which the model to hand was the English public charity school. Indigent children were to be given a rudimentary training which fitted them for basic tasks and domestic service. Though religious groups in the colony made some commendable efforts in this direction, economics dictated that in the early years much of the initiative rested with charitable governors such as King and Macquarie. Indeed it was King's importunings which persuaded the Colonial Secretary to endorse government spending on education in Australia some decades before the home government had become convinced of the need to do the same in England itself.[2]

Whether the church or the governor was sponsor, the world-view of the schools in this period was an amalgam of Christian values and the assumptions of a class-structured society. Strong endorsement was given to cultural values stressing the authority of God, governors, magistrates and clergy; in short, the established order.

The Establishment–Bureaucratic Model

The picture began to change as the number of free settlers increased and religious dissension weakened the value consensus. A demand arose for the provision of schools with a more up-market image, and religious groups made an increasingly significant contribution to these, both by founding a number of schools on the English grammar school model and by providing teachers for many of the private schools which emerged in this period. Such teachers included a number of LMS missionaries repatriated from Polynesia. The Catholic Church, of course, had a special ideological commitment to the idea of providing a Catholic school in every parish.

The same growth in population made it necessary for state governments to begin efforts to fill the gaps in the provision of schooling. The strategy adopted was to set up local school boards to administer schools in which the financial support was provided by fees and fund-raising as well as government grant. By the middle of the century it was becoming apparent that administrative changes were required to put schooling on a more effective footing. In 1851 New South Wales recruited William Wilkins from England to develop a new model.

Wilkins immediately set about to move thinking from the older notion of the state being responsible primarily for emergency mendicant provision to a view that the state should be the main provider of universal education, and should set the standard. He began to build a centralized education bureaucracy and a professionally trained teaching service. Consistent with this, the power of school boards was steadily reduced. A bureaucratic ethos grew up under the shadow of establishment values.

The endorsement of wider cultural assumptions was most clearly seen in the attitude adopted towards the teaching of religion. State education in New South Wales, as defined in the Public Instruction Act of 1880, allowed for both denominational instruction by visiting clergy and instruction by the classroom teacher as part of the 'secular' curriculum. The Act made clear that what was meant by 'secular' in this connection was religious teaching which excluded 'dogmatic or polemical theology'. The aim was to avoid denominational differences, while endorsing what A.G. Austin has called 'Common Christianity'.[3]

It should, however, be noted that, laudable as Wilkins' efforts at improving the efficiency of instruction were, teaching to him was the *administration* of learning. The training of teachers involved practice in classroom control while supervising the rote learning of the syllabus. Theoretical studies included little reference to teaching methodology, much less to the psychology of learning; they consisted mainly of the further study of those subjects which the trainees would be responsible for teaching.[4] At this point curriculum values and administration were very close.

The New South Wales experience was, to varying degrees, repeated in the other states. Victoria, however, challenged the assumptions of the cultural establishment from the outset, and foreshadowed in its Education Act of 1872 a more secularized version of the model we have been discussing. It is time to examine the reasons for this.

The Secular-Bureaucratic Model

The main factor in the Victorian choice was the antagonism towards authority, religious and political, of many of the migrant gold-diggers, whose influence was strongest in that state. There the curriculum was defined as 'secular' in the sense of being 'neutral' towards cultural values and ideologies; an effect achieved, it was supposed, by the simple exclusion of reference in the general curriculum to religion and other controversial areas of belief. Since a curriculum cannot operate in a value vacuum, the Victorian curriculum perforce took on the values of the administrative structure. As in New South Wales, this was coming to be characterized by centralized, hierarchical control, and instrumentalism was the highest value. The basis of curriculum selection was the development of academic subject areas with a view to qualifying for further study or enhanced job selection. 'Getting on' provided an impoverished substitute for the value heritage that Victorian schools were excluding.[5]

The 'secular–bureaucratic' model emerged first, then, in Victoria. Its evolution in other states was due less to the militancy of radical elements in their societies than to the particular form that emergent state secondary schools took at the turn of the century. Secondary education, hitherto regarded as the preserve of private schools, which saw it as their privilege and responsibility to educate the future leaders of society, became the flagship of the reforms introduced in state systems by Peter Board in New South Wales, Frank Tate in Victoria and Cecil Andrews in Western Australia. Each of these innovators was sensitive to the advance of educational ideas in the northern hemisphere: the new interest in educational psychology and pedagogy, the emerging priority of technical education, and the concern, especially in Scotland, to transcend social class boundaries by providing avenues for the able poor to obtain the education they deserved. There was potential here to put the curriculum in touch with cultural movements towards a more democratic order.

Consistent with these ideas, all states eventually followed the innovators in embracing secondary education as part of the government's responsibility. The most able of both sexes gained access to high schools modelled on the grammar school tradition, though some schools went further in embracing scientific areas of study which were not yet common in the private sector. Less able boys could take advantage of technical schools, while girls in this category went to 'domestic science' schools.

A golden opportunity existed to link these developments with ideals of citizenship in a new order, restoring moral vision to the curriculum, but the state secondary schools fell short of their potential in this regard. High schools set out to compete with private grammar schools, with increasing success in the academic sphere. But whereas 'independent' schools were confident of their religious and upper-class roots, which put value into their curriculum (whatever one might think of that value complex), state schools were inhibited by the bureaucratic obsession with value neutrality.

The most serious mistake was to suppose that the instrumental focus enabled such schools to preserve value neutrality. To the contrary, it fostered by default self-interest, the technocratic mind-set and, more recently, consumerism and the one-dimensional consciousness deplored by Marcuse.[6] Church schools, meanwhile, have had their Christian

Democracy and Bureaucracy

objectives diluted by similar goals, and by the additional tendency to endorse social privilege for the few. Neither pattern has been conducive to the production of *public* servants with a strong vision of the common good or the development of a coherent public philosophy.

New Variables in the Post-War Era

The Second World War and advances in radio and television communication pulled Australia into the global stream of consciousness. Australia had hosted the American GI, and her returning servicewomen and men had seen other cultures. A disillusionment with religion and traditional authorities, sharpened by the atrocities of war and the lack-lustre contribution of many military chaplains, led to a general drift away from the establishment values of the pre-war years. In addition, there was a general desire to make a new start. The post-war economic boom focused attention on the attractions of material prosperity, while at the same time making it less necessary to espouse older values of thrift, hard work and the achievement ethic, though these were still paramount for the DPs (displaced persons) and other assisted migrants who came in their thousands from Britain and Europe. At first family solidarity provided a focus for value consensus. Studies in the early 1960s indicated a general aspiration, among indigenes and migrants alike, to get a job and a home, and to have a close-knit family.

The immediate effect of all this in schools was to confirm the instrumental and individualistic goals which had been developing in the previous era. Traditional authority structures seemed at first to be just as firmly entrenched as ever, partly because the administrators of the system were older people whose green years were pre-war. It was this situation that Freeman Butts was seeing when he wrote his seminal *Assumptions Underlying Australian Education*.[7] But there was more change in the air than he had detected.

Many of the new recruits to the teaching services were returned military personnel who were more mature and able to answer back. They were also less committed to the old values, and more inclined to obtain the material and family securities which, during the war years, they had feared they would never be able to enjoy. They tended not to bring love or loyalty into the classroom, but they maintained good order and promoted achievement. They were an ideological time-bomb in education, and their chance to influence policy came when their own children created expansion in state systems which brought in its train a foreshortening of the time-frame required for them to obtain promotion in a centralized system.

Authority Dispersed: The Establishment Challenged

The effects of the post-war baby boom hit the primary schools in the early 1950s and the secondary schools later in that decade. Chronic teacher shortage brought many people into the profession who were young and often not particularly suited to it. This, combined with rapid promotion and the high rate of transfer between schools which it required, produced administrative and curriculum instability. At the same time there was an increasing realization — helped along by the comparisons with America, which were now coming to matter more to Australia — that while industry needed a larger supply of skilled workers, the older patterns of streamed secondary education were hampering the development of many children.

Discussions developed in state after state about the democratization of the secondary school, with the 1957 Wyndham Report in New South Wales and the 1958 Robertson Report in Western Australia setting the pace. It is interesting to study these reports ideologically. The value system of common Christianity is not much in evidence, but there is nothing to replace it. Emphasis is placed on individual development and more equal educational opportunity, which are, from an ideological point of view, instrumental rather than intrinsic values. Subsequent reports have been even more bland in their assumption that only the instrumental values of curriculum need to be talked about. A recent example is the 1983 Beazley Report on state schooling in Western Australia, which is little more than a shopping list rather than a unified vision of where we want society to head.

The increasing youthfulness of the teaching force had another interesting effect. The new breed were products of the prosperous years, who had never known economic depression. There were increasing signs of a leisure ethic replacing the achievement ethic. Even today staffrooms often exhibit this mix, with many older teachers and administrators reared in the Depression years advocating hard work and material security, while many younger teachers project the idea of earning enough to get by so that one can take maximum advantage of one's leisure time and the luxury goods to go with it. The foundations of this phenomenon were laid in the 1950s and 1960s.

Authority Unseated: The Value Vacuum

More profound cultural shifts were also occurring in these years. The sexual revolution reached Australia, and families oriented to material prosperity at the expense of fulfilling relationships had little defence against the youth revolt which was developing. The commercial media contributed to the fragmentation of the family unit by conniving in the invention of a youth subculture characterized by moral permissiveness, a contempt for adult authority, an attachment to commercial entertainments and a vulnerability to the emerging drug traffic. These trends were helped along in the late 1960s by the American trauma over Vietnam, which, by media osmosis, became the shared experience of youth in other countries, whether they were engaged in this conflict or not. Many Australian youth were directly involved, since those chosen for national service by lottery during the war years were drafted to Vietnam.

Such influences created a readiness among youth to embrace the libertinism promoted by the so-called 'Age of Aquarius'. Along with some credible experiments in alternative life-styles and communal living, these was a spirit of hedonism which encouraged the rejection of the old authorities, especially bureaucratic. Charles Reich foreshadowed the emergence of a third level of consciousness which would leave the technocratic mind-set behind and bring freedom and spontaneity of relationships.[8]

In the schools such influences were felt at a number of levels. They helped, for instance, in the diversification of the curriculum into elective areas, and the reduction (to some extent) of the influence of university requirements on the curriculum. They contributed to changes in classroom climate which obliged teachers to establish their authority in more subtle and suppliant ways, because the bluff of authoritarianism without an ideological base had been called. They accelerated the disarray of provisions for religious instruction. They provoked calls for studies which would help the new generation to cope with sex and relationships, family and community involvement, and legal and industrial relations, since these things could no longer be assumed to be in place, or reinforced by patterns in the wider community.

They also added hugely to the complications of role definition in educational administration. The principal found that he — there were still few women at this level — had a wider range of responsibilities, having to identify and set the tone of the school while having fewer endorsements from the wider community of the values he considered it appropriate to promote. He had to lead a staff who were better educated and much less subservient than in previous eras, and expected their views on

From Charity School to Community School

school leadership to count. He had to manage a team expanded beyond the traditional brief by the addition of the paraprofessionals who were needed to handle the health, career and counselling tasks increasingly being remitted to the school. In some states and territories there were also substantial moves towards meaningful community involvement, both in support services and in policy-making. To multiply the principal's problems, the demand for a wider range of options in the curriculum caused schools to grow to sizes where quite different administrative procedures were needed to maintain civil order, scholastic momentum and a sense of being a learning community. Even now no state generally requires applicants for administrative posts to give evidence of having acquired specialist training to understand and manage such a wide range of responsibilities.

The New Conservatism: The Managerial Model

The one thing which, to some extent, kept the lid on the problems which the value vacuum and the administrative nightmare were creating was full employment; but that bubble burst in the 1970s. The vision of Charles Reich lost its substantiality as the hard economic facts — and the removal of the Vietnam conflict as a catalyst of revolt — damped down the natural optimism of youth and raised fundamental questions about personal identity and survival in a competitive society. The new tertiary student generation embraced the vision of the self-centred 'yuppy'.[9]

This brings us to the contemporary era. The economic down-turn has levelled out to some degree, but it seems unlikely that there will be a return in the foreseeable future to former boom levels. This has been accompanied by, and in part has caused, a swing to conservatism in the 1980s. There is political conservatism, paradoxically being implemented by Labor governments in most of the Australian states; and there is cultural conservatism, characterized by a return of competitive achievement-oriented pressures in schooling. Private schools — viewed in the 1960s as somewhat *passé* — now have booming enrolments because they promise better fortune in the job market and in the achievement of a comfortable yuppy existence. This produces a new kind of achievement ethic which retains the self-centred materialism of the leisure ethic, and so public service still runs a very bad second.

Potentially, therefore, schools are likely to have fewer discipline problems because they are seen to be necessary to getting on. Ostensibly, innovation is out, convergence is in. But a kind of cultural lag is prompting the teaching profession to sponsor in some states the introduction

49

of unit curriculum approaches, which promise a better deal for all students.[10] There is tension here between the expectations of profession and community, because unit curriculum strategies appear to break down the streaming that appeals to the socially mobile.

Internal Contradictions in the Model

Paradoxically, unit curriculum may be a useful survival mechanism for schools. The new conservatism, reflected in a public rhetoric which talks about 'the basics', 'standards' and vocational studies, cannot resolve the contradictions in an industrial society which, on the one hand, is increasing the available consumer delights and, on the other, creating through job obsolescence an under-class who will have decreasing access to these delights. It is under-achievers (for whatever reason) who have been creating the most difficulties for school discipline in the past, and the choices made possible by the unit curriculum could help to minimize to some extent the alienation of which they are particularly conscious in the classroom.

It would be naive, however, to suppose that administrative strategies of this kind will suffice to dissolve the contradictions in modern schooling. Alienation is a phenomenon which is not confined to low achievers, nor due only to creaking administrative procedures. Many highly intelligent students are jibbing at the value vacuum in their schooling, the domination of subject-centred thinking in staff, school design and timetabling, and the crassness of the consumerism which, in lieu of higher goals, constitutes the main visible reason for working hard at one's studies.[11]

There are other students who are feeling alienated from schooling, but for reasons which cannot be laid so squarely at the door of the teaching profession. A growing number of emotionally disturbed youngsters, abused or neglected at home, is coming to school with a built-in mistrust of adults and authority. If questions of relationships, self-identity, social justice and community participation are not addressed more deliberately in the curriculum, and in realistic, hard-headed ways which disarm the criticisms that such studies are soft in comparison with the traditional disciplines, then schools can anticipate increasing problems of student alienation and disruption.

Meanwhile, the administrative structures of schools are tottering under the competing demands laid upon teachers. In an important sense they, the ultimate deliverers of the educational experience, are still at the bottom of the bureaucratic pyramid. It is they who have to make policies of devolution and school-based curriculum development work. It is they who have to maintain classroom control in the absence of clear agreements about acceptable sanctions. To their traditional responsibility for teaching has been added in more recent times the burden of continuous internal audit with its concomitant increase in record-keeping. This also involves giving more guidance to individual students in regard to academic performance and career selection, requiring skills which their initial training is unlikely to have addressed. At the same time the most caring teachers are increasingly being importuned by emotionally distressed students who are often in need of skilled psychological counselling.

All these demands are pressing in at a time when Western communities are showing themselves less willing, and sometimes less able, to spend as much on public education as they used to, let alone provide the *additional* resources that such amplified responsibilities require. This is reflected in the increasing politicization of central departmental structures. Needing excuses for the financial retrenchments they are thrusting on public education, politicians are tending to outdo each other in gratuitous criticism of teacher performance, while at the same time reducing the advisory services in central and regional offices which might help teachers to do better.

This last remark may appear to run against the tide of current theorizing, which talks about the need to create smaller administrative units, so that the hierarchical features of bureaucracy can be replaced by participant democracy, with teachers having more jurisdiction over their own professional labours, albeit with increased participation by parents as well. In these circumstances how can there be talk of centralized advisory personnel? But the point is precisely that the emphasis should be on *advisory*, not executive. The substantial reduction of head office staff, in those states where it has already occurred, has taken greatest toll on the advisory echelon, even though many middle management executives have also gone. The local school cannot alone generate the resources to keep up-to-date in every subject area. More professional they may have become, but not omniscient. Advisory services are viable only where some economies of scale have been achieved, and that suggests some measure of consolidation.

Teachers are also finding that financial stringency and the slower rates of population increase are closing the doors to meaningful career advancement. The relatively fast promotion of the 1960s put many people into high positions who are still well away from retirement, and it is probable that the increasing rhetoric surrounding in-service teacher development is meant in part to draw attention away from the unlikelihood of promotional reward for good effort.[12]

In short, the managerial model of educational administration is selling the community short. Without a rediscovery of the common good, and a recommitment to adequate servicing, the public schools may well regress to the status of charity provision for the disadvantaged — which is where our story began — with the best teachers retreating to the private sector.[13]

Authority Negotiated: Towards a Democratic Model

What values, then, should animate the curriculum and administration of schools? Let us acknowledge that a dark scenario is possible. Pluralistic societies have difficulty in supplying common purposes and expectations which might enable school communities to work for the levels of cohesion and cooperation that are needed. The energies of the teaching profession are being diverted — by the self-interest which in Australia substitutes for moral vision, and by the criticisms and withdrawal of services of their political masters — into rearguard industrial resistance. One consequence of these trends could be such an increase in the specificity of job descriptions that little scope will remain for professional initiative and spontaneity. This could be a regressive outcome from current moves for 'award restructuring'. Another consequence could be the further alienation of teachers from the local communities which their schools serve.

Similar reactions could be expected from school principals. Pressed on the one side by frustrated teaching staff, they are simultaneously being put by their superiors in the position of being publicly answerable for what goes on in their schools. In this scenario they will undoubtedly band together for mutual protection and be tempted to develop a tribal ethic instead of a service ethic.[14]

A more optimistic scenario can plausibly be advanced. It will depend on a resolve to solve as many problems as possible *at community level* in preference to issuing edicts from the centre.[15] It will require an initial recognition that the myths of technocratic autonomy and ideological neutrality are false and pernicious. Determined attempts must be made to embed schools more securely in their regional communities through the development of negotiated value charters which cover all aspects from school administration to classroom practice, and from community participation to the roles of paraprofessionals in the school.

Realism obliges us to acknowledge that the prospect of obtaining a value agreement as wide and pervasive as old Christendom, which is what some hope for, is neither plausible nor appropriate. The first step in value negotiation must be to identify the principles which guarantee the democratic middle-ground of Australian society. There are taken-for-granted freedoms of individual speech and action, coupled with general agreements on the desirability of social justice, caring and cooperation, which *can* be fashioned into a minimal, but by no means vacuous, value charter for schools. From such general principles it should then be possible to derive tough-minded guidelines for administration and precise terms of reference for the various contexts in which parents and professionals are expected to interact. It should also not be beyond the wit of people of good will to develop specific agreements about disciplinary, assessment and counselling policies which the school can reasonably expect will be endorsed and backed up in most homes and by the community at large.

If the present value vacuum (and the promotion of self-interest and consumerism by default) is not relieved by such negotiations, then either state schools will lapse into such a vapid directionlessness that public policy will swing resources even further into the private sector (a trend which is already occurring), or they will come under the sway of ideological minorities who have the will to capture the decision-making processes and impose their values on the whole. It is perhaps in Victoria, the state most affected by the neutrality doctrine, that the signs of this happening are most evident, and disenchantment with state schools commandeered by unrepresentative lobbies is increasing the drift to alternative schools.

The author clearly prefers the scenario of state schools developing negotiated value charters at local community level. If this is to be realized, then requiring *each* individual school to form a school board is probably *not* the wisest course. It would seem preferable to identify *regional* communities for this purpose — at least in urban areas — encompassing zones large enough to accommodate *a few* high schools and their feeder primary schools. This facilitates the distribution of specializations among the schools in a region so that there is less need to make high schools as big as they have presently become, and it increases the basis of inter-school comparison which is needed to assist in the moderation of standards.

Such an arrangement also increases promotional opportunities for teachers within that region, instead of making relocation a condition of professional advancement. A distinctive style of educational leadership and management is required to operate this model, which is neither autocratic nor weakly egalitarian. Appropriate protocols need to be developed in educational administration courses to nurture this kind of leadership style, and preference should be given to those applicants for administrative positions who have been prepared to undertake such courses.

Further Issues for Investigation

Various issues remain to be investigated further. The notion of a 'value charter' for a school needs spelling out. Some have argued that the modern Australian community is now so diverse that it is unlikely that agreements of sufficient specificity will be obtainable. At best, it is believed, all that one can hope for is a set of statements of the kind that invite us to support motherhood and apple pie. I would want to claim that there is already enough anecdotal evidence available, for example in the Canberra and New Zealand experiences, to show that people of good will can go a good deal further than this.[16]

Another sceptical reaction is to claim that the push for community involvement has come too late. The community, it is said, is now so absorbed in self-gratification that there is insufficient motivation for public service. Coupled with this, the politicization and industrialization of teachers have gone so far that effective collaboration with the lay public is an illusory ideal. These claims have to be put to further test. Even now every state can produce examples, on the one hand, of some highly encouraging patterns and, on the other, of some failed experiments. At the least we need more action research into the procedures which are most efficacious in achieving the desired results.

A third valid query is whether talk about a value charter implies the authoritarian propagation of the values charter as such in the school classroom. Undoubtedly it does imply that values education is necessary, and that the charter negotiated in a particular region is intended to legitimate some very specific approaches to school administration and curriculum content. At the least students are to be made aware of the importance of values and the impact of world-views and cultural traditions on the society they live in. But what methods of teaching and assessing will be appropriate in the area of values education? We have not been good at this in Australia. How should it be done? It should not be assumed that in asking the question I think either that we have encountered an insuperable obstacle or that we are in the position of having to invent the wheel. There is a considerable and growing literature on values education, admittedly displaying a diverse range of views.[17] We are not without theories to test, but they have not been tested to any great degree in the

Australian context. This query represents, therefore, not a deterrent, but an opportunity.

Notes

1. An earlier era would have substituted for 'mission' such terms as aims and objectives, but in the light of the importation into educational administration of business management terminology more appropriate to the selling of encyclopedias, arising from current political practice at both federal and state levels, which reduces all ideals to economic audits, I seek to remain comprehensible.
2. I have not thought it necessary to provide close documentation of the historical developments which underlie this account. Since the classic pioneering study by A.G. Austin, *Australian Education, 1788–1900* (Melbourne: Pitman, 1961), there has been a steady flow of careful studies filling in the details, associated with the names of such patient scholars as Fogarty, Gregory, Hyams, Lawry, Murray-Smith, Selleck and Turney.
3. *Ibid.*
4. I have discussed these training procedures in more detail in Brian V. Hill (1977) 'Training State School Teachers in New South Wales, 1880–1904' in A.D. Spaull (Ed.), *Australian Teachers*. Melbourne: Macmillan of Australia, pp. 62–80.
5. Lest this judgment be thought too harsh, attention is directed to the symposium on 'Objectivity and Neutrality in Public Education' reported in E.L. French (Ed.) (1964), *Melbourne Studies in Education, 1963*. Melbourne: Melbourne University Press.
6. Herbert Marcuse (1972) *One-Dimensional Man*. London: Abacus.
7. R. Freeman Butts (1957) *Assumptions Underlying Australian Education*. Melbourne: Australian Council for Educational Research.
8. Charles A. Reich (1971) *The Greening of America*. Harmondsworth: Penguin.
9. A contemporary slang term for the young, upwardly mobile professional person.
10. The concept of a 'unit curriculum' is one in which each of the traditional subject areas has been broken up into relatively self-contained modules lasting a term or a semester. Some modules are sequential and oriented to higher study, others to the needs of the early school leaver and so on. Students are encouraged to match their choice of units for study with their real prospects and intentions for the future, rather than taking a more limited range of prestige subjects running through all the years of study in order to produce the final results most conducive to obtaining access to preferred tertiary study or employment. Choice is not necessarily open slather. The Western Australian pattern is to require a minimum number of units to be taken from each of seven 'curriculum components'. These identify major life-concerns such as 'science and technology' and 'personal and vocational awareness'.
11. See C.W. Collins and P. Hughes (1982) *Where Junior Secondary Schools Are Heading*. Melbourne: Australian Council for Educational Research, and Peter

Fensham, Colin Power, David Tripp and Stephen Kemmis (1986) *Alienation in Schooling*. London: Routledge and Kegan Paul.
12 There are some signs that the current industrial push for 'award restructuring' may provide an opportunity for advanced teaching competence to be rewarded.
13 See Brian V. Hill (1988) 'The Brave Experiment: Is State Schooling in Jeopardy?' *Discourse*, 8, 2, pp. 76–96.
14 The possibility is perceptively explored in Margaret Mackie (1977) *Philosophy of Educational Administration*. Brisbane: University of Queensland Press.
15 I have sought to deal with the political realities implied by this recommendation in three articles which were main addresses at a conference of Australian Primary Principals on Community Involvement, published in *The W[estern] A[ustralian] Primary Principal*, 1, August 1985, pp. 5–33.
16 In a book commissioned by the Australian Teachers' Christian Fellowship I recently attempted to identify several very specific areas in which it was clearly likely that tough-minded policy statements could be generated. See Brian V. Hill (1987) *Choosing the Right School*. Sydney: ATCF Books. It may still be an act of faith at this stage to say it *can* be done, but the gamble seems reasonable.
17 Some of my own efforts in this regard are collected in Brian V. Hill (1988) *Values Education in Australian Schools*. Perth: Murdoch University.

Chapter 4

Democracy, Bureaucracy and the Politics of Education

Grant Harman

This chapter aims to explore tensions between democracy and bureaucracy in Australian education from a political perspective. It considers in particular the proposition that in the late nineteenth and early twentieth centuries in Australia government school systems were developed as large bureaucratic systems, but in the last decade there has been considerable divergence from this pattern as attempts have been made to resolve a tension between bureaucratic concerns of consistency, economy and efficiency on the one hand, and emerging democratic demands of participatory decision-making and localized autonomy on the other. In addition, it considers more broadly the extent to which tensions and conflicts in Australian education revolve around ideas of democracy and bureaucracy.

The argument is that the events of the past decade or so with regard to the administration and control of education can be interpreted as a tension between particular democratic ideas and a traditional model of bureaucratic control for education, as developed late last century and early this century in the various Australian colonies and later states. But such an interpretation has limited utility since

> both democracy and bureaucracy are complex concepts with a variety of meanings;
>
> in some senses bureaucratic structures and procedures have been a response to achieve particular democratic ideals, and bureaucracy often works to protect such ideals;
>
> a considerable degree of tension has revolved around competing ideas of both democracy and bureaucracy; and
>
> other factors apart from democracy and bureaucracy are central to recent conflicts about educational governance.

In other words the perspective taken here is that, while the idea of a tension between democracy and bureaucracy has some value in explaining recent conflicts and developments in Australian education, its value as an explanatory device is nevertheless limited, especially if democracy and bureaucracy are conceived as broad 'global' concepts.

The words 'politics' and 'political' are used in various senses in Australia. Sometimes they refer to matters to do with parliament and government; sometimes to matters to do with political parties (i.e. partisan politics); and sometimes to dirty or unfair play in public life. Here I use the terms in a broader sense, as frequently defined by contemporary political scientists, to mean all those processes and institutional mechanisms by which a society attempts to govern itself and resolve fundamental conflicts and disputes. According to Heinz Eulau and James G. March,

> Politics refers to the activities of individuals or groups, from the family to the international organization, as they engage in collective decisions. Although we usually think of politics as involving competing or conflicting leaders, factions or parties, that seek to occupy governing positions in the public arena in order to shape public policies, politics is also found in the government of private associations, business firms, labor unions, churches and universities. (Eulau and March, 1969: 14)

At its core the politics of education is about who runs education and who decides on education policy, about whose interests are being pursued and why, about major conflicts over governance structures and policy, and about how such conflicts are resolved. Understandably, a major focus for the politics of education in Australia is government policy, the roles and actions of ministers and bureaucrats, and the operation of the state and territory education systems. But the politics of education is also concerned with politics within schools, colleges and universities, with interest groups and how they pursue educational objectives, and with broad community values and how conflicts on these are fought about and resolved. In terms of our topic the twin themes of democracy and bureaucracy could be explored across a broad canvas. One interesting exercise, for example, would be to observe tensions between bureaucracy and democracy within teachers' organizations. But space is limited and so our discussion must be selective.

The chapter is structured as follows. First, we will consider the two key concepts of democracy and bureaucracy and their place in Australian education. We will then take a small number of case studies involving

Democracy, Bureaucracy and the Politics of Education

both democracy and bureaucracy to explore in what senses conflict can be interpreted as a basic tension between democracy and bureaucracy.

Democracy and Australian Education

Democratic ideals and ideas about democracy have played quite a significant part in Australian education, but it is important to recognize that over the past hundred years there has been no single democratic ideal. Rather there have been, and are today, many different strands to thinking and aspirations about democracy. The multiplicity of democratic ideals is well played out in Australian education and various conflicts can be interpreted as conflicts between different ideas and forms of democracy. For example, as we will see below, the recent push for greater local participation in school governance can be interpreted as a push for participatory forms of government over representative forms.

Whatever definition we might take of democracy, its full form is seldom found. According to MacIver, 'Democracy is a form of government that is never completely achieved' (MacIver, 1965: 132). 'Democracy' is an ancient political word, which means simply government by the people. In classical Athens, where the word originated, democracy meant rule by the *demos* or people. But in the modern world the word 'democracy' carries with it related ideas about popular government and popular sovereignty, about representative as well as participatory forms of government, and about both republican and constitutional government.

In the ancient world pure democracy was held in suspicion, both by aristocratic philosophers such as Socrates and by proponents of mixed government such as Aristotle. Because democracy involved the rule of the people, and the people included the poor and the unpropertied, some influential thinkers rejected the idea of democracy since it would mean rule by the undisciplined masses. Plato associated democracy with the subordination of reason to passion, while Aristotle identified it with immoderation and instability (Dahl, 1963: 26–7). Some of these concerns have affected our thinking about democracy and how we have structured political institutions. For example, schools have been asked to take on a major role in political education to try to develop an informed public, while various checks and balances have been provided in political institutions to guard against hasty and irrational decisions by the population.

In its early modern incarnation as social contract theory, the democratic ideal challenged traditional dictatorship and the divine right of kings. Its argument was that the ultimate source of all government authority lay with individuals, possessed of both natural liberty and natural rights. In its more modern form, since the eighteenth century, democratic theory concentrated first on extension of the franchise, popular sovereignty, equality of all before the law, elected governments and the self-determination of major groups of people. With the winning of universal suffrage in the West at the beginning of the twentieth century, democratic theory and practice turned to issues of democratic nation-building and then shifted from purely political questions to socio-economic ones, about production, distribution, property-holding and class. According to Barber, in recent times the

> relationship between formal and legal equality and political democracy on the one hand, and the systems economic production and distribution on the other, have ... come to dominate scholarly discussion as well as ideological politics. The 'people's democracies' of the second and third worlds assert their democratic legitimacy in the language of economics, pointing to their putatively egalitarian modes of ownership of capital, production and distribution, their guarantees of employment, and their devolution to public planning, while they neglect or even denigrate the role of multi-party electoral systems, political and legal rights, and parliamentary politics. The older democracies of the West, relying on traditional and legal language, emphasize electoral and civic rights and the formal liberty and equality of the political system; if they associate democracy with economics it is only in as much as they hope to identify the freedom of the private market with the freedom of a democratic political regime, in the manner of Milton Freidman or Frederick Hayek. (Barber, 1987: 116)

Even in Australia over the past hundred years or so there have been different strains of democratic thinking, and different groups have placed particular emphasis on one aspect of democratic thinking over another. Thinking on democracy has often been somewhat confused and seldom well articulated, but it has centred on some key issues. These are set out below.

Who Rules? Behind this question in Australia often lie conflicting theories about human nature and citizenship. 'Democrats' believe that people possess the capacity for self-rule, but others see the need for competence or enlightenment. Around these issues debate about school boards has sometimes revolved. Do members of the community have the competence to take key decisions about the governance of the local school? Are they in the position to make judgments about appointment of a principal and staff? As noted earlier, a good deal of the impetus for social studies curriculum (and in an earlier age for inclusion of civics in the curriculum) has come from a perceived need to develop a well informed and responsible citizenship. Other tensions relate to whether decisions by popular government should be made by simple majorities, and what notice should be taken of substantial minority interests. On various issues about non-government schools, minority interests have vocally demanded concessions.

Within What Limits and Scope? Some groups demand the extension of the powers of popular government, even if this means restricting the liberty of individuals to some extent. In the education domain the debate has often centred on the extent to which compulsion should be applied to various aspects of schooling, and the extent to which the liberty of individuals should be restricted for the good of the total society.

For What Ends? In democratic thinking there is a basic conflict between the interests of the community and the interests of the individual, or more generally between liberty (individual rights) and equality (social justice). This conflict is at the core of many of the policy debates over such matters as equity programs, schemes to give special attention to gifted children and government funding for non-government schools.

By Direct or Indirect Means? The basic choice for democratic government is rule by direct popular methods or through representative institutions. In its early manifestations democracy was generally understood as a form of communal self-government, with direct representation by citizens. In response to the scale and complexity of modern societies, representative institutions were devised, but representative democracy is often criticized as another form of oligarchy or as rule by élites (Pateman, 1970). The pressure for increased community participation in education, especially at local levels, can be viewed as one quest for a measure of direct popular government to supplement representative government.

Under Which Conditions Is Democracy Mentioned? Traditionally there has been a variety of views about what special conditions sustain democracy: small governmental units, liberty and free choice, equality and social justice, public ownership and common goods. Underpinning debates on key issues in education are different views about what is desirable or necessary to sustain democratic government. Rousseau, for example, saw democracy as being dependent on special conditions, including a small state where citizens met face-to-face, equality in rank and fortune and an austerity of life and mores. Some of the thinking about decentralization in the administration of Australian education appears to be in that tradition (Turner, 1960). But other writing about educational administration in Australia had focused on the role of equality and social justice in democracy along the lines articulated by the Canadian political theorist C.B. Macpherson (1973), and so has looked favourably upon public ownership and common goods as foundations for the political and legal equality on which democracy rests. It is likely that a substantial strand of opposition to 'state aid' in the 1960s and 1970s was based on such ideas, although it was seldom well articulated along these lines.

Bureaucracy and Australian Education

With respect to Australian education the word 'bureaucracy' has a number of different meanings. First, it is used in a technical sense to mean a system of administration carried out on a continuous basis according to set rules and by trained professionals. This meaning comes from Max Weber, who was responsible for establishing it firmly as the dominant meaning of bureaucracy in twentieth century social science. Weber noted that administration by professional experts was becoming increasingly prevalent in all political systems across Western Europe, and indeed in all organizations where complex and large administrative tasks were undertaken.

Weber defined bureaucracy as a system of administration with the following characteristics: hierarchy (each official has a clearly defined responsibility and is answerable to a superior); impersonality (the work is conducted according to set rules, without arbitrariness or favouritism, and a written record is kept of transactions); continuity (the administrative offices constitute full-time salaried occupations, with security of tenure and prospects of regular advancement for incumbents); and expertise (officials are selected on merit, are trained for their function, and control access to knowledge and information stored in files). According to Weber, together these characteristics maximize efficiency, and make bureaucracy essential for complex industrial societies (Beetham, 1987: 48; Weber, 1968).

While Weber's classic definition of bureaucracy is that used fairly generally in specialized scholarly discussion of educational administration in Australia, the word 'bureaucracy' has other usages in Australian education. It is frequently used in a derogatory sense, to indicate characteristic vices of administration in many large organizations, such as 'red tape', unresponsiveness, delay. It is sometimes used also to refer to the corps of professional administrators as a social group, especially administrators located in head offices of large education departments. In many discussions about educational administration in Australia bureaucracy is used in a derogatory sense. This has been particularly so in the case of those arguing over the past couple of decades for a greater degree of decentralization and devolution for reform of bureaucratic structures, and for a greater degree of community participation. Bureaucracy has also been used in a derogatory sense by those criticizing particular decisions of education departments.

Apart from this derogatory usage, bureaucracy is sometimes used in Australian education to mean the central office of education departments, or the senior level of officials. The outside view often is that this 'bureaucracy' speaks with a single voice, has its own view of education policy questions and often dominates over ministers. Of course, the reality is different. While there is often a high degree of shared views at senior levels in any large organization, and particularly in one in which outside recruitment at senior levels has not been common, there is often a strong measure of competition and some degree of conflict between different administrative units. Further, over recent years senior officers have complained of their relative lack of power compared to that of ministers (Harman, Wirt and Beare, 1987).

In the main social science disciplines and subdisciplines, there has been active debate over various aspects and characteristics of bureaucracy. In organization theory, for example, a central question has been whether Weber's identified characteristics do maximize efficiency. In sociology one major interest has been with bureaucracy as a new social category, representative of a new middle class distinct from both capital and labour. In economics a major interest has been in the relationship of bureaucracy to a free market approach, while within political science the main interest has been whether bureaucracy poses a threat to democratic principles of open and accountable government. Beetham notes:

> Theories of democracy can be distinguished according to the strategies they propose for overcoming ... [the] problem of bureaucratic power. Elitist-oriented theories stress the role of political leadership and advocate measures designed to secure political control of the bureaucracy, such as the political appointment of top civil servants, or the creation of political advisers to Ministers. Theorists of open government advocate public access

to government documents — on the principle that ministers as well as administrators have a vested interest in secrecy. More participatory theorists look to popular involvement in scrutinizing administration at the local level, on the grounds that the character of policy cannot be separated from the manner of its execution. These positions are not mutually exclusive. Together they suggest that the requirements of a democratic system of administration cannot be simply derived from a general model of bureaucracy. (Beetham, 1987: 50)

In Australian education the debates on bureaucracy generally have not been of a high scholarly or theoretical nature, but they have concentrated on a number of issues. One theme is about efficient operation in a context of growth and complexity in functions. To a large extent the major reports of the last decade or so, up to the recent Scott Reports for New South Wales schools and TAFE, are about the reform of bureaucratic structures to achieve greater efficiency. Other themes have been the reduction of power of senior bureaucrats through the establishment of education commissions, state boards and control of the education system by a statutory body including community and teacher representatives; about more activist roles for ministers with their own staff of advisers; and about efforts to increase community participation and local control through the establishment of school councils, school boards and regional councils.

Democracy and the Development of Centralized School Systems

We now turn to the establishment late last century in each of the Australian colonies of highly centralized, 'bureaucratic' school systems and their development until recently. The history of these school systems has been well documented, but the key question to explore here is whether these systems represented a triumph for bureaucratic thinking over democratic ideals.

Various local and overseas writers of the past three or four decades have been strongly critical of the highly centralized, administrative model that developed in Australia. The writing of a number of Australians (e.g. Turner, 1960) suggests that behind their criticisms was a view that such arrangements were not appropriate in a democratic society, as there was no real role for the local community or region in educational governance.

Some overseas writers, however, were much more critical and more explicit about their concerns. In the 1950s, for example, Professor Freeman Butts of Columbia University in New York visited Australia and was repelled by the high degree of centralization in the governance of education. In his widely read book, *Assumptions Underlying Australian Education*, he criticized the high degree of administrative centralization from several points of view: one was that of democracy. He wrote:

> The basic questions are these: 'are decisions made by a relatively few people in a centralized system more likely to be democratic or undemocratic? Is centralization necessarily democratic or undemocratic? Will an exclusively centralized system of decision-making ultimately serve the cause of democracy in a society at large?' (Butts, 1955: 16)

He went on to ask whether Australians

> miss something of the vitality, initiative, creativeness and variety that would come if the doors and windows of discussion were kept more open all the way up and down the educational edifice. The two-way flow of education ideas might lead to more broadly based decisions, and therefore more democratic ones. (Butts, 1955: 17)

Butts' criticisms were taken to heart by many Australian educators at the time, who tended not to examine too closely the value position from which Butts wrote, or to appreciate the quite fundamental differences between Australian and American social and political attitudes. Similarly, while many Australian educators today appreciate increasingly the factors that operated to produce the highly centralized school systems, they do not always appreciate the social and political forces which gave rise to these arrangements.

The various Australian colonies in the second half of the nineteenth century faced considerable problems of vast distance, limited resources and a thinly spread and scattered population in a society where the role of local government was severely limited. Hence it was not surprising that public education in Australia developed distinctly differently from that in the United States and Britain. What is not often appreciated is that Australian ideas of democracy also developed differently, and these ideas reinforced the pressures towards the use of highly centralized administrative models for education and a range of other government functions. Partridge comments that in the mid-nineteenth century,

> one begins to hear in colonial politics the themes of Australian democracy as it subsequently evolved — a case for the interests and needs of the ordinary man, a distrust of privilege and superiority, an assumption that it was the business of Government to see to the welfare of the common people. Henry Parkes, the dominant personality in New South Wales politics in the seventies and eighties and the author of the important Education Acts of 1866 and 1880, was a radical and a demagogue who cultivated the appeal to the simple rights and needs of ordinary men and women; in his advocacy of state-provided education, he linked State education with the idea of democracy in the sense of looking after the interests and well-being of the common people. (Partridge, 1968: 19)

Butts and many critics of the highly centralized school systems as being undemocratic failed to grasp that the Australian school systems of the nineteenth century were largely in harmony with, and were strongly reinforced by, a particular Australian line of democratic thinking. It was a school system with a high regard for ordinary people and their needs, wherever they might live, that emphasized equality of services across a vast colony or state, that stressed common academic standards, and that provided bureaucratic rules to protect teachers from the whims of local communities. Writing in the late 1960s, Partridge observed,

> Perhaps the least that can be said for Australian public education is that one does not find the disparities between schools of different regions and districts that one finds in the United States or even in the United Kingdom; the quality of schools, the wages, competence and morale of teachers, do not vary according to the resources of a district or the willingness of state, county or district authorities to spend money on public schools. (Partridge, 1968: 66)

Funds for public schools came from the state budget, there was a state-wide teaching service, curricula were state-wide and there were common public examinations and standards. As Partridge has noted, the centralized system was successful 'in developing schools and teaching of a reasonable and uniform quality throughout very large areas and often in universally difficult circumstances' (Partridge, 1968: 69).

American critics like Butts also failed to understand Australian thinking about local communities when they said that the Australian way of administering schools revealed a lack of confidence in the local community. Australian democratic thinking has been concerned with particular ideas of social equity and with particular ideas about the responsibility of government to pursue such goals and to provide for the needs of the population. The same thinking that produced the notion of the basic wage also produced the idea of a minimum or basic standard in education. Above all else, the first objective of public education for nineteenth century colonial governments was to provide a minimum standard of primary education for the mass of children. Later state governments proceeded to establish secondary education and then to extend their concern to tertiary education. But for a long period a basic or minimum education up to the age of 14 years for the large majority of children was at the core of public educational effort. This was the kind of educational provision expected by the great majority of the community. Further, as various writers have noted, the Australian community of the nineteenth century had a great talent for, and liking of, bureaucracy. To a large extent this liking has continued. A.F. Davies observed in the 1960s that Australians 'have a characteristic talent for bureaucracy' (Davies, 1964: 4). 'We take a somewhat hesitant pride in this', he wrote,

> since it runs counter not only to the archaic and cherished image of ourselves as ungovernable, if not actually, lawless people but also to our civics of liberalism which accords to bureaucracy only a small and rather shady place.... But in practice our gift — to be seen in *statis nascendi* at any state school sports — is exercised in a massive scale in government, economy and social institutions. Of course bureaucracy pervades most modern societies — it is the price of complex organization — but Australian demands for security and equality have been unusually strong. (Davies, 1964: 4)

Instead of solving their own problems, nineteenth century Australian communities came to look increasingly to governments to provide solutions on a whole range of problems from selling farm produce and developing transport to providing roads, hospitals and education for their children.

Of course, at times there were tensions between the way the various education bureaucracies worked and the democratic ideals of citizens. Local communities were sometimes annoyed with particular bureaucratic decisions, and often had to lobby hard to get the quality and type of

Democracy and Bureaucracy

educational provision they considered they deserved. But by and large their response was not to demand different administrative arrangements for education, but to try to change or influence particular government or bureaucratic decisions. To a large extent the notions of consistency, economy and efficiency associated with the various education bureaucracies were not at odds with key elements of late nineteenth and early twentieth century democratic thinking. The bureaucratic structures that developed were one response to particular democratic ideals.

Participation and Local Autonomy

Over the past two decades there have been various moves to secure increased community participation in the governance of government schools, and increased local autonomy in control. During the 1960s and early 1970s there was a strong and vigorous push in the ACT to secure not only a school system independent of the New South Wales Department of Education, but a school system without many undesirable 'bureaucratic' features of the New South Wales government school system, and allowing for a high degree of independence for individual schools, for community involvement in governance and for increased flexibility. This pressure led in 1973 to the establishment of the ACT Schools Authority, with a distinctively new and different set of arrangements for the governance of government schools. This pressure for change was not restricted to the ACT, but has been noticeable in a number of states, particularly Victoria. It was also pushed along by the 1973 Karmel Report on schools and by the work of the Schools Commission established by the Federal Government.

The question to address now is to what extent these pressures for change can be interpreted as a tension between the bureaucratic concerns of consistency, economy and efficiency, on the one hand, and democratic demands about participation and local control, on the other. The evidence suggests that this may be one reasonable interpretation, but that it is by no means the only one.

In the case of the movement for change in the ACT there were strong criticisms of the administration of ACT government schools by the New South Wales Department of Education. In particular, there was a feeling that Sydney was too remote, that the ACT had a distinctive character which the New South Wales Department was unable to recognize administratively, and that a more flexible system of education was required. The movement began with the city's Parents' and Citizens' Associations. A letter to the President of ACT Council of Parents' and

Citizens' Associations, signed by ten parents from the Campbell Primary School, expressed dissatisfaction with the education their children were receiving and called for change. This letter listed a number of problems including 'the monolithic, highly centralized structure of the Department of Education in each state, resulting in an approach to children, teachers and parents which is, at best, impersonal, and, at worst, inconsiderate and inefficient' (Blakers, 1978: 31). This eventually led to the establishment of a citizens' committee, chaired by Sir George Currie, which produced an influential report recommending separate control of education and a new 'system of education appropriate to the community and characterized by the flexibility and variety which are a reflection of varying individual needs' (Burnett, 1978: 12). The Currie Report also recommended that schools have a large measure of independence, with a considerable degree of variety being fostered. Each school would have a council representing staff, parents and the education authority to help the principal's administration. A widely representative board would run the system, thus giving the community a voice at highest administrative and policy levels. This approach was supported by *The Canberra Times*, which strongly favoured local community participation and said that 'bureaucrats must be prepared to divest themselves of some of their control' (Burnett, 1978: 15–16). This model was, in essence, the one adopted a few years later when the ACT school system was set up.

Similarly in Victoria in the 1970s and early 1980s there was substantial criticism of aspects of bureaucratic governance and demands for increased participation. School councils were established in 1975, and the reorganization of the Victorian Education Department initiated by the Liberal government in part was driven by demands for increased participation and greater devolution. With the change of government in the early 1980s, the rhetoric about increased devolution and participation continued and was expressed in a number of ministerial papers. One stated: 'The development of a responsive education system can best be achieved by providing participatory and consultative mechanisms not only with the school, regional and central levels but also between these levels' (Blackmore, 1986: 32).

As already noted, the Karmel Report of the Interim Committee for the Australian Schools Commission of 1973 also explicitly argued for increased devolution of administrative responsibility. Its view was that

> Responsibility should be devolved as far as possible upon the people involved in the actual task of schooling in consultation with the parents of the pupils whom they teach and, at several levels, with the students themselves. Its belief in this grass-roots

Democracy and Bureaucracy

> approach to the control of schools reflects a conviction that responsibility will be most effectively discharged where the people entrusted with making decisions are also the people responsible for carrying them out. (Interim Committee for the Australian Schools Commission 1973: 10)

Behind this statement may well have lain particular democratic values, but the argument could be interpreted as one about efficiency and not necessarily anti-bureaucratic.

While this movement of the last two decades can be interpreted as a tension between traditional bureaucratic governance and democratic demands for participation and local autonomy, other elements have been involved, thus suggesting other interpretations. First, the movement for change in part has been a reaction to problems associated with rapid increases in the size of state school systems and with an inability of the traditional bureaucratic structures to cope. In the ACT, for example, the impetus for change came mainly from problems associated with class sizes, lack of adequately trained teachers and administrative inefficiency and insensitivity. Similarly in Victoria, according to Blackmore, the introduction of school councils and other aspects of the initial phases of decentralization and participation by teachers, parents and students 'were largely administrative solutions to a monolithic, unresponsive bureaucracy, with the Regions administering a centralist system' (Blackmore, 1986: 29–30). Blackmore also says that these changes 'served in some ways to defuse the increasing teacher activism and allowed the development of the alternative community schools away from direct responsibility of head office' (Blackmore, 1986: 30). Thus it could be argued that the participation movement was as much a protest about, and reaction to, bureaucratic inefficiency as a clash between bureaucratic and democratic ideals.

Another explanation is that the move for participation and local autonomy was largely a political movement of influential élites to seek more power in the control of education. With increasing levels of formal education and a growing sense of identity, the teaching profession was keen to challenge the power of bureaucrats, from senior levels down to the level of school principal. In various ways the teachers' organizations in each state and the territories from about the 1950s secured formal representation on various departmental committees, but teachers wished for more power. Thus in some states they pressed for education commissions with teacher representation to run public school systems, and at school level for councils or boards having teacher representation to challenge the autocratic power of principals. In addition, various well educated groups active in parent associations pressed for a say. In the ACT, for example, the movement for an independent education authority was largely led by well educated parents active in Parents' and Citizens' Associations. While there was strong community support as measured by attendance at meetings, letters to the press and editorial support from *The Canberra Times*, there was by no means a mass movement. Similarly, in Victoria, while the participation movement was strong, it was largely a movement of well educated élites. Further, in Victoria in 1980, when submissions were called for on the Green Paper produced under Alan Hunt as Minister, many schools and school councils argued against further decentralization and devolution, and particularly against increased powers being forced on school councils. The submission from staff of Elwood Primary School, according to a summary prepared by departmental officers, asserted:

- No evidence that regionalization has improved schools and the education system. Concern that the regions will form an expensive bureaucracy.
- School council members are not competent to select teachers or principals, nor do they have the time. (Harman, 1985: 170)

Similarly, the Regency Park Primary School argued:

- Error in assuming that parents wish to be involved to the degree stated in the Green Paper.
- Even if parents were willing to be involved, they would not be capable of management and staff selection. This would open the way for pressure groups to exert influence on staff and principal. (Harman, 1985: 170)

Thus an alternative explanation is to be found in élite theory and the interest group activities of particular élites.

Another possible interpretation is that the tension was not between bureaucratic characteristics and democratic ideals, but between different ideas of bureaucracy and of democracy. While various professional educators and teachers' associations and community groups were highly critical of many features of the control of schools, most wanted reform and variations rather than the abolition of bureaucratic arrangements along the traditional Weberian model. Some wanted smaller administrative units, some wanted more flexibility and some wanted greater efficiency and responsiveness; but few argued for non-bureaucratic models. Most wanted reform and change of the bureaucratic model. Further, while supporting key elements in the push for greater participation, most of the teachers' unions were suspicious of too much power being given to parents (especially over the appointment of principals and teachers, and over curriculum) and were strongly in favour of retention of state-wide education systems, with a state-wide teaching service. Similarly, with the demand for participation, in many cases the pressure could be interpreted as a tension between participatory and representative notions of democracy.

Democracy, Bureaucracy and the Politics of Education

The major conflicts in the politics of education in Australia in recent years have involved different tensions about democracy and bureaucracy. But it is somewhat limiting to think of the politics of education as simply or mainly a conflict between the characteristics of traditional Weberian bureaucracy and democratic ideals.

The major political conflicts over schools have centred on questions of educational governance (who runs education), on questions about educational processes and educators (what should be taught, how and by whom?) and on the goals and benefits of education (what is the purpose of schooling? who benefits and who should benefit?). Behind these conflicts lie various value positions about democracy and the Australian ideas of fairness, about how a democratic society should organize itself, about the relations in a democratic society between education on the one hand and economy and industry on the other. Behind the conflicts also lie different ideas about bureaucracy and what kind of governmental organization is appropriate, necessary and desirable for the control of public schooling. Thus to a significant extent the conflicts of education politics are about different value positions concerning democracy and bureaucracy. But they are also about other value positions related to such issues as the purposes of schooling, morals, the role of the family, individual liberty and so on. In addition, the politics of education is about the competition for scarce resources and about the efforts of different interest groups and political actors to win more power, position and prestige for themselves. Further, while there are currently strong pressures towards localizing and decentralizing public education, as Connors (1989) has pointed out there are also strong pressures towards centralization and nationalization. The pressures towards centralization and nationalization are influenced by different thinking about democracy, bureaucracy and other values than those that help drive the movement for local autonomy and participation.

One conclusion suggested by this discussion is that in trying to interpret educational politics we need to go beyond seeking a single theory or single proposition to explain events. Political movements tend to be multidimensional in character, and it is often possible legitimately and reasonably to interpret the same complex movement in different ways. We need to explore alternative explanations and assess carefully the evidence to support each in our attempts to find the most reasonable explanation of particular political movements.

References

BARBER, BENJAMIN R. (1987) 'Democracy.' In DAVID MILLER (Ed.), *The Blackwell Encyclopaedia of Political Thought*. Oxford: Blackwell Reference.
BEETHAM, DAVID (1987) 'Bureaucracy.' In DAVID MILLER (Ed.), *The Blackwell Encyclopaedia of Political Thought*. Oxford: Blackwell Reference.
BLACKMORE, JILL (1986) 'Tensions to Be Resolved in Participation and School-based Decision Making.' *Educational Administration Review*, 4, 1, 19–68.
BLAKERS, CATHERINE (1978) 'A Participant Observer View of the Establishment of the Authority.' In PHILLIP HUGHES and WILLIAM MULFORD (Eds), *The Development of an Independent Education Authority*. Hawthorn, Vic.: Australian Council for Educational Research.
BURNETT, CLIFFORD (1978) 'How the ACT Schools Authority Came into Being: A Case-Study of the Records.' In PHILLIP HUGHES and WILLIAM MULFORD (Eds), *The Development of an Independent Education Authority*. Hawthorn, Vic.: Australian Council for Educational Research.
BUTTS, R. FREEMAN (1955) *Assumptions Underlying Australian Education*. Melbourne: Australian Council for Educational Research.
CONNORS, LYNDSAY (1989) 'Futures for Schooling in Australia: Nationalization, Privatization or Unification.' *Occasional Paper No. 13*, Deakin: Australian College of Education.
DAHL, ROBERT A. (1963) *Modern Political Analysis*. Englewood Cliffs, N.J.: Prentice-Hall.
DAVIES, A.F. (1964) *Australian Democracy: An Introduction to the Political System*. Melbourne: Longmans, Green.
EULAU, HEINZ and MARCH, JAMES G. (1969) *Political Science*. Englewood Cliffs, N.J.: Prentice-Hall.
HARMAN, GRANT (1985) 'The White Paper and Planned Organisational Change.' In MURRAY FRAZER, JEFFREY DUNSTAN and PHILIP CREED (Eds), *Perspectives on Organisational Change: Lessons from Education*. Melbourne: Longman Cheshire.
HARMAN, GRANT, WIRT, FREDERICK M. and BEARE, HEDLEY (1987) 'Changing Roles of Australian Chief Executives at the State Level.' In WILLIAM LOWE BOYD and DON SMART (Eds), *Education Policy in Australia and America: Comparative Perspectives*. Lewes: Falmer Press.
INTERIM COMMITTEE FOR THE AUSTRALIAN SCHOOLS COMMISSION (1973) *Schools in Australia*. (Karmel Report). (Chairman: Prof. P.H. KARMEL). Canberra: Australian Government Publishing Service.

MacIver, R.M. (1965) *The Web of Government*. New York: The Free Press.
Macpherson, C.B. (1973) *Democratic Theory*. Oxford: Clarendon Press.
Partridge, P.H. (1968) *Society, Schools and Progress in Australia*. Oxford: Pergamon.
Pateman, C. (1970) *Participation and Democracy Theory*. Cambridge: Cambridge University Press.
Turner, I.S. (1960) 'A Plea for Decentralization in Australian Education.' In E.L. French (Ed.), *Melbourne Studies in Education*. Melbourne: Melbourne University Press.
Weber, M. (1968 ed.) *Economy and Society*. Trans E. Fischoff et al. New York: Bedminster.

Chapter 5

Governing Australia's Public Schools: Community Participation, Bureaucracy and Devolution

Lyndsay G. Connors and James F. McMorrow

In the face of demands for greater democracy, efficiency and accountability, public education structures that have been in place for over a century are undergoing a major reconstruction. These demands have converged into forces for devolution to school communities of responsibilities for aspects of school governance that were previously the preserve of centralized state bureaucracies. For over a century these same demands underpinned the establishment of highly centralized structures and processes for governing public education systems in Australia.

The purpose of this chapter is to examine the context in which this apparent volte-face is being executed, and to explore the educational and political implications for public schooling. It considers the context in which demands for greater community and parent participation in school governance have been accommodated by, and subsumed in, current conventional wisdom about school effectiveness and educational management.

Community participation is specifically about the claims of non-professionals to an active role in shaping educational policy and practice. These include parents and, in some circumstances, students, as well as groups and institutions in the local and wider community.

Various terms are commonly used to describe aspects of community participation in education.

> *Community*: in the context of operating within particular communities, communities may be defined in terms of common characteristics, purposes and interests — geographic, political, economic, racial, cultural, philosophical and religious. 'Community' can also

be used to distinguish 'lay' from 'professional' status. Both definitions of 'community' are valid in particular contexts.

Community involvement: denotes some form or level of inclusion of non-professionals in the operation of a school or system, or both. This may be formal or informal, pro-active or re-active, subordinate or dominant.

Community participation: implies a formal and active role in educational decision-making, ranging from advisory to deliberative. 'Community participation' is the hard edge of 'community involvement'.

Devolution: the focusing of responsibility for the governance of schooling at the local school level.

These terms are recent additions to the discourse of Australian education where, as in other areas of public policy, the tradition of governance and administration has been one of centralized control and provision in the context of Australia's political development as a federation. This tradition was reinforced by demographic and economic imperatives, arising from the size and distribution of the population and the organization of the economic system around state-based power structures, reflecting their colonial origins.

In Australia the introduction of mass elementary education reflected social, economic and humanitarian concerns: the need to control and improve social and moral behaviour, especially in the highly stratified colonial society; the need for a reasonably regimented and literate work force in an industrializing economy; and the liberal, humanitarian and egalitarian demands for mass education as a foundation for individual and social enlightenment and development. From potentially conflicting perspectives these forces converged into a rationale for centralized systems of educational governance, characterized by paternalism, uniformity and regulation.

As compulsory education became an accepted feature of community life from the early part of the twentieth century, parent and citizen organizations began to form around many public schools. These organizations symbolized growing community recognition of the importance of schooling and civic pride in the local school itself. Although precluded from any direct role or authority in their children's education, parents concentrated on fund-raising activities that contributed to the provision of libraries, equipment, school prizes, ground improvements and excursions, as well as to the morale of teaching staff, students and parents themselves. From the 1960s the nature of collective parent action, and the understandings and principles on which it had rested for so long, began to change dramatically. The success of public school systems in producing a literate and articulate 'laity', with corresponding expectations, embodied the seeds of challenge to their governance.

The first effective challenge to paternalistic bureaucracy, however, came from teachers and their professional and industrial organizations. The claims of teachers for a more direct and definitive role in educational decision-making generally opened the way for other challengers, with far-reaching effects on the credibility and legitimacy of education bureaucracies.

Much of the social philosophy and literature of the time questioned the dehumanizing effects of large-scale organizations and provided a rationale for devolving the control of institutions and services to those most directly affected. This found expression in the early 1970s in several public school systems. Regulations expanding the role of existing school councils were promulgated in the 1973 Education Act in South Australia, following the 1971 report, *Education in South Australia* (Committee of Enquiry, 1971). In 1973 the Australian Capital Territory (ACT) Schools Authority was established in interim form. The new authority embodied the principle of devolution of significant decision-making powers to schools, vested in popularly elected school boards. In addition, the ACT system incorporated a central council with parent, teacher and community members, as well as ministerial nominees. In Victoria the Education (Schools Councils) Act of 1975 required all public schools to set up representative schools councils, providing a choice among models which varied in the extent to which they took on decision-making responsibilities formerly exercised at the centre. In other states opportunities increased for classroom teachers and parents to participate in decision-making through less formal structures and processes.

The social and political philosophy which underpinned the devolution of decision-making powers to schools in the public school systems of South Australia, the ACT and Victoria also found expression at the national level during the 1970s. The Whitlam government's agenda of nationally led social reform in many areas formerly the preserve of states entailed community level responsibility for, and participation in, implementation.

It was in these circumstances that the Commonwealth began to establish a more direct role in schooling in response to inadequacies and inequalities in resources and outcomes. The Interim Committee for the Australian Schools Commission, established by the Whitlam government, provided an influential voice for community participation in schooling. In the Interim Committee's report, *Schools in Australia* (1973), the dominant economic perspectives of the expansionist 1950s gave way to social concerns and sociological perspectives which emphasized the needs and interests of the direct participants in schooling (Johnston, 1983: 20).

These values were developed by the policy advice of the Schools Commission in its early years. In particular, it was the Commission's programs for schools, such as the Disadvantaged Schools Program, the Innovations Program and the Professional Development Program, that provided the rationale and the resources necessary to foster and sustain action and debate about community participation. These programs maintained their momentum as agents of social and communal reform throughout the late 1970s and the 1980s. With the return of the conservative Coalition government, however, there began a process of accommodating the concepts and rhetoric of community participation in the notion of individualized choice among diverse forms of schooling.

The dominant economic problems of the 1980s have subsumed these social and philosophical emphases. Public policy in education, as elsewhere, has promoted public expenditure restraint, leading in turn to an emphasis on targeting public funds on specific goals and demonstrable outcomes. The other arm of this policy has been to reduce barriers to private expenditure within the public education system, and to place the authority and responsibility for education management with the 'consumers' rather than the 'producers' of public education. Within education systems the response to economic rationalism has been to promote a form of 'guided democracy': with educational goals, standards and guidelines being centrally determined and monitored; with responsibility for making decisions about how these standards are to be met being placed with local school authorities; and with communities being encouraged to hold schools and professionals accountable on the basis of standardized and comparative assessments of schools' performance.

Community participation in schooling had by the late 1980s become an arm of policies for economic reform, in contrast with earlier social and democratic reformist objectives. Understanding this change requires a consideration of the implications of both the educational and the political dimensions of community participation in schooling.

Educational Implications

Educational arguments for community participation in schooling have developed around a range of themes: home–school relationships, school-community links, the school as a learning community, preparation for democratic citizenship, educational diversity and effective accountability.

These arguments were perhaps most influentially developed in the public advice of the Interim Committee for the Australian Schools Commission, *Schools in Australia*, and of the Schools Commission itself.

Home–School Relationships

Schools in Australia argued that children learned most effectively when there was a constructive relationship between home and school, and that the major influence of parents and home background on children's learning should be recognized and built upon by schools. The Interim Committee argued that action was needed, particularly in schools serving the poorest communities, to break down barriers between home and school and to support communities in articulating the needs of their children and having them met by schools and systems. Public school parent organizations have developed this argument as a rationale for structures and processes that enable parents generally to exert a collective influence on public education policy at all levels — school, system and national — in addition to their involvement as individual parents in the schooling of their own children (Brown *et al.*, 1987).

Community–School Links

The Interim Committee also argued that effective learning required schools to operate within the 'real world' of their local communities. Schools should both make better use of the educational resources of their communities and share their own resources more widely to break down the isolation of schools, teachers and students from their local and wider communities. This view found expression in increasing community use of school buildings and facilities, and in school design incorporating social, cultural and recreational amenities.

The School as a Learning Community

The notion of each school being a learning community developed from the 'progressive' education tradition, which emphasized that students learned most effectively when they related to each other and to their teachers and parents within an 'organic' community (Coleman and Hoffer, 1987; Connell *et al.*, 1982). According to this view, schools needed freedom to create their own holistic environment for learning with a

Democracy and Bureaucracy

coherent relationship between values, resources, curriculum content, pedagogy and school climate. Such a community could be 'open' or 'closed', either interacting with, or withdrawing from, the general community.

Education for Democracy

Part of the educational rationale for community participation in schooling has arisen from the argument that, to learn effectively to become active and informed citizens of a democracy, students need direct experience of democratic processes in the classroom and the school. Teaching and learning processes based on authoritarian relationships among administrators, teachers, parents and students were regarded as inappropriate preparation for active citizenship. Within the classroom, democratic or 'progressive' practices were seen to be consistent with effective learning generally. These 'child-centred' practices emphasized discovery learning, problem-solving, negotiation and communication among teachers and learners. This view embodied a challenge to the centralized control of knowledge that had characterized public education in Australia. It also affirmed the autonomy and influence of classroom teachers as professionals in their own right.

Educational Diversity

Schools in Australia (1973) articulated a view of community participation in schooling that emphasized the pluralist nature of Australian society and the intrinsic value of educational diversity and choice. It argued that no single pattern of schooling was necessarily best, and that highly centralized state bureaucracies had stifled the motivation and creativity of teachers and learners in the public school system particularly; devolution of decision-making responsibility to schools would 'enable a hundred flowers to bloom' (2.10). In particular, the Interim Committee stated that it valued the diversity represented in the existence of non-government schools. This view was reinforced by subsequent reports of the Schools Commission, in which the educational rationale for community participation and devolution of decision-making responsibility was transformed into arguments for parental choice among school (Schools Commission, 1975).

Opposition to centralized bureaucratic control of schooling brought together parents opposed to compulsory schooling, claiming a democratic right to educate their own children at home; those who regarded the bureaucracy itself as unrepresentative of the Australian community and, therefore, resistant to changing social and educational aspirations; and those who believed that the pluralism of Australian society required the development of schools controlled by particular groups in the community to give expression to diverse educational needs and philosophies, including those based on differences arising from social class, religion, ethnicity, race, culture and gender.

Educational Accountability

The forces for community participation in schools in the 1980s reflect the predominance of economic objectives in the context of Australia's declining economic fortunes and the resultant political implications. In this view schooling is characterized as having been unduly controlled and influenced by the 'producers', namely professional educators in schools and bureaucracies, who successfully obtained significant public resources for schools, while resisting traditional forms of public accountability such as inspectorates and external examinations. In contrast, the 'consumer' model for schooling emphasizes the rights of parents, in particular, to determine the value of schooling, to control policy directions through the expression of choice among diverse forms of schooling, and to make professionals directly accountable to parents at school level.

The principal rationale behind this view is that school improvement is most likely to occur where parents are able to move their children freely between schools, since schools unable to convince sufficient parents that they are providing an effective educational program will not remain viable. This 'market' view of schooling requires a flow of information about relative performance and utility, in the form of standardized information on educational performance and outcomes. Devolution of authority to school level, rather than community participation as such, is the means of achieving educational accountability.

The earlier educational arguments for community participation, based on child-centred theories of teaching and learning, were consistent with a range of school–community relationships. They could be used to justify forms of parental and community control, consistent with the view that schooling is fundamentally an extension of the home, where the prior rights and responsibilities of parents in the education of their children prevail. Equally, they were able to justify forms of community level school governance, consistent with the view that schools belong to the wider society. These, of course, were fundamentally political questions.

The arguments did not, however, have any intrinsic implications for either centralization or decentralization of school governance.

By contrast, the new forces for devolution are not based on any particular view of the teaching and learning process, but are derived from notions of individual parental choice, community control and public accountability. The educational arguments for community participation in schooling have been overtaken by political arguments for devolution of school governance, with significant implications for public schooling.

Political Implications

Educational rationales for community involvement in schooling do not exist in a political vacuum. Decisions about education reflect particular values and serve particular interests. They also often represent the outcome of a struggle for influence among various interests in the nature and operation of schooling. For much of this century educational policies have generally reflected conservative values. Senior education bureaucrats, in particular, have generally shared the conservatism of the public service, and of the education profession itself. Post-war expansion in education produced an informed and articulate group of professionals within the community, including within parent and teacher organizations, with more progressive and radical social and educational values. Their political activism focused on the structures that gave power to the bureaucracy, rather than on the political content of particular educational policies.

The politics of community participation in Australian education have varied according to the interests and circumstances of the players: parents, teachers, bureaucrats, politicians and, to some extent, the media.

Parents

Activism in schooling offers parents a direct way of expressing their protectiveness of their own children's educational interests. Association with their children's schooling may be, to some parents, a psychological investment in 'good parenting' and an important motivation for political involvement in school level or peak organizations. Activism also enables committed and articulate parents to influence the nature of their children's education, to win resources from the rest of the community to that end and to protect their children's schools from the infiltration of 'other' educational and political values.

Traditionally, parent involvement in schooling has been regarded in Australia as a kind of civic service, providing personal and social rewards to the participants, as well as material and cultural benefits to many schools. The 'Parents' and Citizens' movement in Australia both developed from and fostered this kind of 'civic' activism, with its inevitable extension into political activism.

It is to be expected that parent activists will bring their own political perspectives to bear in setting the goals and establishing the operating patterns of schools. Thus arguments at school level about such issues as resource allocation, curriculum and financial contributions will reflect the prevailing balance of political opinion. This may include active resistance to changes by defenders of the status quo, who often use the argument that schooling must be protected from overt politicization.

The relationship between parent activism and political motivation is perhaps more open within the peak organizations, state and federal. Major players in these organizations frequently display their overlapping activism with other political organizations, including political parties, typically finding expression in factions formed around clear political positions. In general, however, there is a strong culture of 'non-politicization' in Australian schooling, which has effectively countered infiltration of parent groups by organized political forces. On the other hand, political activists may attempt, by invoking parental status, to gain legitimacy for the advancement of particular ideological views of schooling.

For some, participation in parents' organizations is a means to political activism generally. Parent organizations provide a respectable and socially accepted political training and recruiting ground, particularly for women who continue to have difficulty in gaining access to other organizations such as trade unions, professional lobby groups and political parties. Two Education Ministers, Susan Ryan and Joan Kirner, developed their political base and skills partly through their experiences in leadership positions within the Australian Council of State Schools Organizations.

Teachers

The emergence of teachers as a militant professional group in the 1960s and 1970s focused attention on the relative powers of teachers and the central bureaucracies and inspectorates. The devolution of educational governance was supported by organized teachers, both in principle and as a means of transferring power to themselves. This assertion of the authority of teacher-professionals was justified through the ethic of worker participation and given expression through the principle of devolution, at least for the professionals if not for parents and the wider community.

The intensity of the struggle for this kind of 'professional' devolution, however, led to an alliance, albeit an uneasy one, with activist parents. At least initially teachers were prominent in supporting a fairly general notion of community involvement, an important step in the development of political momentum for devolution and community participation.

The alliance of parents and teachers was soon to be tested when debate moved to more concrete issues, such as curriculum and staff selection. More intrinsic political tensions, such as the opposition of 'Liberal' parent activists to the perceived 'Labor' links of teacher unions, were also soon to appear. These cracks in the educational alliance at school level were important in weakening the influence of both parents and teachers at the important stage of articulation and definition of devolution, leaving the field to others.

Bureaucrats

In the face of the momentum for devolution the typical reaction of senior system administrators was to attempt to manage strategies for devolution from the perspective of their own survival. Such strategies included the reinforcement of the status and role of the school principal as the 'system representative' in each school, the provision of small amounts of discretionary money to divert energy into school level discussion over its distribution, and the establishment of consultative processes, which included community representation, at system level.

Administrators also tried to retain authority through strengthening their claims to professionalism. Significant impetus was given through professional associations to the recognition of educational administration as a legitimate discipline in its own right. Senior educational bureaucrats increasingly attempted to draw their authority more from the profession of education than from bureaucratic structures as such; in doing so, they placed themselves in a more obvious alliance with teachers and their organizations.

The decline in the 1980s of the role of the Director-General of Education marked the development of a more explicit political relationship between education bureaucracies and the government of the day. This occurred in a context of policy directions concerned with economic efficiency and budgetary restraint, and with placing greater responsibility for the provision of educational services on local school communities.

Thus the educational professionals, teachers and bureaucrats, and the parent and community interests concerned with an agenda more directly related to education found their struggle with each other made redundant by organizational restructuring and a fundamental change in the language of the debate.

Politicians

Major parties in Australia have tapped apparent public concerns about educational standards for political purposes. Political rhetoric has consequently developed in terms of transferring power to 'the people', namely parents and families concerned, as consumers, with basic standards and discipline. This rationale for devolution, of course, has a quite different philosophical base from the socio-educational rationale of a decade ago, developed almost entirely by the education professionals.

The current political imperative for devolution also arises from confused and often conflicting community expectations of schooling: the balance between 'academic' and 'vocational' objectives; the social and cultural goals and values underpinning these objectives; and perspectives on the pastoral and custodial roles of schools. The consequent difficulties for politicians in articulating agreed, electorally appealing policies have provided a motivation for transferring some of the odium of controversy and conflict to the school level. Devolution in these terms can be a strategy for relegating to the political market-place the task of determining the nature of educational provision and allocating educational opportunities through encouraging competition and parental choice among schools, and providing incentives for private effort. This strategy is consistent with current conventional wisdom on corporate management, which places devolution of *process* issues in the context of centralized setting of objectives and monitoring of performance through outcomes.

Media

The media have had a significant influence on political debate in Australia about community participation in education. Media commentators have generally attacked entrenched professional and bureaucratic interests, on the grounds that the public interest in education is best protected by limiting the powers of professionals, bureaucrats and politicians in favour of direct popular control at the school level. They have also tended to support moves to deregulate public schooling by advocating dezoning policies to enable and encourage parental choice, diversity and local accountability.

The reasons for this approach by the media to educational issues are complex. For the print media in particular, and to some extent popular radio, there is a vested interest in promoting public debate about the relative quality of public and private schooling which has become, rather like the Royal Family, standard copy. The resultant presentations and opinions reflect the generally conservative attitudes of media proprietors, managers and senior journalists; and the general predilections of their clienteles for upper-middle-class values, appreciative of media articulation of their concerns about educational quality, of support for increased community influence over professionals and bureaucrats and, in some cases, of legitimation of their own substantial investment in schooling outside the public sector.

In the current debate about community participation, the influence of the media has been important in articulating and publicizing popular perceptions of schooling, rather than in providing informed comment on actual education policy or practice. Most importantly, media coverage of, and commentary on, educational issues may have helped to destabilize the context for schooling generally, and for public schooling in particular.

Areas and Locus of Decision-Making

Arguments for community participation and devolution of responsibility for decision-making as a means of accountability can be traced back to the report of the Interim Committee for the Schools Commission (1973): '... responsibility will be most effectively discharged where the people entrusted with making decisions are also the people responsible for carrying them out, with an obligation to justify them, and in a position to profit from their experience.' Such arguments, however, do not address questions about the locus of political responsibility for public schooling in Australia in key areas: goals, curriculum, staffing and resource allocation.

Goals

Despite their fundamental importance for the nature of the schooling provided, there has been little serious attempt in Australia until recent times to make explicit the broad policy goals of public schools and school systems. This reflects the intrinsic difficulty of articulating values and principles and of making explicit assumptions about the 'common good', particularly in an increasingly complex and diverse society. Some of the system statements of goals and objectives developed in the last decade were undoubtedly a response to a perceived need to create a sense of shared educational purpose and to defend public schooling against a growing range of detractors.

At the same time individual schools have also developed formal statements of their goals as a basis for school improvement plans. These school level statements of goals had an unequivocally educational focus. Increasingly, however, systems began to encourage, or even to require, such statements as part of a management-driven press for program budgeting and external monitoring and accountability.

These developments were soon overtaken by centrally determined statements of purposes and goals. In April 1989 the Ministers for Education, at the behest of the Federal Minister and through the Australian Education Council, endorsed a statement of 'common and agreed national goals for schooling'. Despite rhetoric emphasizing the need for all those involved with education — governments, administrators, teachers, students, parents, business and the general community — to develop a shared commitment and spirit of cooperation, this statement was developed without comprehensive consultative processes or formal acceptance by those affected (Schools Council, 1989). This can be seen as a further development of a process of devolving responsibility and accountability for educational performance, while reasserting centralized authority for determining the purposes, priorities, standards and criteria by which that performance would be assessed.

Curriculum

A major impetus for community participation in schooling has been the general argument for school-based curriculum development. During the 1960s evidence began to emerge from education research that through the established, dominant curriculum schools presented a view of the world alien to students from socially subordinate groups; thus they served to reinforce and reproduce prevailing patterns of educational and social inequality. It was this rationale for school-based curriculum development that gave teachers and parents on the left of the political spectrum most cause to support devolution on educational grounds. It was argued that a 'relevant' curriculum was best generated by local communities, working together to construct an alternative to a mainstream curriculum designed to transmit and sustain dominant class values.

By the late 1980s this support for school-based curriculum development wavered, with the realization that student-centred progressivism could result in curriculum ghettos and the exclusion of large numbers of disadvantaged students from the benefits of mainstream education. This led in turn to arguments for a democratic program of common learnings that included the significant experiences of all social and cultural groups and a comprehensive set of intellectual perspectives for making sense of them (Connell, 1987). These arguments for a reconstructed program of common learnings have generally overtaken the earlier press for diverse forms of compensatory curriculum.

Conservative groups, including many teachers and parents, were concerned to preserve established values through a dominant curriculum. They were never supportive of school-based curriculum development. Their general preference for centralized monitoring of standards as a basis for comparing the relative performance of schools and of students implies the existence of a generally standardized curriculum.

There would now appear to be virtually bipartisan political support for a centrally devised 'essential' curriculum for schools. The debate now centres on the nature of that curriculum and on processes for implementation and monitoring, and is occurring at both state and national levels. These forces have converged to undermine the rationale for community participation in developing school curriculum at all levels, but particularly at the school level. In most states measures are underway to rein in the proliferation of courses developed at school level, in some cases through a participatory process.

Staffing

It has been argued that a positive relationship between schools and their communities is more easily achieved where there is community participation in decisions about school staffing, such that teachers and school communities 'choose' each other, on the basis of a mutual commitment to goals, curriculum and pedagogy. The apparent advantages of private schools in being able to appoint their own principals and teaching staff have been invoked in support of this argument.

Despite some opening up of selection processes to community influence at various levels, there has been no significant devolution to local communities of school staffing responsibilities in Australian public education systems. Recent developments in staff selection policies have tended to strengthen the position of school principals and, in some cases, regional directors (Management Review, 1989). Unwillingness to devolve responsibility for staff allocation may be the legacy of the strong egalitarian tradition in Australian public education: the continuing fear that without centralized allocation of staffing existing inequalities among school communities will be exacerbated. It also reflects reluctance to confront, at the level of the school community, the complexities and sensitivities of industrial relations in Australian schools. Neither politicians, teacher unions nor government or parent organizations have accepted an industrial model based on the school, rather than on the level where the employing authority is defined, that is the state government. For these reasons no serious attempt has yet been made in Australia to establish the practical conditions necessary for the devolution of staffing decisions to school communities.

Resources

Arguments for community participation in education have also been based on a view about the relationship between such participation and the efficient and effective use of resources. It is argued, for example, that school communities are best able to define their needs, and then to make decisions about how to allocate resources in response to those needs.

As with staffing decisions, as noted above, recent trends have been in the direction of transferring responsibilities to principals and senior teachers for framing and implementing school budgets. The state governments, as raisers of revenue and providers of resources, continue to retain responsibility for the allocation of funds to regions and to schools, within which school budgets are framed. The devolution of limited financial management to schools, which might include involvement by school communities, is inevitably peripheral to overall resource allocation in systems where teachers are centrally hired and where there is relatively little flexibility to vary their conditions of service.

Resource allocation decisions, therefore, cannot logically be devolved from the locus of power within the political system overall. In Australia constitutional responsibility for the provision of schooling continues to lie with the states. To the extent that this has been challenged, the argument has been about the relative powers and responsibilities of state and federal, rather than between state and local, levels of government.

Participatory Structures

The collectivist political and social ideologies of the 1960s and early 1970s found expression in the establishment of centralized bodies at both national and state/territory levels. These were the Schools Commission, the ACT Schools Authority, the Education Commission of New South Wales and the State Board of Victoria. All began to function in an economic and social climate changing rapidly in the time between their conception and establishment. They were, nevertheless, potentially powerful, particularly through their capacity to promote informed public debate on educational issues. This was a capacity politicians and bureaucrats took immediate steps to limit, through imposition of directive guidelines, the weighting of membership with 'sympathetic' appointees, a general under-resourcing and bureaucratic surveillance. The most influential of these central participatory bodies were, arguably, the Schools Commission, set up in 1974, and the ACT Schools Authority, established a year earlier. Both agencies were despatched in the 1987 federal budget, and replaced by advisory arrangements which severed responsibility for policy advice from involvement in the operation of either schools or school programs.

The Schools Commission's governing legislation provided for openness in policy development, advice and implementation; a membership representative of major educational groups and authorities with a direct interest and involvement in schooling; and an obligation to consult widely and to report publicly. Through its responsibility for running major schools programs, the Commission gained a level of financial and related political weight rare among advisory bodies. As economic conditions deteriorated, however, a Commission set up to provide independent, regular and public reminders of the resource needs of schools was destined to become a political liability. A progressive transfer of Schools Commission programs from the Schools Commission to the then Commonwealth Department of Education and Youth Affairs commenced in 1985. The Commission was systematically isolated from governmental processes and stripped of its resources. Tensions within the Commonwealth portfolio damaged the Commission's credibility and capacity as the government's major source of policy advice on schools. The states had, over the life of the Commission, maintained their reservations about its role in promoting informed public debate, in providing access by community groups to sensitive data, and in providing a means for Commonwealth encroachment in schooling. Predictably, they demonstrated no will to intervene in Commonwealth business by opposing the demise of the Commission. The interest groups, likewise, including government and non-government parent and teacher organizations, raised little public outcry, despite the fact that the Schools Commission had afforded unprecedented access to the development and implementation of public policy at the national level.

In the Australian Capital Territory, until 1973, public schools were run by the NSW Department of Education. In that year the Schools Authority was established in interim form, with a corporate, central governing body, the Council of the Schools Authority, comprising parents, teachers, citizens and the chief bureaucrat. The establishment of a participatory structure, in which parents and the community were to be formal partners for the governance of public schooling, owed much to a coalition between the ACT branch of the NSW Teachers Federation and the local parent organization. The teachers were particularly interested in school level participatory structures as a means of increasing the power of classroom teachers and reducing the authority wielded by principals and the central bureaucracy in the New South Wales system. Teachers thus saw support for the parents' demands for a break from New South Wales as consistent with their own interests.

The ACT Schools Authority was arguably the most powerful of the participatory bodies established at system level in terms of its responsibilities for the actual operation of schools. The fact that it had only part-time members, including its chairperson, was an inherent weakness and a source of tension. Control of resources and the information available to the Council was firmly in the hands of the bureaucracy, whose chief was also a voting member of the Council. A clear sign of irritation by government with the realities of community participation in decision-making came with the decision in 1985 to reduce the size of the Council from fifteen to ten, to decrease the influence of parent and teacher organizations relative to that of the Minister's individual appointees. When the Authority's governing body was abolished in the context of the 1987 federal budget, Hedley Beare, the inaugural Chief Education Officer for the ACT system, outlined the rationale for establishing a central participatory structure: 'Setting up the authority ... governed by a council representative of the community, was an attempt to encourage a sense of public ownership. Parents and the community were to be overt and official partners in the schooling process' (Beare, 1988: 2). He observed that its abolition 'had turned the public schools in Canberra into just another government department.'

A different perspective was provided in reply by Eric Willmot, the current ACT Chief Education Officer:

> Councils of statutory authorities are established to manage institutions on behalf of governments at the policy levels proper to those statutory authorities. Some councils allow themselves to come to be regarded as a kind of people's parliament, quite often arriving at cross purposes with the government that appointed

them. That is at variance with the Australian democratic system, which is a matter of ballot boxes, and not of appointed councils or committees ... what we have seen in the ACT is the Government's reaction to this situation and, in a sense, a consequent regularisation of the purpose of statutory authorities. (Willmot, 1988: 2)

As with the Schools Commission, the absence of opposition from community groups was a notable feature of the dissolution of the ACT Schools Authority: 'Where are the voices of dissent? Where are the teachers who worked so hard to convince their professional and industrial associations of the worth of this system? Where are the parents who helped to build and run it?' (Hughes, 1988: 2).

The ambivalence of parent and teacher organizations to both the Schools Commission and the ACT Schools Authority can be explained partly by the fact that, while such bodies provide access to information and the decision-making process, they also constitute a form of co-option, constraining the freedom of these organizations to pursue self-interest by direct political pressure. In the case of the ACT Schools Authority, the absence of structural links between the Council of the Authority and the other participatory structures, the school boards, confused and fragmented the forces for community participation. The retention of individual school boards in the ACT, combined with the dismantling of the central participatory statutory authority, provides a clear and concrete expression of the new agenda for community participation.

This new agenda focuses on a transfer to school level, within a centrally determined curriculum, industrial relations and fiscal framework, of those responsibilities consistent with the promotion of diversity, competitiveness, productivity and local accountability. Areas of responsibility consistent with this view include: student discipline policies; public relations and promotion of the particular image of individual schools; allocation within schools of marginal, discretionary recurrent and capital funding; and the traditional function of general fund-raising, which would be deregulated in terms of rules governing access and equity.

School boards or councils have become the means for operationalizing the devolution of power from central authorities, accompanied by restructuring and decentralizing of traditional bureaucracies. In Victoria, for example, continuing moves towards 'self-governing' schools followed the recommendations of the Ministry Structures Project Team in late 1986. Similar changes are now underway in other states, notably Western

Australia, New South Wales, Queensland and Tasmania. It has also been noted that, in general, the forms of schools councils or boards established or proposed enabled some community involvement in selection of senior staff, but not powers of hire or fire over teachers, and some local level management of marginal funds. On the other hand, moves at both state and national levels to reassert central responsibility for curriculum guidelines and monitoring of achievement have accompanied these developments.

It is as if the concept of community participation has, for practical purposes, been redefined and reduced to that of devolution, largely through the vehicle of school boards and councils. Experience overseas and in Australia (the ACT and Victoria particularly) raises questions about the social and educational costs and benefits of reliance on this form of community participation as a means of strengthening public schooling. While studies abound of the positive educational effects, for less advantaged groups in particular, of parent involvement in their children's learning, there is little or no evidence of direct benefits from parent representation on school boards. The form of parent participation institutionalized in ACT school boards was described in 1976 as 'participatory impotence' and a facade (Scott, 1976). The report of a management review of the Authority eleven years later (Berkeley and Kenway, 1987: 54) echoed this description: 'The Panel's inquiries indicate that community participation in the election of school board members remains limited in many schools and that the teachers and principals, in particular, often dominate discussions.' The Panel recommended that, 'as long as the Authority continued to subscribe to the principle of devolution', it should provide real opportunities for more community participation and for the development and training of those who become school board members, using resources available for personnel and professional services. This raises the issue of diverting resources from the professional development of teachers, with a long-time commitment to classroom teaching, to the training of parents serving short terms on school boards. Board membership has proved to be unrepresentative in terms of class, ethnicity and gender; it has excluded, in particular, less formally educated parents. The effect in many ACT schools has been to distance the more representative Parents' and Citizens' organizations even further from educational decision-making. To the extent that active and articulate parents have been recruited into the governance of individual schools, the potential pool for system leadership has been fragmented and attention diverted from the operation of the public school system as a whole. This focusing of parents' energies on individual schools, rather than on the more abstract notion of a system, is seen as a strength by advocates of devolution, frequently citing the perceived strengths of traditional private schools in establishing a client relationship with parents. The issue of individual school autonomy is less clear, however, in relation to those non-government schools set up to serve identifiable communities as distinct from individual fee-paying parents. A recent confrontation in the United Kingdom between parents at one Catholic school and diocesan authorities, for example, led to an official statement that those parents who choose Catholic schools for their children must do so with adequate regard to the common good of the community and the balanced provision of Catholic schools for the whole Catholic community (*The Tablet*, 29 July 1989).

The proper governance of a socially comprehensive public school or system requires ways of managing conflicting and competing values and interests, while maintaining a stable and secure environment for teaching and learning. The experience of the ACT is that those pressing for reform, and thereby challenging the status quo, will often be forced to retreat in order to avoid conflict in the school community. Reforms in such areas as equality of educational opportunity for girls, for example, have depended heavily on the authority and leadership of the centre. It is as if the structures of councils and boards at the individual school level have become the substance of community participation. This has the inherent danger of distracting attention from the nature of the public education system itself, and from the philosophical underpinnings of that system.

Conclusion: Implications for Public Schooling

Community participation in schooling continues to be a significant idea within Australian education. It has developed over more than two decades from an ideological base concerned with equity and social justice to one that seeks, through the promotion of choice and diversity, to respond to individual needs and talents. Through the process of devolving responsibilities to school communities affected by critical decisions, current educational and political forces for community participation aim to promote an enterprising and productive, rather than a dependent, culture; they aim to develop local and community-based, rather than societal, accountability structures and processes.

This profound change in the ideological underpinning of community participation in education is reflected in changing perceptions of the nature of public education itself. The history of public schooling in Australia has developed around widely shared egalitarian principles and values, concerned with enabling all citizens to gain equal access to shared and useful knowledge and to develop the skills necessary for them to participate in, and contribute to, Australian society. This has, in practice, developed within an Anglo-Saxon, Protestant and generally socially conservative political and cultural framework. This does not, however, detract from the fundamental importance of these principles to the development of public schooling in Australia.

Devolution of responsibility for educational decisions, as currently defined, intrinsically confronts many of these principles. Devolved systems, by definition, place high value on differences between local communities, rather than on the common needs and objectives of the society as a whole. Devolved structures are designed to address and express the needs of individuals and local communities, rather than guaranteeing the rights of all children to access to commonly valued knowledge. Locating decisions at school level could also have the effect of re-focusing the objectives and operations of schools from the educational needs of all children to the psychological and political needs of some adults, as those adults attempt to gain advantages for their own children in a generally competitive environment, or to use schools and schooling as vehicles for achieving their social and political objectives. As Watt (1989) argues, the devolution of powers to self-governing schools has an ideological meaning.

Forms of devolution that encourage significant differences in resources and curriculum will necessarily result in major educational inequalities between school communities, in provision and in outcomes. A devolved education system is unable to call on a disinterested system authority to prevent gross inequalities. Competition between schools for scarce enrolments will encourage resource differentials, as a basis for real or apparent educational differences or specializations.

The quality of educational provision within public school systems could also be affected by devolution. An emphasis on local decision-making and accountability processes could divert resources and priorities from educational objectives to other concerns, presenting schools with major opportunity costs: the development of financial management capacities; the fragmentation of leadership talent among parents and teachers; and the management of conflict and confrontation at the local level.

It must be recognized that the ideological foundations of the current devolution movement in Australian education, within a broader climate for the privatization of assets and institutions, are redefining the nature of the public school system itself. As in other areas, much of the public debate in this area has focused on political and administrative structures and processes, therefore distracting attention from the more fundamental

Democracy and Bureaucracy

questions of purposes and long-term goals. Because the current political and social framework embodies values, principles and priorities quite different from those traditionally underpinning Australian public education, it is not surprising that the particular mechanism of devolution is difficult to reconcile with the foundational principles of Australian public education. The central argument is more about values and principles than about particular structures and processes, and as such can only be resolved politically.

This is not to say that structures of governance and administration are unimportant. The dismantling of the centralized bureaucracies that have sustained public education in Australia for more than a century will have profound effects on the nature and operation of public schooling. As governments and ministers for education, or their equivalent, continue to confirm their role in setting standards and in monitoring outcomes, alternative central bureaucracies are being established, with expertise and responsibilities closer to the goals of the government of the day than with the education profession. The capacities of these alternative agencies to obtain the necessary knowledge and information to sustain the central government's authority over educational institutions in a devolved system remain to be assessed.

These developments reflect government concern to retain central control over the substantive issues in education. As has been shown in this chapter, there has been no devolution of real power from the centre to local school communities over setting education goals and priorities, the essential curriculum, basic resource allocation, teacher recruitment and industrial relations; nor has there been a major struggle to decentralize these responsibilities to school level. What is more significant is that the 'centre' is being redefined, as described above. The key struggle will be over the nature and composition of the new central agencies, and their relationships with the major political authorities and interest groups and with the devolved structures expected to be responsible to those agencies.

There will continue to be resistance from the recipients of the devolution process if they are given only peripheral responsibilities and are placed under significant pressures to justify their activities within an accountability framework and against centrally determined and monitored standards and guidelines. This is especially so for those community members, particularly parents and teachers, who are increasingly perceiving the current devolution movement to be against their interests, to be inconsistent with their own goals for community participation and to be contrary to the foundations and traditions of public education.

As these tensions are expressed and resolved, perhaps iteratively, through the political process, schooling in Australia at all levels will continue to be characterized by instability. In this climate the notion of community participation as a means to informed, ethical and effective decision-making in education, and to a strengthening of the public education system, will become less relevant as political forces compete with each other for the support of the more powerful interests located around the issues they have created.

References

BEARE, H. (1988) 'Canberra Parents Lose Input to Education.' *The Canberra Times*, 29 January.

BERKELEY, G. and KENWAY, N. (1987) *A Management Review of the ACT Schools Authority: Report to the Minister for Territories*. Canberra: ACT Schools Authority.

BLAKERS, C. (1940) *School and Community. A Review of School/Community Relationships*. Canberra: Australian Council of State School Organizations.

BRADY, P. and POPE, B. (1979) *School-Community Based Decision Making*. Report on the Second National Conference. Prepared for the National Advisory Committee on School Based Decision Making, Canberra.

BROWN, J., CAHIR, P. and REEVE, P. (1987) *The Educational Rationale for Parent Participation*. Canberra: Australian Council of State School Organizations.

COLEMAN, J.S. and HOFFER, T. (1987) *Public and Private High Schools*. New York: Basic Books.

COMMITTEE OF ENQUIRY INTO EDUCATION IN SOUTH AUSTRALIA (1971) *Education in South Australia, 1969–1970*. Adelaide: SA Government Printer.

CONNELL, R.W. (1987) 'Curriculum Politics, Hegemony and Strategies of Social Change.' Macquarie University, Department of Sociology.

CONNELL, R.W., et al. (1982) *Making the Difference: Schools, Families and Social Division*. Sydney: George Allen and Unwin.

DEPARTMENT OF EDUCATION, QUEENSLAND (1989) *Community Participation in School Decision Making*. Information Statement No. 124. Supplement to the Education Office Gazette, 17 February.

HUGHES, P. (1988) 'Where Were the Voices of Dissent?' *The Canberra Times*, 22 February.

INTERIM COMMITTEE FOR THE AUSTRALIAN SCHOOLS COMMISSION (1973) *Schools in Australia* (Karmel Report). Canberra: Australian Government Publishing Service.

JOHNSTON, K. (1981) *Ambiguities in the School and Community Debate: An Analysis of the Past, a New Hope for the Future*. Directions in School and Community Project, School and Communities Studies, Vol. 2, December.

JOHNSTON, K. (1983) 'A Discourse for All Seasons? An Ideological Analysis of the Schools Commission Reports, 1973 to 1981.' *Australian Journal of Education*, 27, 1: 17–32.

MANAGEMENT REVIEW: NSW EDUCATION PORTFOLIO (1989) *Schools Renewal: A Strategy to Revitalize Schools within the New South Wales State Education System* (Scott Report). Milsons Point, NSW: Management Review.

NEW SOUTH WALES DEPARTMENT OF EDUCATION (1987) *The Establishment of School Councils*. Memorandum to Principals. 23 February.
NEW SOUTH WALES DEPARTMENT OF EDUCATION (1988) *Support Document: Schools Councils 1988. Policy and Procedures* (draft).
NORTHERN TERRITORY DEPARTMENT OF EDUCATION (1987) *Towards the 90s. Excellence, Accountability and Devolution in Education*. Darwin: NT Department of Education.
SCHOOLS COMMISSION (1975) *Report for the Triennium 1976–1978*. Canberra: Australian Government Publishing Service.
STATE BOARD OF EDUCATION, VICTORIA (1986) *Balancing Community and Statewide Needs*. Advice on Devolution to the Minister for Education. Vol. 1.
The Tablet (1989) 'Cardinal Baum Lends Support.' 29 July.
WARNOCK, M. (1988) *A Common Policy for Education*. Oxford: Oxford University Press.
WATT, J. (1989) 'Devolution of Power: The Ideological Meaning.' *Journal of Educational Administration*, 27, 1.
WESTERN AUSTRALIAN MINISTRY OF EDUCATION (1986) *Better Schools in Western Australia: A Programme for Improvement*. Perth: WA Ministry of Education.
WESTERN AUSTRALIAN MINISTRY OF EDUCATION (1988) *School Development Plans and School-Based Decision-Making Groups*. Discussion Document. Perth: WA Ministry of Education.
WILLMOT, E. (1988) 'Times Have Changed in ACT Schools and Will Go on Changing.' *The Canberra Times*, 8 February.

Chapter 6

Exploring Trails in School Management

David McRae

In the arena of school management various forms of 'democracy' currently jostle with 'scientific' business management, the 'new managerialism'. The purposes of both are to bring schools into line; in one case with the wishes of the immediate community, and in the other with the wishes of their more evident and distant political masters. Both schools of thought claim that their underlying *raison d'être* is the improvement of performance. In this chapter it is suggested that both streams of thought have fundamental weaknesses and are likely to do more harm than good. In neither case is there a great deal of understanding evident of the nature of teachers' work, or any clearly apparent interest in examining closely schools as institutions to see how they do work, and how they might be encouraged to perform better.

These are broad brush strokes. One thing which can be confidently asserted is that for any generalization made about Australian systemic education, examples can be found which deny its truth. In some systems the 'new managerialism' is being used to wrest back the balance of control from teachers or 'the community'. In others 'democracy' is being used as a weapon to lever open closed systems. The same ideas are at differing points of fashionability and development in different systems. One would expect this to continue cyclically. As a result, however, the following observations will relate more proximately to some situations than others.

Visions of Democracy

It is a mark of how friable things are in education that in 1990 one can be proposing a critique of both participatory and representative democracy as a means of managing schools. In the author's experience they were tender new buds during the mid-1970s which took legislative root and flowered most strongly in the early to mid-1980s. Democracy is, of course, a fluid notion. The forms in which it was described most fulsomely in the 1970s were congruent with the times — everyone should have a say and participate in deciding about everything. I have a strong memory from 1973 where, at a union AGM, delegates sought to outdo each other in inclusiveness, first building parents en masse into school decision-making procedures, then other community representatives, then students, again en masse, then support staff, then cleaners and ancillary staff. Such was the impetus that for anyone to have questioned why would have been heretical, let alone at what point, or how.

The issue was that of rights, and the rhetoric was devoted to the visionary possibilities of what ought to be. How could it have been otherwise when one considers what it was to which that particular movement was responding? Brittle, rigidly stratified, insensitive, uninterested in the real state of what was happening in schools — that was how the bureaucracy appeared, at least from a teacher's perspective at the time. Like many things in education the tenor and style of that bureaucracy had outlived its cultural relevance by ten to fifteen years. The medium for reform was political action. The school was the arena for contestation. The context was Victoria in the early 1970s. The colours were black and white. No other shade was acceptable.

Without any official approval, school administrative committees were established, elected curriculum committees challenged the authority of the school executive, and collegial decisions became more widespread. In addition there was a variety of experimentation with student and parent involvement in decision-making. These 'experiments' (they were not viewed as such) tended to begin not with peripheral issues or matters vetted for relevance but at the core issues of curriculum and school organization.

However good or important an idea, it will stand or fall on its implementation. Now, fifteen or more years later, almost all school systems would claim to have instituted some management practices which could be described as 'democratic'. By and large they tend towards 'representative' models of democracy, partly because those responsible for their introduction (politicians, unionists and even administrators) live and operate in environments where this is the métier, and there is a powerful temptation to reach for and attempt to recreate the known and familiar.

From broad experience of schools in Victoria and close observation of schools in the Participation and Equity Program (PEP) and the Disadvantaged Schools Program, both of which have (had in the case of

PEP) a commitment to broadly participatory democratic management practices, I would say that certain forms of 'inclusive', 'democratic' school management will always fail. Further, most of the forms of 'democratic' management I have seen produce results which consistently include poor decisions, energy wastage, diffusion of focus for the school's task, and a decline in teacher morale through increased vulnerability and downgrading of professional skills and expertise. I believe they can disguise increasingly covert and isolated processes of decision-making and be destructive of collegial support, or produce the antithesis of democracy.

It is also pointless to try to disguise this difficulty: control of a school includes control of the budget. About 90 per cent of school budgets are spent on staffing. Only the most modest inroads have been made into locally controlled staffing for government schools in Australia. While the major proportion of funds and resources comes from a central source, schools will be at least as accountable to that source as they are to the express wishes of the local community.

Those who claim that failures in 'democratic' school management can be put down to failures of will and imagination may be right. I think not. I think there are weaknesses beyond the well known failure to excite popular enthusiasm for school decision-making work. Following are three which appear to matter.

What Are Teachers For?

First, 'democracy' as it has been commonly implemented in schools misunderstands the nature of both 'role' and 'accountability' in school settings.

Clearly, parents have rights with regard to the education of their children, and their opinions and attitudes are of considerable consequence. Equally clearly, students' points of view should be taken seriously and encouraged. 'Democratic decision-making procedures' as they have been institutionalized appear to inhibit rather than promote these results.

Among the *Guidelines* for the Participation and Equity Program was the following:

> The whole school community must be committed to proposed improvements. Parents are more likely to feel confidence about proposed changes when they have been able to influence the process throughout.... Teachers, parents and students should be represented in decision making through a democratic process

which ensures that changes being made in schools have the support of broadly-based parent, teacher and (where these are developing) student organizations. (CSC, 1983: paras 3.17 and 3.18)

The *Guidelines* go on to counsel against 'tokenism': 'Experience in several Australian systems indicates that the establishment of formal participatory structures is necessary but not sufficient for real participation to occur; resources must also be provided to develop the capacity of young people and inexperienced parents to contribute to school planning and policy. For teachers, being able to collaborate with students and parents is part of professionalism today' (*ibid.*: para. 3.40).

Initiatives in these areas were most popular in South Australia and Victoria because schools are ministerially directed to include parent and student representatives on formally established school councils with wide powers. But it did not matter where they occurred or under whose authority, the sought-after results from participatory, democratic, representative, decision-making structures were most difficult to achieve. The reasons most commonly advanced are that both students and parents felt threatened by the apparent expertise of teachers who did not go out of their way to help them; that no variations were allowed in meeting procedure to help people unused to this style of operation; and that no efforts were made to prepare members of either group properly for their role. This is not supported by the evidence.

Nationally there were several hundred in-service courses conducted in each year of the PEP, all at least partly directed towards inducting parents into the mysteries of 'schoolishness'. Nayano Taylor's study of PEP committees in South Australia (Taylor, 1986) suggests that the unfriendliness of other members was the least frequently occurring problem referred to by parent and student members of committees. PEP programs produced a stream of publications about meeting procedure and ways of making participants feel comfortable, and there was consistent evidence of their use. Effort went into ensuring that jargon was kept to a minimum and that minutes and reports were written in straightforward language.

The real reasons seem to relate almost entirely to the differences in role of the 'decision-makers'. Neither students nor parents were directly responsible for seeing their decisions carried out. Both groups had difficulty in keeping in touch with their 'electorates', if such existed. Both were troubled by the time commitment necessary for full involvement. The significance of the change from 'student as member of a class' or 'parent of a student in a class', under the control, legally if in no other way, of a teacher, to 'student or parent as powerful committee member' has not been properly investigated.

To perform their work, teachers are not elected. They are employed. They are paid to do work for which they have been trained. They are selected, one might hope, on the basis of their suitability to perform that work. They stand in a particular relation to an employer. To perform their role in schooling, parents are not elected. They are conscripted (mostly very willingly) by the provisions for compulsory education. They are not selected. While there are instances where their interest extends to the school as a whole, their primary interest is focused on an individual or individuals within it. They are, by and large, neither trained nor employed to run schools. To perform their role in schooling, students are not elected. Again they are conscripted (again mostly very willingly) by the provisions for compulsory education. By definition, they know less, and are less mature and experienced than their teachers. No matter how much variation there is in individual cases (and in my experience it is considerable), these differences in role, stake and status will distort the 'democratic' quality of decision-making in school forums.

If it is unlikely that representative committee work will ever become a widely acquired taste, it is equally unlikely that the word 'democratic' can be applied to its operation in schools in anything other than a limited sense. It is a clumsy and often ineffectual means of determining opinion, particularly as access to the 'electorate' is limited and difficult.

The Significance of Leadership

Second, 'democracy' as it has been commonly implemented in schools misunderstands the nature and significance of school leadership.

The position of principals in many school systems still remains unclear, forcing them to rely increasingly heavily on their own personal resources and authority. That is at least partly a result of the movement to 'democratize' schools. In Victoria, where secondary principals are locally selected, the role statement indicates the number of masters the principal can be expected to serve:

> The principal as spokesperson, representative and school community leader occupies the central and pivotal position within the school. The principal carries out the dual role of being both the representative of the Ministry of Education and thereby

responsible to the Chief Executive, and also being executive officer of the school council, responsible to the school council for the implementation of council policies and decisions on all matters within its jurisdiction.

The principal carries ultimate responsibility for the administration and organization of the school, though this responsibility is to be exercised in consultation with the staff.

On the surface this job description is a recipe for the production of wimps, tyrants or broken men and women. The wimps are busy following up the myriad directions that it is possible to garner from all those sources of authoritative advice, and equally busily trying to avoid the inevitable conflict which will arise. The tyrants have grown impatient with any form of collegiality and consultation, and impose their pivotal spokesperson's will over their domain. The broken men and women oscillate between each position.

Principals have to be allowed to be effective leaders. Their role is to stand at the crossroads of a school and direct the traffic, which is mostly flowing towards that same intersection, uncertain at times of the degree of authority which may be exercised, not always confident of the direction to take, making mistakes and picking up the pieces when 'accidents' occur. It's a tough job.

Discussions of effective schooling consider the role of the principal to be vital. Why? To provide effective and strong leadership. This can mean that principals throw their weight behind decentralized decision-making and 'democratic process'. Sometimes this results in anomalous behaviour. 'I bullied the staff into acceptance of democratic decision-making', confessed one principal interviewed during my study of the Participation and Equity Program (McRae, 1989: 134). Paradoxically, wherever I observed this sort of behaviour occurring (and it was reasonably widespread), the result tended to be an increase in the authority of the principal and the centrality of the role assigned to him or her in the school; not a 'democratic' flattening of the patterns of authority, but a steepening of the pattern of charismatic leadership (and a happier school because of the way those participating felt they could contribute to decisions, and the way in which those contributions would be both valued and enacted).

This led me to believe that it was necessary to make a distinction between collegial contribution to decision-making (another characteristic of good schools) and the sort of democratic decision-making where on every issue 'the numbers have it'. The latter generally seemed to do more damage to the fabric of the institution than to repair and support it.

Schools Go Fast

Third, 'democracy' as it has been commonly implemented in schools misunderstands how schools must operate, and the absolute requirement for both speed and efficiency in decision-making.

Large group involvement in decision-making is commonly a characteristic of democratic process. I have regularly observed two effects of this procedure in a school context. The first is its inability to produce decisions, whatever 'techniques' are used, leading to confusion and frustration. This is claimed in the literature to be a staging point in a longer-term process which takes many years to develop. Apart from the fact that school communities turn over quickly and inexorably, the negative effects are too common and too pronounced to lead me to believe that if you wait long enough it will 'turn out'.

The second effect is an outcome of the first. While the large group stews over matters ranging from details of curriculum policy to the colour of rubbish bins, power becomes centralized in a small group who either cannot or will not wait. This has led me to this hypothesis: the larger and less efficient the group apparently involved in making decisions, the more frequently decisions will be made less openly by a small group or by an individual.

A school won't wait. There is very little 'down time' in a school. You cannot turn them off for six months while you retool, and you certainly cannot turn them off for six months while you decide how you're going to retool. The following case study illustrates some of the features of what I believe happens where poorly framed inclusive operations gather heads of steam.

No fewer than eight working parties were set up at this school during 1985 to produce papers on various aspects of desirable change. Each committee contained staff, student and parent members. Parents were also involved through a large-scale network of neighbourhood meetings, for which some parents were trained as group leaders. At least one member of staff attended each meeting. There were several hundred meetings all told. These informal 'committees' spent many hours working over their particular topics and presented their reports towards the end of that year. In 1986 the work focused on three main areas: curriculum/structures, discipline and equity.

The curriculum structures working party provided the main event. The curriculum/structures committee was established with twenty-one members: three students, three parents, fifteen teachers, including the principal and the two assistant principals, with the PEP coordinator as chairperson. Every faculty was represented, and meetings were held once every fortnight after school. The aim was to develop an outline for a new school curriculum in two months. This deadline was extended by two months and then by four months.

The first proposal was for a curriculum which would provide 'common, compulsory and diverse experiences' to be drawn for Years 7 and 8 from six areas. 'Too radical' was the response. How would both sequential and discrete courses fit? Choice might not increase or might still follow gender patterns. Streaming for maths was stressed as a necessity. The timetable would be a problem. How would teachers cope? The proponents of the idea found a model of a timetable that used vertical grouping and a more complex grid to enable more choice through adding additional 'lines' which would be available to students. The students could choose their subjects each semester, after which the timetable would be constructed.

Then major worries began to surface in some faculties about diminished status. The social studies faculty did not wish their offerings to be relegated to elective status. By the end of term there was a feeling of exhaustion and disillusionment among members of the committee. The principal became cautious about the proposal, believing that the parents were, by and large, satisfied with the existing curriculum. Four further curriculum models were presented, two based on a core/elective structure and two on a 'common' structure. All courses were to be of semester length, presented within the borrowed concept of the 'grid' timetable.

In the discussion that followed one teacher suggested that most staff could cope with whatever was decided as long as it was decided quickly. However, nothing was decided: discussions had become circular and to some extent acrimonious. As a result the school executive (the principal and the three assistant principals) decided to abandon this form of decision-making. A new subcommittee, comprising the school executive, the PEP coordinator and a parent, a student and a staff representative, was to produce a new curriculum structure. If no consensus was reached, a vote would be taken with the principal having the casting vote. The non-negotiable decision would then be taken back to the full subcommittee for discussion and, if necessary, negotiation of details.

This news was received with some ambivalence. Some were glad that a final decision would be made, some were angry with faculty groups for having put their interests before those of the whole school. Others were annoyed about losing control of the decision. Most reflected on the breakdown of a process in which there had been such initial confidence. The School Board eventually overturned the decision of the steering group, and a core/elective structure was introduced in 1987 for Years 7 and 8. In 1988 it was to be extended to Years 9 and 10.

Ainslie Hudson, from whose description of this situation I have drawn as well as my own experience of the particular school, concludes:

> Certainly the need for consensus within this relatively large group inhibited imaginative and innovative response and led to the adoption of a very conservative approach to structural changes .... The level of expertise in curriculum and related issues and the level of readiness for change varied enormously. As there is no reason to believe that this school was atypical in this, the problems of the committee call into question the whole basis of participative decision making in a situation, such as curriculum redevelopment, where agreement has to be reached on more than underlying principles and objectives. The conclusion reached therefore is that there are certain fields where specialized expertise is a pre-requisite for efficiency and effectiveness, and where large committees are not conducive to decisive action. (Hudson, 1987: 32)

Her comments take us back to the discussion of role. Ignoring the 'render to Caesar' principle of ascribing clear responsibilities for making decisions related to the genuine interests and (where relevant) the expertise of those involved seems to be the core problem. The actual interests and needs of the various parties rather than those conjured up by the rhetoric have been passed over.

If participatory processes are going to work, it is essential that issues are vetted for relevance and interest to the participants. You ask parents about uniform and discipline policies; you talk with them about the general directions that curriculum and assessment should take. You ask students about matters which are in their sphere of interest and appreciation. In some cases the advice of those groups should be sought; in others they should make the decision. This prospective variety cannot be legislated for. A single model of decision-making will not work for schools of all histories, sizes, geographical locations and student age groups.

The 'democracy' movement was a direct response to an unsatisfactory situation, and its ambitions were of the finest. That it has not succeeded in practice can be put down to a number of factors, including the utopianism and idealism of its genesis (thoroughly characteristic of education), and the fact that the mechanisms used to introduce it were clumsy, bland and badly focused. But the primary reason has been a failure to understand that while schools are, in an extended sense, governed, they are not governments.

Organisms or Pyramids?

The radical reason for the failure of 'democratic' school management is, as far as I can tell, identical with that which will cause the 'management' movement to fail: an unwillingness to understand, appreciate and respect the work schools do and the ways in which they operate.

In their study of what makes for an effective company, Peters and Waterman characterize the shared beliefs of the school of 'scientific management' as follows:

- Big is better because you can always get economies of scale. When in doubt, consolidate things; eliminate overlap, duplication, and waste. Incidentally as you get big, make sure everything is carefully and formally coordinated.
- Low cost producers are the only sure-fire winners. Customer utility functions lead them to focus on cost in the final analysis. Survivors always make it cheaper.
- Analyze everything. We've learnt that we can avoid big dumb decisions through good market research, discounted cash-flow analysis, and good budgeting. If a little is good, then more must be better, so apply things like discounted cash flow to risky investments like research and development. Use budgeting as a model for long-range planning. Make forecasts. Set hard numerical targets on the basis of those forecasts. Produce fat planning volumes whose main content is numbers. (Incidentally, forget the fact that most long-range forecasts are bound to be wrong the day they are made. Forget that the course of invention is, by definition, unpredictable.)
- Get rid of those disturbers of the peace — i.e. fanatical champions. After all, we've got a plan. We want one new product development activity to produce the needed breakthrough, and we'll put 500 engineers on it if necessary, because we've got the better idea.
- The manager's job is decision making. Make the right calls. Make the tough calls. Balance the portfolio. Buy into the attractive industries. Implementation, or execution, is of secondary importance. Replace the whole management team if you have to get implementation right.

- Control everything. A manager's job is to keep things tidy and under control. Specify the organisation structure in great detail. Write long job descriptions. Develop complicated matrix organizations to ensure that every possible contingency is accounted for. Issue orders. Make black and white decisions. Treat people as a factor of production.
- Get the incentives right and productivity will follow. If we give people big straightforward monetary incentives to do right and work smart, the productivity problem will go away. Over-reward the top performers. Weed out the 30 to 40 per cent dead wood who don't want to work.
- Inspect to control quality. Quality is like everything else; order it done. Triple the quality control department if necessary. Have it report to the President. We'll show them (i.e. the workers) that we mean business.
- A business is a business is a business. If you can read a financial statement, you can manage anything. The people, the products, and the services are simply those resources you have to align to get good results.
- Top executives are smarter than the market. (Peters and Waterman, 1982: 42–4)

For reasons of space I will have to direct readers to other sections of Peters and Waterman's book for their compelling analysis of why these beliefs are a recipe for failure, and the authors' quite simple analysis of their practical effect — you go bust. What ought to bring a wry smile to the face of anyone keeping abreast of current changes in education is just how closely these recipes for failure resemble those changes.

This sort of managerialism is about the importance of control and quantification. These are reconciled tactically by stiffening line management and increasing quality control. The workforce is more prescriptively ordered (with the lumps smoothed out), while 'hotshots' (from whatever background, but always 'managers') are inserted at the top.

Peters and Waterman are writing about large business corporations, but there are obvious parallels with education systems. Each government education system is among the largest industries (by both budget and workforce) in their respective states. They are all organized (nominally) with head offices establishing policy, with branch offices supervising its implementation and with outlying providers, assisted by unattached service organizations, delivering the product. Customer relations are of crucial significance to effective performance, and increasingly they are industries operating in a competitive climate. (One of the most interesting 'beliefs' above is the second: 'survivors do it cheaper'. With the shift of students towards the private sector [more than 7 per cent over fifteen years], one can see that at least some clients relate 'expenditure' to 'quality'). There are outstanding performers and problem areas. The product is clearly harder to shift in some areas than others, yet a core of committed workers chooses to operate in such situations.

However, the differences between business and education are equally notable. In state education (as in health and welfare) there is little choice of clients. This has a distinct effect on the performance of the industry as a whole. This sort of education is a state-owned and run industry, and is therefore subject to a much higher degree of direct political influence. It is also subject to indirect political influence, being 'chock-full' of ideology.

In education it is very hard to relate the fiscal bottom line to performance. A balanced budget means virtually nothing in terms of 'company performance'. The total per capita sum expended can increase mightily, as it has in the last twenty years, without anyone being able to put the result in a box, take a picture of it, or write it down on paper. (It would be possible to do a great deal better in this area if teachers themselves were less fearful and negative about attempts to do so. This is somewhat odd given that examples of such data almost always show a steady improvement in performance, without necessarily being precise about causes.) This problem of identifying performance is one of the most marked in education. There is no balance sheet that will express it adequately, nor is there ever likely to be one which is entirely satisfactory because of the diffuse quality of the industry's 'mission'.

But rather than dampening the relevance of Peters and Waterman's analysis to schools, these differences tend to cement it. The characteristics of excellent (best performed, not most genial) companies extracted from their research become even more pertinent. Successful companies, they say, assume that the situation they are managing will produce both ambiguities and paradox. They manage on that basis rather than a 'rational' planning model. (Please note that this is a two-sentence summary of a thirty-page chapter and forgive its inadequacy.) Flexibility and speed of response are therefore of optimum importance. This is much harder to obtain in an area like education, which is marked out as much by beliefs, job performance very closely related to personal identity, and habits and expectations, which are the products of twenty, thirty or more years of experience, as anything else.

I had intended to suggest that the appropriate management model for systemic education was the antithesis of what occurs. Schools, which are flexible and consistently changing, I was going to say, should be stable, consistent and conservative, matching their function, which at its core is stable, consistent and conservative, and almost dramatically plain — the care and nurture of the intellectual and social behaviour of young people. Central administrations, which tend to be stodgy and inflexible, should be able to respond to the needs of their outliers with flexibility, speed and appropriateness. However, the situation is not like that. Remembering the helter-skelter of senior administrators shifting ground constantly to meet political demands (only some of which will come from either the customers or the deliverers of service), the intransigence of middle management and the difficulty of changing some teacher behaviour, that suggestion is far too bland. It is a simple picture. It is full of ambiguity and paradox.

Excellent companies have a bias for action. They will give something a go on a small scale to see how it works before large-scale and costly implementation. To do this, education systems risk the charge of 'guinea-pigging', but there have been periods in the past when central administrations were both more experimental themselves and more sympathetic to divergent local initiatives than they appear to be at present. One of the main reasons that this has occurred is the institution of agreements between unions and management about working conditions, the 'iron sums' that significantly reduce the flexibility, and the good will, to be found in schools. It is also partly because of the vastly increased political intrusion into management, and partly because with the advent of computerized information systems it is now possible to know much more quickly and accurately what schools are doing (at one level at least).

Excellent companies stay close to their customers. They study their needs intently at first hand. They are less inclined to tell them what they need (as both schools and education systems do perpetually), than to find out what they want. One of the reasons for the 'democratic movement' referred to above was to repair shortfalls in this area. But the 'demos' turned out not to be the people, the actual mums and dads, but the representatives of tightly tuned lobby groups with their own idealized and abstracted requirements. There is no doubt that school staffs are significantly inhibited by both central administration and lobby groups in their capacity to respond to local need.

Excellent companies encourage autonomy and entrepreneurship. Here we enter deep water. The issue of entrepreneurship is discussed elsewhere in this book. My own view is that it is entirely characteristic of good principals, less so of good schools. However, I would like to say something about autonomy and link it to the next of Peters and Waterman's characteristics of excellence: productivity through people, prizing and caring for your workers.

Teaching as a profession has undergone a significant slide in status during the last twenty years for a number of reasons. One is the tendency of our society to judge the worth of work by the financial reward which accrues to it. In teachers' case that has seen a marked relative decline. One is the structural shift in the nature of the workforce with the increase in size, importance and status attached to the service and communications industries in the private sector. One is that the rise of credentialism has increased the visibility of the highly competitive nature of upper secondary schooling with the resulting effect of an increased number of disappointed parents. Beyond that there have been only limited attempts by systems, commonly instantly undercut by other measures, to try to raise the morale of their workforces and to indicate that teachers' work is valued. Unions have been complicit in this through their lack of imagination in proposing possibilities for career restructuring which reach beyond wages and conditions.

Despite the fact that all system-generated restructures claim to start from the point of delivery of service, there has been almost no thinking about the real consequences of that. The outcomes always seem to be biased towards organizational diagrams which start beyond the school. It seems that results of devolution have been to increase the power of the centre to control larger and larger areas of teachers' work and school organization.

After examining a formidable range of research, Sam Sieber concluded that the following three things motivated teachers (this is a paraphrase of a lengthy passage):

- autonomy — the freedom to control tasks and conditions, and to have beliefs legitimated;
- the opportunity to sate aspects of professional appetite — satisfying professional curiosity, improving professional skills and applying them to new areas, general professional enlightenment;
- prospects for improvement of their role efficiency, to do the job better with less stress. (Sieber, 1981)

The capacity to act autonomously ('professionally' perhaps) was considerably ahead of the others. It is this very capacity that the 'new management' theorists and actors are seeking to limit; but that cat is out of the bag: once autonomy and self-management have been established only a tyranny will retrieve it. What is horrifying is that employers think so little about their workforce that they seek to undermine the essential reason that their workers enjoy their work, and make no effort to use and capitalize on that information.

The last of Peters and Waterman's observations is that excellent companies have 'simultaneous loose–tight properties'. By this they mean that some aspects of the company's culture are so strong and so well entrenched that no one would think of questioning them. They are often slogans ('Service before all else', 'We start and finish at the customer'), sometimes they are almost unstated but always understood (like much of that which is cultural). They are the means by which corporate loyalty is generated and maintained. They allow people to join in and be part of something, and yet maintain their autonomy and sense of individuality. Control of one's own destiny is to be found in the 'loose properties'. The sense of the job brief is: 'You understand what we are trying to do; now get on with it, doing the best you can.' That is the ethos being promoted.

Where does one find that in education systems? In various places at various times a good deal of work has been put into persuading parents and the general public that education systems have a plan and a purpose. Has the same sort of work been put into explaining that simply, effectively and credibly to those who work in schools, who are actually supposed to be doing the work? What sort of effort has been put into building up corporate loyalty? In my experience I cannot think of one such campaign, nor can I even think of any tentative measures recently directed to this end. The only related thing that springs readily to mind is the effort from both employers and employees which has gone into the promotion of adversary relationships.

In Conclusion

Schools are not governments, and they are not businesses either. They are schools. They are the sharp end of what education systems do. Without them there are no education systems. However much lip-service has been paid to these ideas, action has not proceeded on that basis. Contention has been not so much about effective and appropriate management but about who has the right to control schools and the degree of interference which can be exercised over their work — a quite different question.

The implications for action have not been spelt out, but they must include:

- establishing new sorts of relationships between management and workers, recognizing the characteristics and needs of both;
- pushing responsibility down and tying it off, leaving it there;
- encouraging politicians to stay out of management, to operate on ends not means, and to establish policy and to check performance against the goals of that policy;

- reducing rhetoric and paying more attention to implementation and the genuine effects of implementation; and
- trying to balance the interest in what ought to be with an increased understanding of what is.

References

COMMONWEALTH SCHOOLS COMMISSION (1983) *Participation and Equity in Australian Schools: The Goal of Full Secondary Education.* Canberra: Commonwealth Schools Commission.

HUDSON, AINSLIE (1987) *Participation and Equity Program in ACT Government Schools 1986: Case Studies and Overview.* Canberra: ACT Schools Authority.

MCRAE, DAVID (1989) *Teachers, Schools and Change.* Melbourne: Heinemann Education Australia.

PETERS, THOMAS J. and WATERMAN, ROBERT H. (1982) *In Search of Excellence: Lessons from America's Best Run Companies.* New York: Harper and Row.

SIEBER, S. (1981) 'Knowledge Utilization in Public Education: Incentives and Disincentives', in R. LEHMING and M. KANE (Eds), *Improving Schools: Using What We Know.* Beverley Hills, Calif.: Sage Publications.

TAYLOR, L.V.N. (1986) *Committees: Parents, Students and Teachers Working Together.* Adelaide: Participation and Equity Program, South Australia.

Chapter 7

Democracy, Bureaucracy and the Classroom

Garth Boomer

Democracy and the Classroom

In dealing with the relationship or tension between democracy and bureaucracy, I want to begin at the micro level with a consideration of the classroom, asking the question: 'What might a democratic classroom look like?'

At once I am confronted with the difficulties of the portmanteau word 'democracy'. It is a word commonly invoked by people of quite different political/ideological persuasions and carries with it strong emotional and moral force. Very few people wish to be perceived as being undemocratic. So, when people use the term 'democracy', they beg a deeper question: 'What kind of democracy?' or, more searchingly, 'What vision of the ideal society is being implied?' It might, for instance, be a kind of Darwinian/meritocratic democracy, in which all citizens have legally equal access or equal opportunity to the goods of society, but where the top prizes go to the swift and talented. It might be a small 'l' liberal democracy in which the individual has rights and opportunities to choose from diverse offerings; the right to vote and the right to be different. Or it might be a 'social justice' democracy in which the state in the interests of the relatively powerless requires affirmative action or positive discrimination aimed at equalizing the distribution of society's wealth and rewards.

For the purposes of this exploration I shall construe democracy as a regime devoted to ensuring that all citizens have a voice and a say in how their own lives are to be conducted, how local affairs are conducted and, collectively, in how the nation is to be governed. I would, therefore, wish to stress the social justice/social responsibility aspects of 'democracy'. It is upon this base that I shall construct a description of the ideal democratic classroom. I shall then posit what an ideal democratic bureaucracy might look like, before confronting a few realities.

Unequal Power

The 'democratic' teacher realizes that he/she has an unequal power relationship with the class and that this cannot be undone. There is institutional power, carrying with it sanctions and rules made by the institution; and there is experiential/knowledge power, a superior understanding, in most cases, of that which is to be learned and tested. Now various democratic gestures can be made to alleviate the worst effects of such powers, and the democratic teacher will make them while at the same time realizing that he/she cannot give his/her power away.

For instance, the school rules will be built jointly with the students and then applied not by the teacher alone, but by the class community. They will also be monitored by the class community and modified from time to time. In this way the classroom will mirror the democratic process in the enactment of laws in the wider society. While such a regime is more democratic than the laying on of rules framed by the teacher, it should be recognized that even if a 'one-person-one-vote' system applies to the making and following of rules, the teacher will still have undue influence because of all the other powers which he/she has. A word from the teacher seeded informally, in the context of the overall value set which will permeate the teacher's presentation of self in the classroom, can profoundly mould and direct class opinion. Many progressive or self-styled 'democratic' teachers are unaware of the pervasiveness and subtlety of their own reserve powers and, for this reason, often work under the illusion that they are more 'child-centred' than they really are.

Where a teacher is aware that these reserve powers will operate no matter what measures are taken to alleviate them, then it is likely that the powers will be wielded more healthily. The teacher will be better attuned to the facts that at the deepest levels we teach what we are and that what we are is far from straightforward. A very aware teacher will know, for instance, that despite ourselves we carry various forms of personal/societal/educational contamination into the classroom. For instance, male teachers carry with them their socialization as males, deep-seated orientations towards men and women, such that even the most aware and vigilant of men will catch themselves from time to time in undemocratic or unequal behaviours. This is a good thing. By admitting and demonstrating reform of the self, the teacher is promulgating what we might call 'internal democracy' — the capacity to recognize unhealthy coalitions of 'constituents' in the mind and to liberate and activate hitherto silenced or oppressed mental minorities.

Teachers also carry with them, to a greater or lesser extent, accumulations of educational habit which, undetected, may work to undermine conscious attempts to be democratic. There is in schools deeply sedimented behaviourism (the mind as *tabula rasa* to be imprinted), 'transmissionism' (knowledge as 'stuff' out there to be transmitted and acquired) and 'ableism' (the notion that some children are born more able than others). These 'isms' have been infused into the culture and heritage of education to such an extent that they are largely transparent. The accumulated habits and traditions of schooling are institutionalized in textbooks, examining systems, arrangement of furniture, reporting procedures, reward systems and so on. Taken together, the 'isms' account for strong totalitarian and fascist tendencies in schools, since they are projected from a view of the human brain as 'given' and 'imitative'. That is, they deny the young human being as constructor of knowledge, and they valorize the teacher/authority as didactic, controlling, shaper, moulder and initiator of the imitative young. If democracy is about hearing, allowing and strengthening the voices (and thus *minds*) of the people, then it must be recognized that intending democratic teachers will need to develop highly perceptive ways, first of recognizing and making opaque hidden 'terrorism' in schools, and, second, of mobilizing an array of techniques for opposing and, if possible, routing the enemy.

In relation to the joint framing and setting of rules, as but one example of a democratic classroom, it can be seen that an idea which would be quite widely applauded by enlightened citizens outside schools is easier said than done, given the way schools and society have evolved.

Recent post-modernist writings go far beyond my simple analysis, to cast considerable doubt on the question of choice and agency. Let us assume that a class comprises some Aboriginal children, some recent arrivals to Australia of non-English-speaking background, some children who have been taught to be seen and not heard at home, and a mixture of boys and girls. What will it mean if this class, encouraged by a 'democratic' teacher, votes on a set of class rules? Clearly, each voice in the classroom will not be equal. Each individual will 'choose' out of a complex personal context which will be more or less empowering. Is it not possible that the rules will have already been 'written' by the dominant regimes in society, by the traditions of schooling, by well worn notions of how people behave in school? Is it not likely that the choice offered, on examination, is merely a way of co-opting the class into the culture of schooling?

Democracy and Bureaucracy

How does the teacher who recognizes the inequality of the voices and votes in the classroom begin to redress the injustice? Paradoxically, it would seem that in order to produce some of the preconditions for a more healthy democracy, the teacher must wield power, intervene, take affirmative action and question the very bases of democracy as it is practised in society (the classroom writ large). The teacher will need not just to *recognize difference* among class members, but to act deliberately to have that difference heard and validated. The boys need to hear the different perspectives of the girls. Somehow all must come to recognize and redress the devastating effect of racism on the Aboriginal and non-English-speaking students.

What might have been seen as a fairly simple business (rule-making) is, in fact, hugely complicated. As soon as 'democracy' is unpacked and shown to be highly problematic, the major dilemma of the teacher is revealed. To teach in a liberating way that recognizes the legitimacy of the brains and voices of all students, the teacher must eschew harmony and go far beyond the cosmetics of conventional democratic practice, which through the 'ballot box' may serve to entrench existing power differentials and injustices.

No wonder that many highly aware and committed teachers, while recognizing much of the argument above, opt not to take on the ingrained system. No wonder that those teachers who do think things through in this way, and decide to become active fighters for a deeper level of democracy, have to be both tough and strategic in order to prevail against traditional, conservative practices, on the one hand, and harmonizing, 'progressive' practices, on the other.

The Ideal Democratic Classroom

I have surely argued myself to the point of saying that the key feature of the ideal democratic classroom will be its *persistent* questioning of the idea of democracy; its *insistent* probing of the notion of fairness and equality. Having said this, I believe that a healthy, if not ideal, democratic classroom would also have the following features.

Explicitness

Before students are taught to argue, negotiate and vote, a precondition for the classroom is a high level of explicitness. For most of their years at school children are compelled to attend. Already a key tenet of democracy is undermined. This needs to be confronted and stated. From the teacher's point of view the state (through the Ministry or Department) has made certain aspects of the educational program mandatory. On these matters there is no choice. Children should know this explicitly and be told *why* the state deems it non-negotiable. Teachers have personal styles, idiosyncracies, preferences, biases and values. These will have a huge effect on the classroom regime, whether implicit or explicit. It is better that they be explicit. At least they can then, as the children gain confidence in questioning, be subject to scrutiny and evaluation. At least such explicitness renders the power figure a little less invulnerable and is a gesture in the direction of power sharing.

The school itself has written and unwritten rules. If the children are to have a chance of transforming the school for the better, they need to know where it stands (officially and unofficially). Schools are riddled with secrets about how to live successfully in them. Those of us who graduated successfully no doubt learnt most of these secrets over time. We learnt what pleases teachers, what kinds of answers were rewarded, how to anticipate what might be in a test and so on. Some students learn these secrets more readily than others. (I suspect parents or older siblings of some children are very good informants.) The democratic teacher will arrange to teach deliberately the secrets of schooling on the basis that information is power and some students are not getting it.

Negotiation

Within the non-negotiables outlined above the democratic teacher will institute a kind of educational socialism. Individually and collectively, *we* have to make our way. *We* have to live together productively. *We* have to share responsibility for our collective achievements and well-being. The teacher cannot, and should not, try to divest him/herself of the ultimate responsibility for what is achieved, but it should be absolutely clear and constantly reiterated that *the teacher cannot learn for the students*.

Fundamental to deliberate learning is the *intention* to learn deliberately. Intention to learn can be motivated through external reward-and-sanction methods, and under such a regime students, having begun because they 'had to', may come to be intrinsically committed or intrigued by their learning. Learning will be at its best and most efficient, however, where through negotiation (or simply out of personal desire or necessity) the student intends, agrees, undertakes to work to some end.

Depending on a range of contextual, situational, age-level, time constraint matters, teachers are able to open the curriculum to more or less negotiation ranging from allowing students to choose, say, which of several assignments they will do, through to the detailed co-planning of a full unit of work covering content, processes, outcomes and evaluation. Ideally, a visitor to a democratic/negotiating classroom ought to find each student able to articulate what is going on, why and to what ends (including how things will be valued and assessed). Ideally, personal or group intention to learn will be so powerful that students will be highly self-reliant and self-regulatory, 'discipline' coming from the contracted and 'owned' job to be done.

A warning needs to be issued about negotiation. The techniques of negotiation, in classrooms as in society, can be used by the relatively powerful to increase their own power. Clever teachers can co-opt and colonize students' minds through securing allegiance won through versions of negotiation, which are in fact 'pseudo' and illusory. My litmus test for the true negotiated classroom is, therefore, to ask whether the teacher has these attributes:

a commitment to children becoming more and more self-reliant and socially critical;
a genuine belief in the child as constructor of his/her knowledge;
a genuine and demonstrated capacity to be persuaded away from certain designs after due argument;
therefore, a degree of vulnerability.

Questioning

While I have not seen definitive research, I feel confident that most teachers would agree that from Year 1 to Year 10 self-initiated question-asking in our schools atrophies. (Students in Years 11 and 12 start asking more questions of a certain kind as they collude with the teacher in the quest to pass external examinations.) Even the most casual observer will attest to the almost ferocious question-asking capacities of children aged up to 5, young adventurers in a complex, bewildering and infinitely intriguing world. For various reasons schools seem to act as lobotomizers of questioning. Quickly the school genre becomes one of teacher asking (usually questions where the answer is known) and students answering. Apart from relatively trivial procedural questions, such as 'how wide should the margin be?', the questions arising out of puzzlement, wonder or confusion become increasingly rare. Children are more likely to ask their peers than the teacher how to tackle a problem. Asking a question in class seems to carry certain kinds of stigma. To ask may be to be considered either dumb or sycophantic. It may also be to annoy a teacher who does not appreciate being derailed from a particular train of progress.

Whatever the reasons, and I suspect the main reasons are to do with power and control, one of the most undemocratic features of schools in the Western world is their dearth of student questioning. Cynics might observe that this is precisely the role of schools: to socialize the young into relative harmony, compliance and quiescence.

The democratic classroom will be one in which the teacher minimizes his/her questions, ensures that the learners are plunged into difficult and challenging territory, and then waits to have his/her knowledge commissioned. If he/she cannot answer the call, then he/she becomes an information broker indicating where an answer might be found. This means that teachers would voluntarily consent to de-escalate their arms build-up. The teacher question is one of the key pieces of educational artillery. The democratic classroom is dedicated to strengthening the battery and fire power of students.

Reflection

Schools, especially secondary schools, tend to be twitchy places. Learning tends to be fragmented into lessons and subjects. Even in primary schools where, structurally, there is the opportunity for integration and 'interdisciplinary' work, the tendency is to assume relatively short attention spans and to divide work into 'bite-sized' chunks and exercises.

The test or assignment is the 'power' end of the curriculum. Students and teachers work to what is valued, so any scholar interested in power and influence in schools should look primarily at how the 'testing regime' works. Who sets the tests? What is valued? Who sets the evaluation criteria? How is the test marked? What kind of feedback is provided? Asking such questions puts one at the heart of classroom politics. This is where power is most naked.

My thesis is, first, that the more the curriculum is fragmented (and then tested in fragments), the less likely it is that the learners will reach deep understanding which might inform action in their own lives; second, the less involvement students have in setting and evaluating tests, then the less they are likely to learn from the results.

Accordingly, my democratic classroom would be one where the

interconnectedness of learnings (even in subject-oriented secondary schools) would be emphasized and where major assignments would require synthesis and the demonstration of 'grand' as opposed to 'petty' control of information and ideas. The classroom, consistent with principles of negotiation, would also be one where students and teacher together plan the assignment or test in relation to what is to be learnt, establish the evaluation criteria, co-evaluate the product and reflect upon how to do better next time.

This classroom would not see knowing what is to be in the text as cheating, but as totally consistent with deliberate learning. How can one deliberately learn if one does not know what is being deliberately valued? Of course, the teacher again finds the arsenal depleted. Teachers have kept enormous power by using secrecy about testing. No doubt, it has given all of us teachers plenty of kicks in the past to surprise the young with an unanticipated question.

The question of reflectivity is crucial to the democratic classroom. Having set tests and assignments (with or without negotiation), there is a strong drive in schools (because of the 'we-must-cover-the-course' panic) to mark the test, give it back and move on quickly to the next unit. Now, if improvement and increased learning power depend on explicitly evaluating the quality of what has been done in order to do better next time, our schools could be unwittingly disempowering students by giving them cryptic feedback and no time to reflect on their achievement (or lack of it). How many students across Australia are in the habit of going straight to the grade or mark and then filing the test in the waste-paper basket? If the answer is 'most', what an indictment of learning and what a waste! All that work waiting for some powerful, clarifying, consolidating reflection is passed over because of an uncivilized and misdirected urge to get on with the course.

Reflection will not just apply to assignments in the democratic classroom. The democratic teacher will render problematic the whole life of the classroom community and its curriculum. On a wide range of fronts time will be made available to stop and take stock. How well did that lesson work? How can we improve our group work? Are we not doing enough talking? Which students are not being heard? Why?

The democratic classroom will have many other features besides the four selected. It will involve parents; it will be productive and interactive; it will value collaboration; and it will take action to improve the school community through the channels available.

The Educational Bureaucracy

By bureaucracy in education I mean essentially the enabling/directing superstructure by means of which the system is managed and resourced. Within schools there is a mini-bureaucracy, but I shall speak of the central and regional conglomerations of power which act outside schools.

I shall begin by posing the question: 'What kind of bureaucracy would best serve the democratic classroom described above?' Answer: 'One which is *explicit, negotiated, questioning* and *reflective*.' In other words the principles underpinning the democratic classroom should be congruent with the principles underpinning the bureaucracy. Having said that, I should hasten to problematize the notion of 'bureaucracy'. In the first place there are strong temptations to reify, to turn a highly complex ensemble of individuals into a thing — the bureaucracy. Those outside the bureaucratic structures, particularly teachers, are most prone to depict '*the* department' as a wilful, mechanized creature or, rather, machine. 'It' decides to do things to schools; 'it' is uncaring, unresponsive, ill-informed, etc.

The reality, of course, is that the bureaucracy comprises layers of human beings, more diverse than the usual label of 'grey public servant' would suggest. Especially in education in Australia most of those in key power positions have been teachers; since they have come to power over time, they are likely to have different educational 'persuasions' and, if one could unearth them, different political allegiances. In other words 'the bureaucracy' is by no means a homogeneous gathering of like-minded public servants. Depending on issues being considered, there are various currents of power, ebbs and flows of influence, blockages, coalitions and disjunctions. Rarely does anything flow immaculately up the bureaucracy or down. Various kinds of 'noise', deliberate or unintended, distort, deflect, hold or transform messages and intentions.

The most powerful force acting on the bureaucracy is the 'political will', which will be in varying degrees in tension with the educational will, as felt by either the schools or the bureaucrats. By definition, within the wider democracy it is the role of the bureaucracy to carry out the wishes of the people as interpreted by the minister of the day on behalf of the government.

Followers of *Yes, Prime Minister* will have some comprehension, albeit caricatured, of how ministerial will may be gently or not so gently opposed or transformed by people in bureaucracies, but those who live in educational bureaucracies in the 1990s in Australia will surely attest to the power and implacability of political desire. It is easy to argue that in terms of democracy this is a good thing. The people who have voted a government in would want it to assert its mandate. They would want education governed by their representatives, not by career public servants. In this regard Australian education has undergone major shifts of influence over the past decade. Once the Director-General of Education called a wide spectrum of shots. Now the Minister covers the major 'waterfronts' and requires a chief executive to make things happen. There has been a growing political dissatisfaction with the built-in inertia of bureaucracies and schools. They have been seen to have such 'cultural lag' that governments, mainly galvanized by the need for education-based economic reform, have been intervening directly and dramatically to enforce restructuring, which, at least in the rhetoric, will require more democratic decision-making within parameters set by government.

The Ideal Bureaucracy?

When one talks of the ideal educational bureaucracy, it needs to be in the knowledge that any bureaucracy is complex, subject to conflicts and not autonomous, unseverable from the government of the day on the one hand, and the schools on the other. In a very real sense the bureaucracy will be, and can be, only as democratic as the government of the day. It does have limited, but demonstrated, capacity to resist the worst or best effects of any government, but it is, by function, in the end a servant of the people's elected regime. It can be, and is, affected by the constituency it manages and, in turn, it affects schools and teachers. Contrary to the 'inertia' notion referred to above, educational bureaucracies in Australia over the past thirty years have tended to force innovation and to be pro-active, giving the lie to the image of the bureaucracy as a conservative and quelling influence.

Briefly applying the four features of the democratic classroom to the bureaucracy, I would make these observations.

Explicitness

The system would, according to this criterion, make quite clear what is non-negotiable, what is policy and what is to be evaluated. Criteria for evaluation of schools, teachers and the system itself would be explicit. Roles and responsibilities of officers at all levels would be spelt out. Curriculum guidelines would be supported by explicit exemplars of what is to be valued. The system's values, mission and plans, both long- and short-term, would be known by all in the system. The criteria for the allocation of resources, especially social justice criteria, would be available as a means of scrutinizing and critiquing all decisions made.

The first step in the creation of a dynamic, democratic bureaucracy is the establishment of clear statements about where it stands, making it at once comprehensible and vulnerable (to critique according to its own standards).

Negotiation

Having clarified and stated the non-negotiables, the bureaucracy will establish procedures to blur distinctions between 'the bureaucracy' and 'the workers', and to develop a unified, organic, mutually interdependent system in which meaning, tasks and evaluation are shared and negotiated. Consultation and negotiation must be genuine, and the bureaucracy should be subject to the same litmus test as the negotiating teacher with respect to intentions and capacity to make changes in the light of discussion.

Just as teachers cannot give away their power, so the Director-General and his/her public servants cannot give away their key powers. They are increasingly devolving and delegating some powers, but not key powers. One would hope that, in an ideal system, the Director-General would have the accumulated wisdom gained through negotiation and discussion to make the best decisions on behalf of the whole system. One must remember, however, that the Minister in this ideal set-up is also collecting wisdom. In the perfect world the intelligence of the Minister and the Director-General will be perfectly congruent and all good will flow to the system.

Questioning

The perfect bureaucracy would *at all levels* encourage hard questions about what we might do, what we are doing and what we have done. The ethos would be one of civilized dissent within a cooperating democracy. The system's continuing health will depend on its negative capability, the capacity, having acted, to be critical in the interests of higher quality next time.

The hard part is how to encourage constructive questioning *within* the ranks, rather than potentially destructive criticism outside the organization. The fundamental task of the system must surely be to secure itself from outside predators. Its questioning of itself from within should make it powerfully able to enter into non-defensive dialogue with those who would critique from without.

Reflection

The work of the ideal bureaucracy from policy formulation to program development and projects should be seen as a series of action research endeavours, subject to the classic action research cycle of problem → reflection → hypothesis → action → reflection →. Plans should be 'rolling' plans, built on the presumption of change and modification in the light of action in the field.

The system should healthily oscillate between tight construing/action and loose construing/speculation, so that it builds into its processes *anti-entropic* strategies for renewal and revitalization. The bureaucracy should model, for the whole system, well-based action and reflection upon action.

Some Realities

Stepping back from the 'shoulds' and 'oughts' of an ideal world, one is confronted with certain lessons from experience and history about bureaucracies and classrooms. Just as classrooms and schools carry many unexamined assumptions, rules and habits, so do educational bureaucracies. Systems of filing and routing of memoranda; complex delegations; funnel-like decision-making patterns; learnt tricks in covering the backside; decision avoidance by using the bureaucratic run-around; anonymity assurance techniques: all these can cohere to reinforce the outsider's view of the bureaucracy as a machine which takes on its own life and denies the humanity and agency of those within it. The term 'fighting the bureaucracy' reverberates with many who live within one. The frustration which individual officers feel when their ideas or contributions are rejected or swallowed by 'the beast' can lead to dispirited paper shuffling and entropic 'public servantitis'.

Inertia

With all the attempts in Australia in the last two decades to reform educational bureaucracies, usually in the direction of decentralization and 'flatter' organization charts, it can be seen that after 'shake-ups' systems are still likely to resettle in a hierarchical mode with regional offices tending to be replicas of the central bureaucracy from which they have been spawned. This is understandable, since most of the key actors in the reformed bureaucracy were socialized and rewarded under the old bureaucracy; unless they themselves are reformed, they will tend to reproduce old behaviours in new structures.

So it is at classroom and school levels. Recent studies of educational innovation in the USA indicate that while there have been many surface level shifts, fads and fashions, the fundamental teacher–student relationship has not changed and that a transmission model of teaching, didactic and teacher-focused, has remained entrenched and largely inviolate for more than a century.[1] I am sure that a similar study in Australia would yield similar results. If this is true, one can only conclude that educational bureaucracies have been singularly unsuccessful in recent times, if one is to judge them by their espoused doctrines as given form in policy statements and curriculum guidelines. Here the rhetoric *and the advice* are saying that teachers should adopt project, inquiry methods, employ group work and in various ways throw more responsibility onto students for the management of their own work. My conservative estimate, based on personal observation, textbook sales, student testimony and dialogue with teachers over many years, is that perhaps 10 per cent of our teachers are in this mode. Bureaucracies come out badly as change agents if change is the *real intent*.

Another way to view this phenomenon of mismatch between bureaucratic rhetoric and school action is to see the system's espousals as 'decoy discourses'. These discourses attract attention away from the *actions* of the bureaucracy in terms of resource provision, teacher promotion and deployment, assessment and examining systems, accountability and monitoring procedures, and decision-making structures. The decoy gives an appearance of modernity, defusing much of the energy of radical or reformist lobby groups.

But this analysis would be to credit bureaucracies with extremely Machiavellian motives. The reality is more likely to be that bureaucracies, like politicians, find it easier to say than to do, so that well-intentioned policies simply founder on the embedded rocks of custom. These rocks, of course, serve to protect the privileged and powerful, and in many ways, are the insurance policies of those with vested interests against the vicissitudes of party politics. That is, a version of democracy which protects the already and traditionally powerful permeates the structures of bureaucracies. While almost all actors within the bureaucracy may individually have reformist tendencies, the system carries within it containing and conservatizing rules and structures.

The Need for Reform

This may help to explain the recent phenomenon of what I have called the ministerialization of education in Australia. Mainly for economic reasons, but for cultural and social reasons as well, Australia has to reconstruct itself. We are faced with the cumulative consequences of cultural and economic lag, not just in schools but also in business and industry. Indeed, industry has been no different from bureaucracies in its inability to effect reformed work practices and new dynamic forms of corporate management. A few industries have led the way, but most lag behind and cling to outmoded practices and procedures. Politicians acting in response to economic pressures are intervening, hoping to win the collaboration of industries, agencies and bureaucracies in short- and long-term plans for reform.

In the field of education ministers are intervening in ways which were not evident a decade ago. It is as if governments, which in the past have been pleased to let the inertia of educational bureaucracies preside over safely conservative schools, now *really* want a change. There are signs that politicians are frustrated by the Sir Humphrey style bureaucrat and wish to appoint people with a *will* for change as sought by the government of the day. As never before, our bureaucracies are being rocked and restructured. Democracy, if you like, assuming that ministers act for the people, is saying that our schools and the bureaucracies that run them, are not keeping pace. Bureaucracy and democracy, in this regard, are well and truly in tension.

If one looks more closely at the will and motivations of politicians, it is not hard to find a perplexing schizophrenia which, no doubt, reflects the confusions of the electorate. While we need to produce more skilful, flexible, communicative and collaborative people who are self-starting and self-reliant, it seems that we fear social dissolution. Simultaneously we want to shock our schools into a new entrepreneurialism which will unleash initiative or potential *and* yet control them, restore order and conformity in classrooms which have returned to the basics. At the same time as schools are called to be more aware of, and responsive to, the modern 'world out there', they are under pressure to reassert a nineteenth century academic curriculum. Public examinations, which are prime agents for ensuring that half our human resources fail, are being reaffirmed, while politicians also call for schools to ensure that all young people get a worthwhile and challenging education. All this boils down to the conclusion that when it comes to saying what kind of classrooms and schools they want, our politicians, and the employers who influence them, only dimly know what they mean. Democracy, mediated by the politicians, is sending education bureaucracies decidedly mixed messages. Given the containing forces which already exist within educational bureaucracies, it might be posited that the nett effect of political intervention at this time will be negligible where it should count — in the micro communities of classrooms. The push-me-pull-me nature of political intent is likely to be absorbed and neutralized; not, however, before a good deal of restructuring and upheaval has occurred. The eventual response of teachers is likely to be to continue to do what they have been taught to do.

From Rhetoric to Action?

Democracy, however defined, has been fully realized nowhere in the world. Australia is but one flawed democracy. Here certain voices are amplified, certain voices are muffled. The will of the people is manipulable and manipulated. The corruptibility of democratic ideals is evident at all levels of society. Self-interest, backed by money, swamps the self-interest of the poor.

One way to interrogate a 'democracy' is to ask: 'In whose interests is it operating, socially, economically and culturally? How are its rewards distributed?' That is, to ask the economic questions. There is also the 'regime' question: 'Who is controlling and who is inventing?' These questions bring us quickly to the heart of education because they are questions that we would wish to apply to any classroom or any educational bureaucracy that purports to be democratic:

> Does each student/participant have an equal voice?
>
> In whose interest is the classroom or bureaucracy operating?
>
> What things are rewarded and who gets the rewards?
>
> Who makes what decisions?
>
> Which people have their inventions/learnings recognized and encouraged?
>
> Which people are controlled and silenced?

These are the equity or social justice questions which education systems have been asking of themselves with fluctuating intensity over the past two decades.

There are signs that energy and enthusiasm for the rhetoric of equality are on the wane, perhaps because the urgency of the 'economic imperative' has drowned out the 'welfare' voices and because the last decade or so could be seen as all talk and very little action. The slogans of 'equal opportunity' and 'equal access' (and others like them) have tended to become hollow mockeries — chest-thumping, self-righteous decoys deflecting attention away from a relatively unchanged reality.

A more optimistic interpretation is possible. While debate about equity and democratic schooling has been largely conducted at the system policy/guidelines level, important advances have been made not only in changing the official discourse, but also in some cases in securing new legislation. This has legitimized and supported reforming actors in the systems and schools so that some changes in practice, if patchy, have occurred. Systems which have operated largely on a 'bully pulpit' model may now be ready to give systematic teeth to their espousals. The attention may have turned from merely saying to doing. It might even be seen that equity has an economically dry face. We are culpably wasteful of our human resources, and the consequences of social alienation and economic deprivation of some groups, in terms of long-term social disruption and crime, are patent. We can no longer afford to be undemocratic in the valuing of our people.

Conclusion

This chapter has ranged across a wide field in an attempt to raise issues of bureaucracy and democracy as they contend in education. Four features which might be sought in schools and in bureaucracies have been suggested. Brief explorations of the context and the realities which will render this difficult have been offered. In conclusion, it is suggested that it is, however, worth reaching for the unreachable.

Note

1 L. Cuban (1984) *How Teachers Taught: Constancy and Change in American Classrooms 1890–1980*. New York: Longman.

Chapter 8

Democracy and Bureaucracy: Curriculum Issues

Christine Deer

At the heart of the educational debate about the curriculum is the question of who should control it. Should the power lie with the centre, that is to say the ministers of education and their supporting bureaucracies? Or should it be with the schools and their local regions? At this level parents and other members of the local community can share with teachers decisions about education. There is continuing tension as to which group should have the control and what the balance between the two should be.

The definition of the word 'curriculum' is itself contentious. It comes from a Latin word meaning 'race-course', implying a set course to be 'covered'. However, there are many different definitions of the term and each implies different values. Marsh and Stafford (1988: 3) summarize four of these definitions (see Table 8.1). Each of these definitions poses problems. It is notable, too, that the second and third definitions imply that the word 'curriculum' is more than content, as there is an emphasis on the process of learning.

Changes in the debate in Australia in the last few years at federal and state levels are increasing the emphasis on education for employment, particularly in science and other technologically related industries. To achieve national goals of a better educated, technically literate and more flexible work force there is more emphasis on control of the curriculum by the centre and a decreasing emphasis on control at the local or school level, sometimes referred to as 'the periphery'. Table 8.2 summarizes the essential differences between centralized and school-based curriculum development.

Historically, in Australia since the 1880s the power has been with the bureaucracy. The Head Offices of the Department of Education in each state issued syllabus documents to teachers who used these to plan their

Democracy and Bureaucracy

Table 8.1 Curriculum Definitions and the Problems They Pose

Curriculum definition	Problems posed by the definition
1 Disciplined study of 'permanent' subjects such as grammar, reading, logic, rhetoric, mathematics and the greatest books of the Western world	Does the state of knowledge change? If so, should this not also be reflected in the curriculum? What is the significance of such knowledge to the learner?
2 All the experiences the learner has under the guidance of the school	Do all experiences (planned and unplanned) count as curriculum? Which experiences are unique to the school?
3 All planned learning outcomes for which the school is responsible	Is it possible for teachers to separate means from outcomes? Does it exclude unplanned, but actual, learning experiences?
4 An event to which the various elements of the environment (physical, psychological, social) make a contribution	Is it manageable to try to consider all these elements? Does it create a static image and downplay the processes (in some cases hidden curriculum aspects)?

Source: Marsh and Stafford (1988: 3).

Table 8.2 A Comparison of Centralized and School-based Curriculum Development

Point of comparison	Centralized curriculum development	School-based curriculum development
Teacher role	Selected teachers participate in curriculum decision-making	Most teachers in a school participate in curriculum decision-making
Teacher commitment to decisions made	Variable	Teachers who participate in making decisions more likely to be committed to implementing them in spirit in which intended
Use of resources (personnel with various expertise, time, reference materials)	More resources able to be marshalled centrally	Limited resources available to single school
Relation of curriculum to individual school needs	Curriculum developed on basis of generalized student needs and interests	Curriculum developed in line with needs and interests of specific school

Source: Deer (1985: 32).

teaching programs. Each state employed inspectors to visit teachers on a regular basis to assess whether they were carrying out the instructions of the Head Offices. The centre controlled the curriculum because it prescribed what should be taught, and it used the inspectorial system in an attempt to ensure compliance with centrally issued instructions. At the beginning of the 1970s there was a devolution of power in some states, particularly Victoria. There schools — teachers, parents and in some cases students — were given the opportunity to devise their own curricula for the compulsory years of schooling. In the past ten years of increasing financial constraints, with less money for all areas of government, there has been growing pressure for more efficient use of government resources in education. There has been a redefinition of the relationship between the centre and the periphery, with the centre taking greater control. At both federal and state levels government policies are leading to more centralized control of the curriculum.

In Australia, however, whether there has been more emphasis on centralized curriculum development or on school-based curriculum development, the 'competitive academic curriculum' (Connell et al., 1982) has remained the dominant and most prestigious curriculum in schools. The Schools Commission (1980: 6) stated that 'ability displayed in bookish ways remains the most seriously valued ability in schools.' Over time this curriculum has been developed by central authorities with assistance from teachers in both government and non-government schools, representatives from tertiary institutions and parents. Ashenden (1982: 9) describes it as having four defining characteristics:

1 a hierarchically organized body of knowledge, derived from academic disciplines as propounded in universities;
2 a pronounced separation of learner from content and of learning from action;
3 a way of organizing the appropriation of knowledge by individuals in competition with each other;
4 a curriculum which imposes a common pace and sequence to be followed by all learners.

This curriculum has been followed by those desiring tertiary entrance, which has become increasingly more competitive as the number demanding tertiary entrance has outstripped the supply of places. Competition for entrance to the most remunerative professions has been one factor in establishing the status of this curriculum.

Other curricula existing in schools, variously labelled vocational or technical curricula, have been considered by the majority of the community as of lesser value. Students completing this type of curriculum tend to go on to Colleges of Technical and Further Education (TAFE) or to join the work force without further study.

No matter where the power for determining the curriculum lies, it is important to consider what should be the outcome of the process of schooling for the students. McKinnon (1982) states that the outcome should be to give students

> power to negotiate with the world that comes from knowing how, knowing why, knowing where to go, and knowing how to act. They need, before they even consciously want, a growing power over their own circumstances, so that they may take a hand in the decisions that shape their future, and become citizens in the full sense of that term.

This outline of student needs is a useful basis from which to consider curriculum issues. The outcome of whatever curriculum is devised should be to give students power over their own circumstances so that they become 'citizens in the full sense of that term'. The implications of this argument are that there must be a balance between centralized and local control of the curriculum, that schools need a centrally developed framework in which to work, but they must also be given the opportunity to develop a curriculum that suits the particular needs of their students.

One question fundamental to all such discussions is: what knowledge is of most worth? Yet a second question, which should be considered equally important, is: how can this knowledge be brought alive for students (Schools Commission, 1980)? How can knowledge be at the one time compulsory yet compelling for all students? Answers to these questions are, again, part of the political agenda, owing to the dramatic changes in retention rates that have occurred in the 1980s in Australia.

Changes in the Curriculum Required by Changes in Retention Rates: Historical Overview

Changes in retention rates alter the school population quite dramatically and demand, or should demand, revisions in the curriculum. Universal primary education was achieved in Australia by the 1920s. In New South Wales (NSW) automatic progression to secondary education became a reality in 1938 (Bessant and Spaull, 1976: 162), but only a minority completed five years of secondary schooling. Those who did tended to go

Table 8.3 Apparent Retention Rates to Year 12 for All Students by State, 1979–1988 (percentages based on July data)

Year	NSW	Vic.	Qld	SA	WA	Tas.	NT	ACT
1979	34.7	32.0	37.7	36.9	34.2	25.7	22.2	69.6
1980	32.8	32.5	38.6	38.8	34.0	26.9	20.1	66.6
1981	32.9	33.1	38.7	38.9	35.1	26.7	18.0	67.9
1982	33.7	34.3	42.1	41.0	37.4	21.9	18.2	72.5
1983	37.5	38.8	47.2	47.6	40.4	24.7	20.6	72.2
1984	41.4	43.3	53.1	50.1	45.5	27.6	26.4	79.8
1985	41.7	45.4	55.1	51.2	47.5	28.7	30.1	77.1
1986	44.4	46.8	57.5	54.8	50.3	30.3	34.1	77.7
1987	47.1	52.5	62.5	60.2	54.4	33.0	40.7	79.0
1988	51.3	56.9	66.9	66.6	59.2	37.6	45.0	81.4

Source: Commonwealth Department of Employment, Education and Training (1989).

on to tertiary studies. The Wyndham Report (Report of the Committee Appointed to Survey Secondary Education in New South Wales, 1957) extended secondary schooling in NSW from five to six years by 1967. As a result the majority of students completed four years of secondary schooling, about 10 per cent stayed to complete six years and a smaller percentage of these students went on to tertiary study. Compared with that first Higher School Certificate (HSC) group of 1967, retention rates have risen, not only in NSW, but across Australia.

Table 8.3 shows the rise in apparent retention rates for the ten-year period 1979–1988. In 1979 for Year 12 these ranged from 22.2 per cent in the Northern Territory to 69.6 per cent in the Australian Capital Territory (ACT). In 1988 they ranged from 37.6 per cent in Tasmania to 81.4 per cent in the ACT. The change in retention rates in the Northern Territory is dramatic. It is the result of a deliberate policy to improve the senior secondary curriculum so that it is attractive for students to complete their senior secondary schooling in the Territory rather than going south to do so. It is also the result of the lack of localized job opportunities. The power of successful curriculum changes is shown by the increased retention rates in the Northern Territory. There are also dramatic changes in Victoria, Queensland and South Australia.

Other factors have also helped to increase rates. For example, the availability of a credential in Year 11 in South Australia and Victoria increased retention rates in these states. It is worthwhile for students to stay at school longer because they gain documented recognition for their extra time at school. Community acceptance of the idea that more education leads to increased employment opportunities has been a factor in increasing retention. It is notable that Australia has lagged behind other countries in this matter.

Braithwaite and Baumgart (1987: 107) found that many staying or leaving decisions 'were made quite early' in students' secondary careers. In fact 27 per cent of students in their Australia-wide research indicated that they made their decision before Year 7 and a further 35 per cent before Year 10 (1987: 80). These decisions were influenced by many factors including 'the students' educational and career preferences, school performances, family economic situations and job availability ... student ambitions appeared to be the greatest influence upon continuation decisions' (1987: 106).

The experiences students have under the guidance of the school do play a part. In their conclusion Braithwaite and Baumgart (1987: 108) state:

> The 'real' obstacle [to continuation] may be the lack of perception among some families about the benefits of continuation into Years 11/12. Politicians, school and educational authorities strongly urge continuation but the potential benefits for students have not always been clearly spelt out. Publicity could emphasize the potential long-term financial supports available through SAS (Student Assistance Scheme) and the success of AUSTUDY.

Financial considerations are a factor in increasing retention rates. The decision of the federal government to stop payment of the dole to 16- and 17-year-olds in 1987 and reduced employment opportunities have helped increase retention rates.

Table 8.3 is important because it reveals a change in the population remaining for post-compulsory schooling. As a result the currently constructed competitive academic curriculum is no longer suitable for the wider range of abilities, aptitudes and attitudes of students now continuing in the post-compulsory years of schooling. Figure 8.1 shows the retention rates to Year 12 for all schools and for boys and girls separately from 1967 to 1988. Figure 8.2 shows the rates by gender in all Australian states and territories in 1988. The differences in the retention of boys and girls are clear; they are caused partly by the differing availability of jobs for boys and girls, but also by the ambivalence teenage girls have about their future lives (Poole and Beswick, 1989).

The Schools Commission (1980: 6) argued that there was a need to re-examine 'the current intellectual and institutional assumptions which currently govern the compulsory years' [of schooling]. The individual school, however, does not have sufficient strength to create this change, which can only be effectively introduced from the centre. Some have also expressed concern, see, for example, Collins and Hughes (1982), that the

Democracy and Bureaucracy: Curriculum Issues

Figure 8.1 Apparent Retention Rates to Year 12, All Schools, Australia, 1967–1988

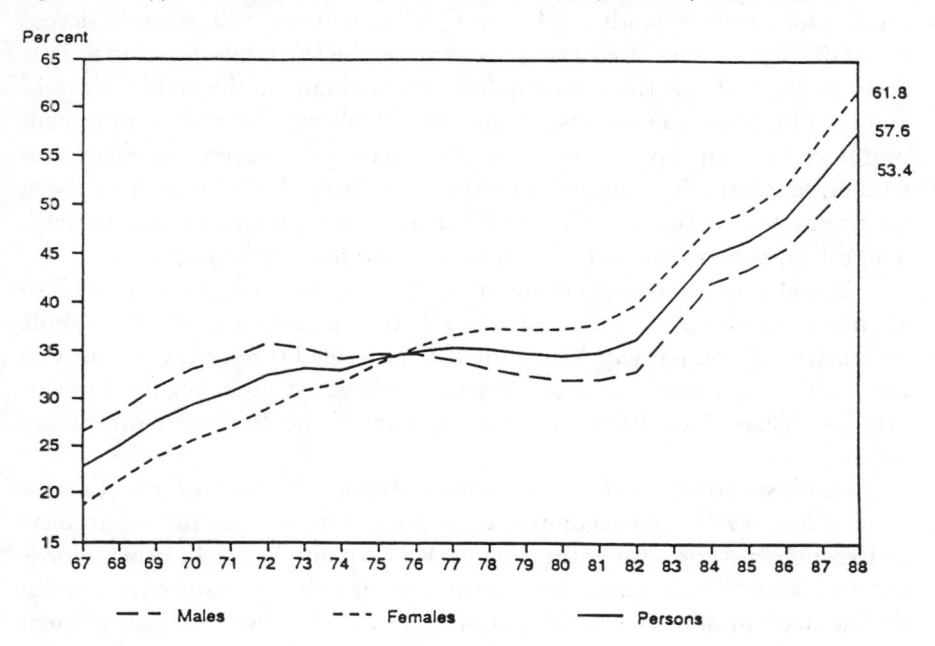

— — Males   - - - Females   —— Persons

Figure 8.2 Apparent Retention Rates to Year 12 by Gender, All States and Territories, 1988

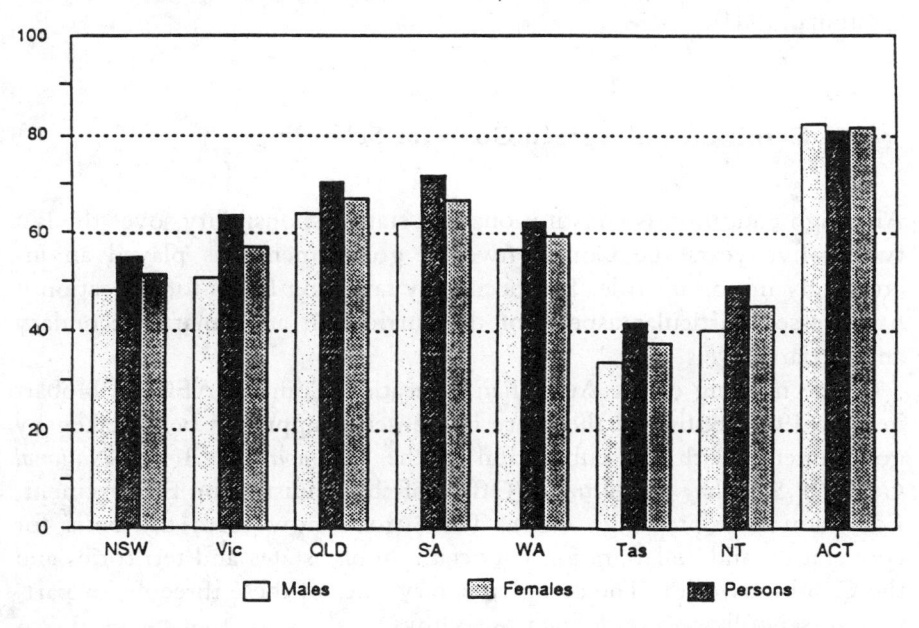

☐ Males   ▨ Females   ▨ Persons

Source: Retention and Participation in Australian Schools (1989) *Monograph Series No. 2*. Canberra: Australian Government Publishing Service, July.

137

competitive academic curriculum is not even appropriate for all students bound for tertiary study. Education bureaucracies and schools across Australia have been attempting to change the curriculum so that it is appropriate both for the new population remaining to the end of Year 12 and for the changes in society, such as the emphasis on equal employment opportunities for boys and girls, the increased interest in Australian studies, particularly changes regarding the way Aborigines have been represented, and the growing technological complexity of our society. There is also growing interest in Asian and environmental studies.

In addition, there has been concern that the curriculum in Years 7 to 10 needs revision, so that there is a better articulation for the whole secondary school, namely Years 7 to 12. This need is felt very strongly in the ACT, where the formation of senior colleges in 1976 left the curriculum for Years 7 to 10 unchanged (Report of the Review Committee, 1983).

In New South Wales the Carrick Report (Report of the Carrick Committee, 1989: 155) recommends that there be 'curriculum continuity' and emphasizes the importance of the K–12 continuum. In other words another government-appointed committee has shown its concern about the curriculum at *all* levels of schooling (see also Education Department of South Australia, 1981; Northern Territory Department of Education, 1983; Report of the Committee of Inquiry into Education in Western Australia, 1984).

Common and Agreed Goals for Schooling?

Although education is constitutionally a state responsibility, over the last twenty-five years the Commonwealth government has played an increasingly important role. By specifically targeting funds for education it has stressed particular aspects of the curriculum at primary, secondary and tertiary levels.

The meeting of the Australian Education Council (AEC) in Hobart in May 1989 confirmed the more instrumental approach being taken by governments with the publication of the *Common and Agreed National Goals for Schooling in Australia* (Office of the Minister for Employment, Education and Training, 1989). These goals now form the basis for cooperation and collaboration between schools, states and territories and the Commonwealth. The complementary roles of these three major partners in schooling were defined as follows:

Schools
The Schools are responsible for the provision of excellent schooling by means of a curriculum which reflects local needs and aspirations within the framework of common and agreed national goals. This is achieved through the development of effective partnerships between parents, students and teachers.

States and Territories
The States and Territories have the constitutional and major financial responsibility for schooling.

Commonwealth
The Commonwealth, along with States and Territories, has a significant role in identifying national priorities for schooling. The Commonwealth contributes to the funding of schooling, has financial responsibility in the areas of higher education and contributes to industry training.

It was also stated that:

Ministers look forward to future development and refinement of these goals in response to the changing needs of the community. The goals will be reviewed from time to time by the Australian Education Council (AEC), using consultative processes involving both government and non-government schools, parents, teachers and the community.

The instrumental role of the Commonwealth is clear. There is now, in the determination of the curriculum, a greater concern for the societal goals of education than in the 1970s.

This approach contrasts markedly with the *laissez-faire* approach of the 1970s and early 1980s in some states, notably Victoria. However, as the 1990s begin, Australia has a much better educated teaching profession. Teachers have gained considerable expertise in school-based curriculum decision-making. In many schools, through the operation of the Disadvantaged Schools Program (DSP), the Innovations Program of the School Commission and the Participation and Equity Program, teachers and members of the school executive have worked in cooperation with the parents of the students they teach and, in some cases, with the students themselves to change their school's curriculum so that the curriculum empowers the students, giving them 'power to negotiate with the world' (McKinnon, 1982).

The increase in expertise at the local level means that there can be no return to complete centralized control of the curriculum based on pre-1970s practices. The federally funded programs of the 1970s and 1980s have shown that expertise for decentralized curriculum-making exists and that it allows school communities to take account of local needs in deciding what knowledge is of most worth and how to make that knowledge compelling for students.

There are now moves to develop overall goals for schooling in Australia. Recently, The Honourable John Dawkins, the Commonwealth Minister for Employment, Education and Training, met all state Ministers for Education with a view to develop a national curriculum policy. Dawkins (1988) has written of the responsibility of the Commonwealth government to provide national leadership and determine priorities for schools; schools are responsible for:

> preparing young people for fulfilling personal lives and active membership of the community;

> preparing all students to take their place in a skilled and adaptable workforce in which further education and training throughout their working lives will become the norm; and

> playing their part in overcoming disadvantage and achieving fairness in our society. (Dawkins, 1988: 4)

Another consideration in the aims of schooling relates to the kind of society we want. If Australians decide the answer to this question, there is a clearer idea of the kind of schooling Australia needs to achieve its desired society. At present the various state Ministers for Education, led by the Federal Minister, are making this determination. Current discussions led one cynic to describe it as a society where students will leave formal education 'knowing the price of everything and the value of nothing'.

One major change in the school population since the 1960s has been the increasing ethnic diversity. The curriculum, therefore, has to address the issue of a common culture. The Schools Commission (1980: 12–13) stated:

> How are we to take into account the differing cultural strands associated with students' differing backgrounds and the different

circumstances which they will encounter in their adult lives in an unequal, stratified and varied society? There are structures of power and reward which affect all social groups some more favourably than others. But there are also beliefs and presumptions which provide evaluative frameworks within which the distinctive orientations of sub-groups can be examined and within which public issues can be discussed.... Schooling cannot uncritically endorse the values and beliefs of either majority or minority groups.

This issue has not been resolved. A resurgence of public debate on immigration signals that a single direction will be difficult to find and implement.

In some states and territories of Australia there is a professional administrator who heads a bureaucracy of professional educators who advise the Minister for Education or Chief Education Officer. More and more these bureaucrats under ministerial direction are determining what should be the aims for the curriculum and thus its broad outlines. Two statements published by the former NSW government indicate this trend: *What Our Students Learn at School* (NSW Department of Education, 1987) and *The Primary Purpose: A Curriculum Handbook for Primary Schools and Their Communities* (NSW Department of Education, 1988). The change from previous eras is considerable.

Today the political parties in power are endeavouring to enunciate comprehensive programs of improvement; they are determining the direction the curriculum is to take, using their powers as our democratically elected representatives. Jecks (1971: 141) raises the following key questions in regard to the exercise of power by the Minister:

> To what degree is he influenced by a party platform? What is his status in Cabinet? Is he likely to lean heavily on his departmental advisers? To what extent can a casual comment by the Minister, for instance on homework, commit his department? The question 'Who determines educational policy?' must be answered differently at different times and levels. Educational policy and practice is a composite process, the resultant of many forces. The prime factor is the state, but the state does not speak with a single voice. Legislative action is not necessarily the initiating agency in Australia for a new situation to first emerge in fact.

Legislative action is becoming the initiating agency in Australia for changes in the curriculum. Dawkins (1988) makes the case for a curriculum that is relevant to our times with a common framework across states and territories and a common approach to assessment. Part of this concern has been generated by population mobility. Figures quoted in the *Sydney Morning Herald* of 28 July 1988 show 450,000 Australian children change their addresses every year. But part has been generated by what Dawkins sees as fragmentation of effort in curriculum development and assessment in a country with a relatively small population. The states have been invited to join with the Commonwealth government in an effort 'to strengthen the schools'. At Commonwealth and state levels legislation is proposed and has been promulgated in some places to change the curriculum in a way that reduces the options in the senior years of schooling. In 1990 it is the ministers and their advisers, with responsibility for education, who are changing the curriculum rather than the professional bureaucrats.

Over the last twenty years there has been a waxing and waning of public interest in education. Today public interest is again increasing, and curriculum issues are assuming a prominent place in the media. In the early 1970s education was a matter of great public interest and debate. There was great concern for principles of equity, and at the national level there was increased spending on education. As a result schools were given more money to spend on programs they had devised and democratization of the curriculum increased. The introduction of the Innovations Program and the DSP under the Whitlam Labor government gave power and responsibility for curriculum change at the local level. Groups of teachers in a school applied for funds to develop programs specifically designed for the students they taught. From the mid-1970s the fortunes of the nation declined and with increases in unemployment and growing deficits these programs in particular, and schools in general, were seen as not having 'delivered the goods'; funds to the states and territories and hence to schools were cut. Now as the 1990s begin there is revived public interest in education, with employment as a focus. More significantly, however, the public is now better educated and more articulate.

Curriculum Issues in Selected States

Vigorous public debate on the latest changes in education in New South Wales followed the election of a new government on 19 March 1988, uniting previously disparate groups such as students, teachers and their unions, the NSW Teachers' Federation and the Independent Teachers' Association, the Federation of Parents' and Citizens' Associations and the Catholic Education Commission. These groups were united in opposition

Democracy and Bureaucracy: Curriculum Issues

to changes being instituted by Dr Metherell, the Minister for Education and Youth Affairs in the Liberal/National Party government headed by Mr Greiner. Although the new government proposed changes in education as part of its election platform, the pace of change and some of the changes produced a public outcry.

One of the problems with education is the multiplicity of goals; some of these take longer to achieve than others, so that there is a tendency to work first on the more easily achievable goals and leave the longer-term goals to the 'too hard basket'. Inevitably tensions arise, as they have done in New South Wales with the election of the Greiner government. It came to power in March 1988 with a mandate for change to the Higher School Certificate (HSC). This it promulgated immediately, thus affecting students in Years 11 and 12 who had already begun their studies for this final external school examination. Normally all changes to the HSC are announced two years in advance, so that students can take account of such changes in their subject choices. This time lapse allows schools to inform parents of the proposals, to make the necessary changes in their curriculum offerings and to arrange relevant staffing changes. Here is a clear case of a minister directing the bureaucracy and the schools to implement such changes immediately, arguing that the changes being imposed are the result of a democratic decision by the people. There was little attempt to understand the implications at the classroom level, and there was a failure to take advice from those responsible for administering education.

Whether these changes will have the effects desired by the government remains to be seen. Some say there will be a fall in retention rates in NSW schools as a result of a greatly increased emphasis on education for the academically able. In other words, the competitive academic curriculum is being reinforced as the most important. At present English is the only compulsory HSC subject, but there are proposals for mathematics, science and a language other than English, preferably Asian, or a social science to be compulsory subjects for the external HSC examination at the end of six years of high school. While the education department bureaucracy under the previous Labor government had moved to liberalize the curriculum, the Liberal/National Party government has moved to restrict it, using the need to maintain and increase standards as its reasons. It is, however, true that despite the existence in many schools throughout the state of curricula that were alternatives to the competitive academic curriculum, it is the latter that is most highly esteemed.

The Report of the Carrick Committee (1989) in New South Wales was presented in September and represents a change in process: there was widespread consultation in its preparation. It proposes changes that will affect the curriculum, for example, a new Board of Studies to cover all years of schooling from Kindergarten to Year 12, highlighting the view that education is a continuum and that there should not be the separation that currently exists. This recommendation is similar to moves in other states such as Victoria.

The publication of the Carrick Report, of the *Discussion Paper on the Curriculum in New South Wales Schools* (Ministry of Education and Youth Affairs, November 1988) and of the *Report of the Ministerial Working Party on the State Language Policy* (December 1988) shows that the NSW government is concerned to provide interested persons with an opportunity to comment on its proposals for changes in the curriculum.

Responses to the discussion paper on the curriculum were used to prepare the White Paper entitled *Excellence and Equity New South Wales Curriculum Reform* (Ministry of Education and Youth Affairs, 1989) which was released in November. It is notable that approximately 1000 responses were received indicating strong professional and public interest in curriculum issues. From 1992, as a result of these responses, the curriculum will be defined in terms of key learning areas, six for primary education and eight for secondary education. These are as follows:

primary education
- English
- mathematics
- science and technology
- human society and its environment (including modern languages)
- creative and practical arts
- personal development, health and physical education

secondary education
- English
- mathematics
- science
- human society and its environment
- modern and classical languages
- technological and applied studies
- creative arts
- personal development, health and physical education.

This framework allows continuity between primary and secondary levels of education (Ministry of Education and Youth Affairs, 1989: 14–15).

The recommendation in the Carrick Report (Report of the Carrick Committee, 1989: 1) for a Board of Studies 'responsible for curriculum development for all the years of schooling and serviced entirely by its own curriculum and administrative structures' conflicts with the central executive structure proposed in the Scott Report (Management Review: NSW Education Portfolio, 1989: 20) for a Director of Curriculum and Education Programs. The Scott proposal would allow the continuation of NSW Department of Education concern with the curriculum, while the Carrick Report would set up an independent structure. This issue concerning the curriculum will be resolved by the government.

In Victoria there have also been great changes to the control and organization of the curriculum, creating enormous upheavals. There is, however, an emphasis on consultation and on collaboration compared with the increased emphasis on competition in New South Wales. The Victorian changes have drawn on strategies used by the Schools Year Twelve and Tertiary Entrance Certificate (STC) group which began work in 1976 in seven schools. By 1986 it involved ninety-seven schools with an estimated enrolment of 2400 students (Freeman, Batten and Anwyl, 1986: 3). It was developed because of the perceived failure of the competitive academic curriculum for some students, particularly those from low socio-economic backgrouds. Freeman *et al.* (1986: 14–15) summarize key aspects of this curriculum.

FIRST AND FOREMOST
The three-way relationship between the teacher, the student and the content to be covered can best be thought of as an alliance between teacher and students, for successful learning.

MATTERS OF PRINCIPLE
1 Classes should be organized on the basis of:
   * close student-teacher and student-student interaction
   * co-operation rather than competition
   * heterogeneous grouping
   * commitment to the success of all students.

2 Units of work should:
   * be challenging
   * be worthwhile
   * reflect the diverse character of society
   * achieve a balance of action and reflection
   * integrate theoretical and applied knowledge.

Democracy and Bureaucracy

By 1988 the Schools Division of the Victorian Ministry of Education was committed to providing a broad general education for all students from Preparatory to Year 12. The Blackburn Report (Ministerial Review of Postcompulsory Schooling, 1985) stressed this objective for the postcompulsory years; it has now been taken up by the notion of curriculum frameworks (Ministry of Education [Schools Division], Victoria, 1988a). These frameworks will guide the development of curriculum and school organization and set out nine areas of learning frameworks: the arts, commerce, English language, languages other than English, mathematics, personal development, science, social education and technology studies. To assist schools in using these frameworks, a *Support Kit* (Ministry of Education [Schools Division], Victoria, 1988b) has been provided. Thus the central authority is providing the curriculum framework, while recognizing that schools need assistance in implementing the framework and also that school communities are best placed to 'plan, develop and implement a curriculum that meet the needs of all students and that of the society in which they live' (Ministry of Education [Schools Division], Victoria, 1988a: 6).

The contrasts between the Victorian and New South Wales scenes are marked. In Victoria there has been more involvement of teachers and students in designing appropriate curricula. Furthermore, the outcomes are recognized by, and are acceptable to, the tertiary institutions. Yet, although aspects of the STC model are being used in Victoria as a basis for linking the worlds of school and work (Ministerial Review of Postcompulsory Schooling, 1985), changes are being brought in very quickly and are causing tension and dislocation for people at many levels of the teaching profession as well as in the educational bureaucracy itself.

In South Australia also there are changes in the organization and control of the curriculum. In contrast to both New South Wales and Victoria, these changes are proceeding more slowly and with more public support. The smaller size of the population, and of the educational bureaucracy, is a significant factor in obtaining acceptance of the changes. The total population of South Australia is only 1,420,000, while in New South Wales it is 5,753,000 and in Victoria 4,303,000 (Australian Bureau of Statistics, 1989). Nevertheless, there is consultation in South Australia and no desire to change all at once. Thus there has been time to gain support. In South Australia there is a procedure that allows curriculum resource materials and guidelines to be developed and then trialled in schools. The results of these trials are organized by a project officer. Cooperation between the schools and the Regional Office and with the Head Office in Adelaide is emphasized. This process is an important means of gaining teacher support for curriculum change (Harisun, 1989).

Democracy and Bureaucracy: Curriculum Issues

At the federal level the Minister for Education, Employment and Youth Affairs, Mr Dawkins, has proposed that there should be a core curriculum for schools that will include increased emphasis on science and technology. Across Australia most states and territories have spelled out plans that emphasize a core of subjects that are required learning for all students. The Gilding Report (Report of the Inquiry into Immediate Postcompulsory Education, 1988) from South Australia sets out subjects to be completed in the post-compulsory years. Table 8.4 summarizes what were defined as key areas of learning by the Curriculum Development Centre (CDC), and by the Northern Territory, South Australian and Western Australian Education Departments at the beginning of the 1980s as given in the Report of the Committee of Inquiry into Education in Western Australia (1984).

Table 8.4 shows a remarkable similarity in the areas of knowledge considered to be of most worth by bureaucracies across Australia. There is little dispute about 'the general parameters of the kinds of understanding and skills which should be central to the curriculum of all schools' (Schools Commission, 1980: 18) for at least the compulsory years of schooling. Most teachers, parents, employers and other members of the community would agree with the identification of these areas. There is, however, dispute about what should be taught within these areas, how it should be taught and what should be required in the post-compulsory years of schooling. Here the tensions between bureaucracy and democracy are strong.

Assessments, Examinations and Credentials

Just as there are discussions about what knowledge is of most worth and how this knowledge can be made to come alive for students in the schools, there are also differences of opinion about how systems should go about determining whether the desired outcomes of schooling have been attained. One of the fastest ways of effecting curriculum change both in content and in classroom practice is to change the assessing, examining and credentialling practices. In the ACT and in Queensland there are no external examinations. In the ACT at the end of Year 12 students receive a Secondary College Record which details the courses studied and the grades obtained. These may include registered courses approved by the School Board, accredited courses approved both by the School Board and by the Accrediting Agency within the ACT Schools Authority and tertiary accredited courses which are also acceptable to the Australian National University and hence for entrance to other tertiary

Democracy and Bureaucracy

Table 8.4 Key Areas of Learning Defined in Five Reports

Curriculum Development Centre (1980)	NT (1981)	SA (1980)	Tasmania (1980)	WA (1984)
Communication	English language	Language studies	Language	Language and communication
Social, cultural, civic	Social and cultural	Human society	Social studies	Social studies
Mathematics	Mathematics	Mathematics	Mathematics	Mathematics
Science and technology	Science	Science and computer education	Science	Science and technology
Health education	Physical education Health education	Health education Personal development	Physical education Health education	Physical and Health education
Work, leisure, lifestyle	Life and work skills	Transition education	Life problems	Vocational and personal awareness
Art and crafts	The arts	The arts	The arts	Practical and creative arts
Environmental studies		Environmental studies		
Moral reasoning and action beliefs				
	Computer education			

Source: Committee of Inquiry into Education in Western Australia (1984: 51).

institutions. In NSW by contrast, as already mentioned, there is an external examination at the end of Year 12. It was changes to the valuing of subjects on the Higher School Certificate that partly caused the public outcry in NSW in 1988. Abolition of the proposed Certificate of Secondary Education and a return to the HSC were further causes for public debate. The Greiner government also announced plans for yearly statewide testing of literacy and numeracy skills at the end of Years 3, 6 and 10. These Basic Skills Tests began in 1989 for Year 6 students and a small sample of Year 3 students.

The certificate which students receive at the end of their schooling currently serves many purposes. It is a certificate showing what students have achieved. While it has already been noted that not all who complete six years of secondary schooling want to go on to tertiary studies, in some systems the credential received is designed to include information to serve this purpose. It also provides information for employers.

A study in New South Wales by Roseth and White (1987) showed that employers, given a choice of four possible documentation packages that school leavers could be given, considered the most useful package or folio of documents to be one which contained an externally issued certificate, a school report and a school reference. Roseth and White (1987: 45) conclude that 'employers are eager to have a great deal of detailed and comprehensive documentation to aid them in employment selection processes.' The Greiner government implemented such a package for the 1988 school leavers with sponsorship by the National Roads and Motorists' Association (NRMA).

Baumgart's (1988) *Reports and Records of Achievement for School Leavers* provides an Australia-wide overview of the issues related to student assessment and system level evaluation. Eight broad issues are raised in the papers in this collection: standards-based assessment, certificates and records, moderation and comparability, the states' different areas of study, student–teacher relationships, the need for teacher development, schools and TAFE, relating newer forms of assessment to other changes and certification and selection. Baumgart emphasizes that at the school level there is 'a concern with specifying standards of performance and recognizing successful achievement', while there is still a need to refine 'our conceptualization of criterion-based assessment and the implications for its use in formative and summative evaluation and reporting.' He makes the point that system level guidelines will be needed for schools to report records of achievement and 'moderation will need to satisfy dual functions of ensuring students and providing comparability of standards across schools' (1988: 7). In addition, Baumgart states (1988: 8): 'It is imperative that changes we make to assessment and reporting give due recognition to achievement across all areas of study. Not to do so will result in distortions in curricula, with some students opting for unsuitable courses or facing frustration and failure.'

Bailey (1988: 205), in his contribution to Baumgart's collection, makes an important point about multidimensional knowledge, that is, the recognition of people covering both 'wide knowledge or breadth of knowledge' or 'deep knowledge or deep understanding'. It is important to assess these different types of knowledge and, in doing so, to build on the work of the last fifty years:

> in establishing reliable, fair, valid and repeatable procedures of evaluation, or to develop systems of evaluation which are

theoretic or depend wholly on specific decisions, avoiding the use of general principles and underlying concepts. Our past assessment practices may have resembled the man looking for his watch under the streetlamp because the light was better there; that does not mean that we should turn the light out and grope around in the dark. It would be better to try to improve the lighting everywhere. (Bailey, 1988: 210)

Conclusions

While curriculum changes are occurring throughout Australia, plans for their implementation are not also automatically being presented. Change involves us all in using extra energy; it can cause pain because it is much easier to retain the status quo or, as Rudduck, (1984: 66) writes, 'the comfortable cradle of convention'. In issues related to curriculum it is insufficient simply to develop new policies and mandate their implementation. Fullan (1982) emphasized that governments have a role in education to protect minorities and to be concerned about quality and equity in education because these problems are unlikely to be addressed at the local level. Yet governments and their associated bureaucracies cannot order curriculum changes and then automatically assume that they will take place 'behind the classroom door'. It is well known that it is difficult to manage change in a single classroom; it should be obvious that to manage change at state or national level is even more difficult. 'Policy-making is both more compelling and more exciting than policy implementation. There are overall, many complaints and few satisfactions' (Fullan, 1982: 216).

In discussing change at the central or government level Fullan (1982: 250–6) suggests five broad guidelines; these form a valuable backdrop for the information presented in this chapter. The first relates to the distinction between compliance and capacity.

1 Governments should concentrate on helping to improve the capacity of other agencies to implement changes.
2 Governments should be clear about what the policy is and spend time interacting with local agencies about the meaning, expectations and needs in relation to local implementation.
3 For any new policy, governments should see to it that they or someone else is addressing and looking at the program development and in-service assistance needs.
4 Government agency leaders should take special steps to ensure

that their own staff, especially those who have the most direct contact with the field, have the opportunity to develop knowledge and competence regarding the policy and program, as well as in how to facilitate implementation.
5 An explicit implementation plan is needed to guide the process of bringing about change in practice.

Some states have at least set out a timeline for implementation of the various changes: in Western Australia (Ministry of Education, undated) a proposed timeline stretches from 1987 to 1992; in New South Wales the Scott Report (Management Review, NSW Education Portfolio, 1989: 38–9) sets out a timeline to 1994. *Excellence and Equity* (Ministry of Education and Youth Affairs, 1989: 73) similarly proposes time for the changes to be made with the study of a language other than English. This will become mandatory for the School Certificate for the 1996 Year 7 cohort. The time necessary to identify and prepare sufficient language teachers is recognized.

Doyle (1986: 394), in discussing classroom organization and management, makes the point that classroom settings have distinctive properties. One of these is 'history': 'a common set of experiences, routines and norms ... provide a foundation for conducting activities.' Rapid change creates tension for teachers and students, whether the change is directed to more or to less centralized control. The way changes in the curriculum are introduced affects the way they will be received; this fact deserves more consideration by bureaucrats concerned with change in the Australian curriculum today. However, in terms of Fullan's (1982) guidelines for governments implementing change, it is only at the end of the 1980s that governments in Australia have begun to put into practice such plans. Ministers and their teams of bureaucrats have found it easier to develop a policy than to spend time and energy planning its implementation.

There is still a need to consider both the horizontal and the vertical articulation of the curriculum from the first year of schooling to the last. There is still a need to determine what is the best balance between centralized and local school control of the curriculum. I am convinced that there should be some centralized control because I do not consider that individual school staffs have the time, the resources or the energy to have entirely school-based curriculum development. There is already broad agreement on the areas of learning that are important. Implementation has always been a matter for the local school, but if there is to be a national core and national assessment policies, as proposed by Dawkins, then schools need assistance with the provision of school level resources and professional development for staff to implement that core. A core curriculum should not consume all the available school time, and there should still be a place for school-developed options that suit the needs of individual communities.

Acknowledgment

I wish to thank my sister, Pat Spring, the Editors and John Braithwaite for their comments on an earlier draft of this chapter and Jo-anne Moise for her typing.

References

ASHENDEN, D. (1982) 'Curriculum and the Reform of Australian Schooling.' *VISE News Bulletin*, 31, 7–15.
AUSTRALIAN BUREAU OF STATISTICS (1989) *Monthly Summary of Statistics*. Australia ABS Catalogue No. 1 1304.0 (September). Canberra: Commonwealth Government Printer.
AUSTRALIAN EDUCATION COUNCIL (May 1989) *Common and Agreed National Goals for Schooling in Australia*. Canberra: Office of the Minister for Employment, Education and Training.
BAILEY, M. (1988) 'Dimensions and Modalities in Evaluation.' In N. BAUMGART (Ed.), *Reports and Records of Achievement for School Leavers*. Canberra: Australian College of Education.
BAUMGART, N. (Ed.) (1988) *Reports and Records of Achievement for School Leavers*. Canberra: Australian College of Education.
BESSANT, B. and SPAULL, A. (1976) *Politics of Schooling*. Carlton, Vic.: Pitman.
BRAITHWAITE, R. and BAUMGART, N. (1987) *Staying or Leaving: Commonwealth Financial Assistance to Secondary Students*. Sydney: Macquarie University, School of Education, Centre for Research in Education and Work.
COLLINS, C.W. and HUGHES, P.W. (1982) 'Where Junior Secondary Schools Are Heading: Research and Reflections.' *Australian Education Review No. 16*. Hawthorn, Vic.: Australian Council for Educational Research.
COMMITTEE OF INQUIRY INTO EDUCATION IN WESTERN AUSTRALIA (1984) *Education in Western Australia* (Beazley Report). Perth: Government Printer.
CONNELL, R.W., ASHENDEN, D.J., KESSLER, S. and DOWSETT, G.W. (1982) *Making the Difference*. Sydney: George Allen and Unwin.
CURRICULUM DEVELOPMENT CENTRE (1980) *Core Curriculum for Australian Schools: What It Is and Why It Is Needed*. Canberra: Curriculum Development Centre.
DAWKINS, J.S. (1988) *Strengthening Australia's Schools: A Consideration of the Focus and Content of Schooling*. Canberra: Australian Government Publishing Service.
DEER, C.E. (1985) 'Curriculum Development.' In N. BAUMGART (Ed.), *Education: A Map for Introductory Courses*. Sydney: Novak.
DEPARTMENT OF EMPLOYMENT, EDUCATION AND TRAINING (1989) *Retention and*

Participation in Australian Schools, 1988 Update. Monograph Series No. 2. Canberra: Australian Government Publishing Service.

DOYLE, W. (1986) 'Classroom Organization and Management.' In M.C. WITTROCK (Ed.), Handbook of Research on Teaching. 3rd ed. New York: Macmillan.

EDUCATION DEPARTMENT OF SOUTH AUSTRALIA (1981) Into the 80's: Our Schools and Their Purposes. Adelaide: Education Department of South Australia.

FREEMAN, M., BATTEN, M. and ANWYL, J. (1986) Brunswick East Symposium 'Towards Universal Secondary Education — the STC Experience'. Brunswick East, Vic.: Brunswick East High School Council/Distinction Printing.

FULLAN, M. (1982) The Meaning of Educational Change. New York: Teachers College Press, Columbia University.

HARISUN, M.E. (1988) Personal Communication (Assistant Director, Western Region, Education Department of South Australia).

JECKS, D.A. (1971) 'Major Aspects of the Organization and Administration of Australian Education.' In A.G. MACLAINE and R. SELBY SMITH (Eds), Fundamental Issues in Australian Education. Sydney: Novak.

MCKINNON, K. (1982) 'Pity the Poor Kids.' VISE News Bulletin, 31, 3–6.

MANAGEMENT REVIEW: NSW EDUCATION PORTFOLIO (1989) Schools Renewal: A Strategy to Revitalise Schools within the New South Wales State Education System (Scott Report). Milsons Point, NSW: Management Review, NSW Education Portfolio.

MARSH, C.J. and STAFFORD, K. (1988) Curriculum Practices and Issues. 2nd ed. Sydney: McGraw-Hill.

MINISTERIAL REVIEW OF POSTCOMPULSORY SCHOOLING (1985) Report Volume 1 (Blackburn Report). Melbourne: Victoria Ministerial Review of Postcompulsory Schooling.

MINISTERIAL WORKING PARTY ON THE STATE LANGUAGE POLICY (1988) Report of the Ministerial Working Party on the State Language Policy. Sydney: Government Printer.

MINISTRY OF EDUCATION (SCHOOLS DIVISION), VICTORIA (1988a) The School Curriculum and Organization Framework: P–12. Melbourne: Ministry of Education.

MINISTRY OF EDUCATION (SCHOOLS DIVISION), VICTORIA (1988b) The Frameworks Support Kit: Professional Development Resources for Curriculum Framework. Melbourne: Ministry of Education.

MINISTRY OF EDUCATION AND YOUTH AFFAIRS (1988) Discussion Paper on the Curriculum in New South Wales Schools. Sydney: Government Printer.

MINISTRY OF EDUCATION AND YOUTH AFFAIRS (1989) Excellence and Equity New South Wales Curriculum Reform. Rydalmere, NSW: Sydney Allen Printers.

NEW SOUTH WALES (1957) Report of the Committee Appointed to Survey Secondary Education in New South Wales (Wyndham Report). Sydney: Government Printer.

NEW SOUTH WALES DEPARTMENT OF EDUCATION (1987) What Our Students Learn at School. Sydney: Government Printer.

NEW SOUTH WALES DEPARTMENT OF EDUCATION (1988) The Primary Purpose: A Curriculum Handbook for Primary Schools and Their Communities. Sydney: Government Printer.

NORTHERN TERRITORY DEPARTMENT OF EDUCATION (1983) Northern Territory Schools: Directions for the Eighties. Darwin: NT Department of Education.

OFFICE OF THE MINISTER FOR EMPLOYMENT, EDUCATION AND TRAINING (1989) *Common and Agreed National Goals for Schooling in Australia*. Canberra: Office of the Minister.

POOLE, M.E. and BESWICK, D.G. (1989) 'Girls' Expectations.' In G.C. LEDER and S.N. SAMPSON (Eds), *Educating Girls: Practice and Research*. Sydney: Allen and Unwin.

REPORT OF THE CARRICK COMMITTEE (1989) *Review of NSW Schools* (Carrick Report). Sydney: Ministry of Education and Youth Affairs.

REPORT OF THE COMMITTEE APPOINTED TO SURVEY SECONDARY EDUCATION IN NEW SOUTH WALES (1957) *Report on Secondary Education in New South Wales* (Wyndham Report). Sydney: Government Printer.

REPORT OF THE INQUIRY INTO IMMEDIATE POST-COMPULSORY EDUCATION (1988) *Inquiry into Immediate Post-compulsory Education* (Gilding Report). Adelaide: SA Government Printer.

REPORT OF THE REVIEW COMMITTEE (1983) *The Challenge of Change: A Review of High Schools in the ACT*. Canberra: ACT Schools Authority.

RETENTION AND PARTICIPATION IN AUSTRALIAN SCHOOLS (1989) *Monograph Series No. 2*. Canberra: Australian Government Publishing Service, July.

ROSETH, N. and WHITE, I. (1987) *Documents for School Leavers: What Employers Want*. Sydney: New South Wales Department of Education.

RUDDUCK, J.S. (1984) 'Introducing Innovation to Pupils.' In D. HOPKINS and M. WIDEEN (Eds), *Alternative Perspectives on School Improvement*. Lewes: Falmer Press.

SCHOOLS COMMISSION (1980) *Schooling for 15 and 16 Year-Olds*. Canberra: Schools Commission.

Sydney Morning Herald (1988) 28 July, p. 4.

WESTERN AUSTRALIAN MINISTRY OF EDUCATION (n.d., c. 1986) *Better Schools in Western Australia: A Programme for Improvement*. Perth: WA Ministry of Education.

Chapter 9

Accountability in Changing School Systems

Clive Dimmock and John Hattie

Setting the Scene: Pressures for Accountability

Most governments of Western nations are facing a common problem in the 1980s: how to respond to the rising expectations of their electorates for more and improved services, while those same electorates have made it clear they will not accept tax increases. Indeed their expectations for reduced taxation are pushing governments into seeking new and different ways of meeting the continuing and growing demands placed on them. The Government of Western Australia's White Paper, *Managing Change in the Public Sector* (1986) stated the problem as follows: 'Additional services must be funded both at the expense of other services and by improving efficiency in the delivery of continuing services' (p. 1). These public sector responses spell the need for change in government and public sector administration. They have given rise to what the same White Paper called 'the wave of public sector reform which has been sweeping Australia and the rest of the Western World' (p. 1). Education systems, along with other public services, are increasingly expected to undertake ongoing review, become more flexible and responsive to change, and utilize community resources in an effective and efficient way.

This heightened awareness of the need for more effectiveness and efficiency in the public sector, and in education in particular, can be attributed to a number of pressures, most important of which are economic and demographic forces. Increasing demands for more education, for more places to be made available in schools, colleges and universities can only be met by improved efficiency and/or reduction in existing services, given the static or declining resource levels supported by governments.

A second powerful force has been the tide of 'managerialism' which has spread across the private sector to affect public services such as education. In the same way that private businesses have been driven by a greater concern for managerial effectiveness and efficiency, so have public sector institutions such as schools. Successful management of such institutions is regarded as a sine qua non for organizational effectiveness, just as it is in the private sector. Corporate management is increasingly viewed as having as much relevance for the running of educational enterprises as for private companies. The parallel is brought closer into focus by the thriving private sector within education which has been run more along corporate management lines than government schools.

A third force is political. Throughout much of the industrialized world, including Australia, a widespread distrust of large bureaucratic institutions has become commonplace. This perception centres on the suspicion that large public sector organizations in particular are increasingly remote from, and thereby unable to provide a responsive service to, the client, consumer or customer. In education systems this phenomenon has brought forth policies of decentralization, with the management and administration of schools appearing to pass incrementally from large central ministries to district offices and even down to each school. To the extent that control is exercised from the centre, accountability can play a vital role in establishing relations between the centre and each school. In some education systems decentralization is presently more apparent than real. Critical decisions to hire and fire staff and to decide salary loadings are often retained at the centre, while heightened publicity campaigns to foster the appearance that the critical decisions related to the curriculum are decentralized can mislead people into exaggerating the actual powers and responsibilities devolved. If accountability to the centre is then stiffened, the outcome may result in a form of recentralization.

Besides the trend towards decentralization there have been two other important and related politico-social changes in Australia and Western education systems. The first has been a loss of confidence in the opinions of 'experts', including governments, and a corresponding belief in lay opinion. The second is the rise of 'participative democracy as individuals band together to advance locally-based initiatives ...' (Government of Western Australia, 1986: 3).

Accompanying decentralization has been the birth of the so-called self-managing or self-determining school concept (see Caldwell, 1986, 1988). In Western Australia, for example, the Ministry of Education's publication, *Better Schools in Western Australia: A Programme for Improvement*, depicts this trend thus: 'Whereas once it was believed that a good system creates good schools, it is now recognized that good schools make a good system. Accordingly, the efficiency and effectiveness of the system can be improved only if schools have sufficient control over the quality of education they provide' (p. 5). More specifically, the case for devolution of responsibility to schools is elaborated in terms of the greater exercise of teacher professionalism, the increased likelihood of more meaningful decisions about the educational needs of each student and, finally, the closer matching of school programs with the wishes and circumstances of their local communities.

The past decade has also witnessed a growing concern on the part of parents, employers and others over falling educational standards. Many diverse groups argue that standards of schooling have fallen and, moreover, that new curricula brought in by state governments in Australia (e.g. the unit curriculum in Western Australia) represent a dilution of academic standards. The criticisms of the old curriculum centred on its lack of relevance for contemporary society; the problems with the new focus on its superficiality in breaking subjects into separate units of study, lack of coherence and difficulty of administration.

As a consequence of these economic, demographic, managerial, political and curricular trends, each of which has compounded and reinforced the others, the traditional structures of public sector organizations such as government school systems are increasingly viewed as inappropriate. It is argued that more adaptive structures are needed which recognize that change is a continuous feature of contemporary society. Restructured education systems should consequently reflect the managerial, economic and political forces shaping their adaptation. They need to:

become more flexible in their working arrangements,
be more adaptive to changing technology,
become more efficient and effective,
become more responsive to changing community needs,
initiate programs themselves,
facilitate the activities of non-government community-based groups (Government of Western Australia, 1986: 3).

The Problem of Educational Accountability

While the foregoing arguments present the context within which pressures for public sector accountability have grown, there are quite specific conditions which help inform the problem of accountability in education. The first of these conditions is that while education is regarded as a public service and is mostly financed out of public revenue, it is 'offered in institutions which are largely closed to public scrutiny and difficult to supervise from the outside' (Kogan, 1986: 17). Teachers have a good measure of autonomy even in so-called centralized systems of education. In schools they have a captive audience for at least twelve years, since students are obliged to attend between the ages of 5 and 16. Parents and others outside the school find it difficult to cross the boundaries of the school to appreciate a detailed picture of the complex social, affective and academic world which is their child's school experience. It is all the more difficult for parents and other outsiders to scrutinize the educational experience of a child in a large secondary school, when that student is taught by many different teachers in the course of a school year and experiences a broad curriculum incorporating so many subjects. The relationship between teacher and student is highly interpersonal, making it difficult for parents and others to become involved.

While public scrutiny from the outside has been difficult at the individual student level, it has been equally difficult at the whole school level. One reason has been the absence of generally accepted performance indicators or measures of school effectiveness, against which parents and others could compare the effectiveness and success of different schools. That schools are extremely difficult organizations to supervise from the outside is one of the compelling reasons for the recent trend towards decentralized self-managing schools. One explanation for the difficulty of outside supervision besides the absence of agreed performance indicators is the sheer numbers of schools in relation to the number of central office administrators and district superintendents whose job it is to supervise. The growing difficulty of administering schools from centralized bureaucracies has undoubtedly encouraged the trend to school-based management in a number of education systems, including Australia.

There are also other more subtle reasons for the difficulty of outside supervision of schools. Education is a publicly provided system which is carried out by individual practitioners who are regarded as professionals. Teachers are at one and the same time both publicly employed and practitioners of their profession. The former places them in a bureaucratic relationship with others; the latter gives them certain individual discretion and autonomy. There are other tensions in teacher accountability which Kogan (1986) summarizes as arising between 'the private and the public, the individual and the collective, rights and duties, discretion and prescription, and responsibility and accountability' (p. 18).

Present Accountability in Education

Definitions of accountability and its associated concept, evaluation, abound. Before attempting a description and analysis of present accountability in Australian school systems, a clarification of the term is justified. Two connotations of the term have been espoused — the 'weak' and the 'strong' (Kogan, 1975). In its 'weak' form it is argued that teachers in Australian government schools have been, and presently are, 'accountable'. They are accountable in the sense of being 'answerable' to those who appointed them, and to those who have authority over them. However, a teacher's awareness of accountability in this sense is partial at best, since it is not dependent on any formal mechanisms, and teachers may be 'answerable' in name only and not in practice.

Doubts about the equivocacy of this 'weak' form of accountability have given rise to an alternative 'strong' form. Kogan (1975) defined accountability as 'the duty to render an account of work performed to a body that has authority to modify that performance by the use of sanctions or rewards.' Implicit in this definition of accountability are three distinct elements:

1 the ascription of specific tasks, responsibilities and duties;
2 the duty of those assuming responsibility to render an account to a person or body in authority;
3 the right of those to whom an account is given to exercise intervention in the form of rewards and sanctions.

This is a more formal, systematic and comprehensive form of accountability than mere 'answerability'. It has more challenging implications for those being held to account, and indeed for those holding others to account, than simple answerability. It provides an extremely helpful analytical framework for assessing the extent to which teachers and others are presently held to account in Australian school systems.

While Kogan's definition focuses on the task elements of the accountability process, the East Sussex Accountability Project reported by Becher, Eraut and Knight (1981) clarified the second of the three elements above, namely, the diverse constituencies to whom teachers should render accounts. Three different types or forms of accountability are distinguished, depending on the constituency receiving accountability. Thus teachers are or should be accountable to:

1 their clients, namely parents and pupils   moral accountability
2 their colleagues and themselves   professional accountability
3 their employers and political masters   contractual accountability

The key questions are: Who is accountable to whom? For what are they accountable? How are they accountable in Australian government schooling? What levels of accountability already exist?

The individual teacher generally acknowledges that (s)he is answerable to the principal and to colleagues for carrying out duties responsibly and efficiently (Watson, 1978: 14). But should teachers also be held accountable for the way they interpret the curriculum? Although many state governments provide syllabus guides and recommended textbooks, there is still a significant residual component left to the individual teacher's discretion. Part of this discretionary component centres on the hidden curriculum and the ways in which the teacher presents teaching material, and the values and beliefs implicit in the teacher's approach. Another part centres on how the teacher approaches the subject matter and examinations, as well as what s(he) finds acceptable in the behaviour and manners of the children. Should the teacher be held accountable for these aspects? Many principals accept some degree of responsibility for such areas, but how far the school as a whole is responsible for behaviour, manners and academic subjects chosen for study or examination purposes, and how far these are the responsibility of parents, is not at all clear.

The boundaries between teacher and parent responsibilities have never been clarified in detail. This will almost certainly become an issue in future as parents and others become more participative in school councils. In Western Australia, for instance, the government introduced in 1987 the unit curriculum which requires students and their parents to make curriculum choices at the age of 13. Some subjects have to be dropped at this age in order to fulfil the requirements of selecting units from different sections across a broad curriculum. Although the Ministry of Education has published booklets to help parents and students choose, the information on courses is woefully inadequate. These booklets also invite parents and students to discuss subject choice with the school if they have difficulty. In fact, in all too many cases when parents have sought advice and information from senior school staff on curriculum choice within the unit curriculum, they have found the detailed knowledge they are looking for hard to find, and the advice rendered has often been disappointing and unhelpful. The issue at stake is how far the teacher and school are responsible for a student's choice of subjects, as opposed to the student and parent? And what if advice sought from the school on such matters by students and parents is deemed to be inadequate, misleading or unhelpful?

In highly centralized education systems such as in France or Sweden the issue does not arise to the same degree, since teachers are civil servants and thus bound by regulations. The ministry of education lays down detailed rules concerning the curriculum, time allotted to each subject, textbooks to be used and even conduct in classes (Watson, 1978:

16). Nor does it arise in Russia or China, where ministry regulations exist for all these, but in addition teachers' notes detail only the answers which are politically acceptable. In the USA states such as California and Tennessee are more prescriptive in guiding teachers and students through curricula than is sometimes realized. The same conclusion is true for the more centralized Australian school systems.

In respect of Kogan's three elements of 'strong accountability', teachers in Australian schools are, at most, only partially accountable. Most do not have detailed job specifications or duty statements spelling out their duties, responsibilities and tasks ascribed to them. There is instead a 'general awareness' on the part of teachers in regard to teaching duties, but extra-teaching areas of school work are much more equivocal. Second, the duty of teachers to render account is also ambiguous. To whom should account be rendered — to the head of department, to the principal, to the school council, to parents, to students — to all of these? In what form should the account be given? Teachers meet with parents to discuss children's academic progress or behavioural problems. Teachers may report to their departmental heads or principals when they experience problems of either a professional or personal nature. Those teachers who seek promotion may periodically be accountable to the ministry when they are inspected and interviewed, at which time they are expected to give account of their achievements. Nonetheless, such occasions do not constitute a full or even acceptable accountability. They occur periodically, as and when circumstances necessitate. They are not built into the system; they are not routine or regular. Teacher completion of children's reports for parents to see at the end of each term or school year is one of their few regular routine accountability functions, and these reports are about students, not teacher, performance. Otherwise, very few teachers are expected to submit written or even oral reports of their practices, problems and achievements to anyone.

The third element of Kogan's model of accountability is the right of those to whom accounts have been rendered to intervene. Naturally, if few accounts are being rendered, it is difficult for others to intervene in response. The right of parents, or indeed of principals, to intervene in the work of teachers is problematic. If students fail to perform to expectations, blame is usually put on the student, rarely the teacher. Teachers generally possess considerable professional discretion and much privacy in their classroom activities. In most cases parents have direct access to their children's teachers, but the principal is often protective towards the teaching staff in this respect. Some principals even act as 'gatekeepers' in deciding who is allowed into the school. Principals themselves often feel uncomfortable about approaching teaching staff who they suspect are falling short of expected standards of performance. This is attributed to the lack of more objective evidence on the teacher's performance, personal weaknesses on the part of principals and the absence of adequate management processes in schools to deal with such situations. The inability to 'hire and fire' is one disempowering factor handicapping principals in this respect. Similarly, the rarity of reward interventions whereby principals and senior staff fail to recognize good teacher performance is partly explained by the lack of formal incentive schemes (such as bonus pay) in education, but does not explain why so few words of praise are uttered.

In some Australian states the advent of school councils on which parents and local community representatives sit to approve and legitimize school development plans has thrown into doubt the relationships of teachers, principals and ministry. Is it the principal or school-based decision-making group which runs the school? A Western Australian Ministry of Education Discussion Document (1988) attempts some clarification: 'The school-based decision-making group does not have power or authority over the teaching staff of the school, nor in the supervision of the teaching–learning programme' (p. 5).

Recent trends towards school councils have not only brought accountability to the fore; they have made lines of accountability more confused. There is a sense of moral accountability which teachers owe to students and parents, but no clear guidelines as to where this begins and ends. Most commentators agree that it is a fair principle of accountability to hold people accountable only for those things over which they have control. But how much control do individual teachers have over students' academic results as opposed to their own teaching skills, processes and methods? Most agree that teachers have more control over the latter, and should therefore be held accountable for these processes. However, many groups, including governments and parents, want to hold teachers accountable for products or outcomes, that is, academic results achieved by students. Hattie (1988) has provided some clarification to the process/product dilemma by arguing for the measurement of student outcomes to be taken into account, and that the measures taken need to be selective and valid.

As far as professional accountability of teachers is concerned, there is no professional body of teachers in Australia with an established code of conduct or set of ethics or professional standards. Nonetheless, there are self-imposed standards which most teachers set themselves based on expectations of the teacher's role. These include teaching preparation, behaviour towards and quality of relationships with students and equity in allocating resources.

In respect of contractual accountability teachers have at most only limited awareness of this. Although their salaries are paid by their state government, and they may be moved to other schools by their employer and assessed at times of promotion, most teachers perceive their job as generated from within the school in which they happen to be working. Teachers feel themselves more directly answerable to the people with whom they are in closest proximity, that is, their local school environment. Even if teachers fail to honour their teaching commitments by long periods of sustained absence from school or through incompetence, experience shows that it can be very difficult for employers to remove them from their post, especially if they are supported by a powerful teachers' union.

Turning to the school principal, what accountability characterizes incumbents of this position? Traditionally Australian school systems have been regarded as centralized, which places the principal in a line management position acting as the agent for the centre. Thus as far as implementing government policies is concerned, principals have been accountable to their central office administrators and politicians. This is a form of contractual accountability.

Principals might also be seen as accountable in a professional sense to their colleagues, although whether their leadership style is autocratic or democratic would affect their accountability. The principal is responsible for the management and internal organization of the school and its resources. With increasing decentralization of school systems in Australia, the principal is becoming more responsible for financial management and budgeting, the general philosophy, ethos and values of the school, public relations and contacts with the media, consultation and involvement with more local and in-school decision-making groups. Professional accountability of principals is likely to be enhanced in situations where corporate and team management are to the fore.

In devolving systems of school administration in Australia (see Beare, 1983; Chapman, 1987) the principal becomes accountable to a wider, more diverse set of stakeholders. Accountability to the government and central office as well as to teaching staff and students exists as before, but additional accountabilities are brought into play with school councils and district superintendents. While recent structural changes are increasing the stakeholders to whom principals are expected to render accounts, there is still equivocacy over the fine detail of such accountability. Few principals have detailed job or duty statements, a system of rendering accounts to the wider group of stakeholders has in many cases to be worked out, and intervention by those stakeholders in the form of reprimand or reward is certainly not customary. Is it generally recognized how difficult it is to remove principals from office, even if they can be moved from one school to another?

If the difficulty is acknowledged of holding individual teachers and principals accountable, how difficult is it for whole schools to be held accountable? To date the record is not good. The question of making the whole school accountable is of interest and concern to central office administrators, politicians and parents. The relative lack of accountability in the past is explained by the difficulty of evaluating schools and making valid comparisons of performance between them. Given the dearth of data available, the uncertainty of those interested in evaluating them and the complexity of variables involved, it is not surprising that little effort has been invested in holding whole schools to account. However, research on school effectiveness and improvement is now growing rapidly and this situation appears likely to change in the next few years (see below).

Away from schools, superintendents may be seen as answerable to their ministries, who in turn are accountable to their electorates. Since some of the chief administrative posts in ministries are political appointments, they too may be seen as accountable to politicians first and to the electorate indirectly. However, since there are usually many other issues involved at election time, this cannot be seen as a rigorous form of educational accountability. The chief administrators can always justify their policies behind the 'claim of obedience to their political masters' (Watson, 1978: 18).

The school council, composed of parents, local community, students and teachers, is expected to generate accountability from schools and teachers, but is itself only loosely accountable to the extent that some of its members may be elected by the teaching and parent bodies. This elective status may, or may not, carry with it representative functions. A great deal more could be elaborated on this issue. Much the same argument can be mounted in the Australian school context as Watson (1978) has argued in the English system: many people may talk about accountability in education, but there is often no clear definition of what it means, no machinery or clearly defined lines of accountability within Australian education systems, and 'the further away from the classroom one gets the more blurred do the areas of accountability become' (p. 18).

Accountability at present is often perceived to be patchy and random. It is almost exclusively unidirectional, meaning that it operates top–down in the hierarchical chain, but not bottom–up. Thus teachers are expected to be answerable to principals, principals to superintendents, school council and ministry, ministry to electorate. Little is ever mentioned about ministry accountability to principals, and principals' accountability to teachers. Moreover, teachers are viewed in terms of their accountability to parents, rarely vice versa. However, pressure for more overt formal accountability in school systems has continued unabated in the late 1980s in Australia. A response is evidently being made, and this will shape the administration and management of Australian school systems in the 1990s.

Two Models of Accountability

Many regard a metaphor adopted from the world of business (accountability) with circumspection when applied to education, where objectives are inevitably less clear than in industry. While there are many models of accountability, it is helpful to polarize two: bureaucratic and democratic (Lawton, 1980). Bureaucratic accountability is one-way. Those lower in the hierarchy are accountable to those higher up. One of the best known examples is the Michigan State Accountability System. Its six features typify the bureaucratic model of accountability:

1. common goals are defined and
2. translated into specific objectives,
3. schools are assessed on their ability to meet these objectives,
4. alternative teaching delivery systems are tested and some are advocated,
5. through a specially constructed system of evaluation and assessment results are published,
6. feedback from the results guides the state and local practices.

According to Sockett (1976), 'the teacher is contracted to perform a service, according to agreed upon terms, within an established time-period and with a stipulated use of resources and performance standards.' The focus is on results obtained for resources used. If the teacher fails, that is, if the pupils do not perform, then the teacher has broken the contract and the resource providers can intervene to change the policy or replace the teacher (Pring, 1978: 253).

In this system the teacher is accountable to the public or taxpayer. The teacher is not so much accountable to students or parents or even professional colleagues, but is de facto accountable to system level administrators, acting in the role of 'accountants' or 'auditors'. Student performance is assessed against prespecified objectives measured by standardized tests. Test results are published so that school performances can be compared, and 'improved test scores result in bonus payments to teachers, or increased grants for schools' (Lawton, 1980). The shortcomings and dangers of overreliance on such data hardly warrant mention.

Behind the bureaucratic model of accountability is the assumption that measuring a child's performance is a fair way of evaluating a teacher's effort and competence. Other factors connected with teaching performance are excluded. Evidence tends to show that where testing is heavily emphasized, teachers concentrate less on what is important and more on what is likely to be in the test. The result is a narrowing of the curriculum. Thus bureaucratic accountability is instrumental, utilitarian, hierarchical and product-oriented.

By contrast, the concept of 'democratic' accountability is predicated on the idea of individuals and groups in education exchanging, negotiating and reciprocating accountability. Accountability flow becomes multi-directional — upwards, downwards, lateral, horizontal — in a system of education comprising diverse groups with different functions. This means that teachers are accountable in two directions, 'upwards' for resources and delegated responsibilities and 'downwards' to pupils; the principal is accountable 'upwards' to the school council and district superintendent and ministry and 'downwards' to teaching staff. Above all, democratic accountability means reciprocity, so that principals be accountable to ministry and in return the ministry be accountable to principals. Hence an example of reciprocal accountability would be where the principal, on behalf of the school, agrees to implement certain curriculum changes, perhaps a more vocationally-oriented syllabus, but in return the ministry is accountable for resourcing the school adequately to make such changes possible.

'Democratic' accountability tends to be more intrinsic in its inspiration, more professionally geared in the sense that it provides teachers with certain powers and rights in relation to administrators, and it emphasizes process as much as product. Its significance is that it places obligations on governments and administrators to support teachers and schools in implementing the changes which those same governments and administrators have initiated.

Which of these models of accountability — bureaucratic or democratic — is recognizable in present Australian school systems? Neither pattern is well developed or established. However, given the traditions of centralized control which are difficult to shake off (Smart, 1988), and the perceived lack of support to schools from central ministries pursuing policies of restructuring, most teachers would argue that there are more elements of bureaucratic than of democratic accountability. There have been indications of 'democratic' accountability, such as attempts to establish more participatory forms of decision-making in schools, and embryonic resource agreements and performance indicators which are undertakings by ministries to resource a school to a specified extent in return for that school achieving certain targets. However, these targets remain dubious as accurate indicators of performance.

In the main, more elements of bureaucratic accountability are discernible. Preference for student assessment and exam results as quantifiable measures of a school's performance are clearly apparent. Thus concern for product appears to be taking precedence over process. Moreover, lines of accountability seem to be establishing themselves as top–down, one-way, with ministries keen to be seen by their electorates as running efficient and competitive schools.

The Future Shape of Accountability in Government School Systems in Australia

The accountability choice that ultimately has to be made in Australian school systems is between centralized education systems, based on bureaucratic central accountability with teachers as closely controlled employees, and decentralized systems, based on the concept of delegation with teachers enjoying a large measure of discretion and professional independence, yet subject to a 'democratic' model of accountability.

Given the present restructuring in most Australian government school systems towards decentralized control, the appropriate model of accountability to develop would seem to be democratic. This, after all, reflects the same principles and reasons as underpin the case for decentralization, namely, participation of community in school-based management and a shared partnership in the running of schools. However, while endorsing and espousing policies of school decentralization, most states have as yet done little to encourage processes of democratic accountability at an operational level.

Instead, there are many signs of bureaucratic accountability appearing. For example, in most Australian states there is no longer a close system of inspection. Indeed, in Western Australia subject advisers have disappeared. A vacuum has been created between the central administrators and schools. Consequently, the American experience seems likely to repeat itself in parts of Australia. In the absence of a professional advisory field-force, the central ministry develops top–down 'objective-referenced' tests to measure the performance of pupils and schools against state-set objectives. The vacuum between central bureaucracy and schools is bridged by product-oriented measures, such as standardized tests, which can be set across the school age profile at ages 7, 9, 11, 13 and 15.

Management Processes and Techniques

It seems reasonable to assume that neither the expertise nor the human resources presently exist at central ministry level to conduct more systematic accountability operations. Indeed, it is doubtful whether the resources or expertise exist at district or regional office level after the restructuring which has recently taken place in many states. This fact, when considered together with the argument that the school should be the 'prime institution' for accountability purposes (Kogan, 1975), means that the focus for accountability should be the school level. If this is accepted, then it is tempting to argue that the key to implementing workable and desirable accountability systems is predicated on management processes and procedures operational particularly, but not exclusively, at school level. The importance of management in accountability surprisingly has been overlooked by many observers. We argue that the following are fundamental prerequisites for accountability to operate in Australian school systems:

1 appraisal schemes, involving duty statements and job specifications at the individual teacher level;
2 team reviews, involving evaluation of departmental or sectional groups of staff;
3 whole school evaluation, covering general across-school issues, including policy matters, finance and overall performance.

The theme common to all three is evaluation, and all three forms of evaluation demand careful management to function well. It is difficult if not impossible to operate accountability without a prior stage of evaluation. Since accountability must entail the rendering of an account, then information and evidence have to be gathered before an account can be rendered. Evaluation is the means by which information and evidence are collected, sorted and appraised, and subsequently may be used in rendering accountability.

Management at school level is the generic set of skills and processes necessary to marshal resources effectively to achieve targets and objectives. Its importance in the accountability field lies not only in its concern to make both evaluation and accountability happen by instituting appropriate procedures and allocating suitable resources, but also in its ability to incorporate all three levels of evaluation enunciated above.

At the most basic but critical level is management's ability to enable each and every teacher to feel accountable for their performance. This is especially important in teaching, a profession largely practised by teachers working individually. Unless systems of accountability can be sufficiently fine-tuned and specific so as to spotlight individual performance, there is little hope of ever rewarding good teachers and administrators or of offering help to those whose performance is below par. The mechanism for evaluation at the individual level is appraisal. When appraisal works well, it reviews each person's duties and responsibilities, assesses performance against agreed criteria, and estimates the potential of each member of staff, including principals. Senior managers at school level should be concerned with determining duty statements for staff, assessing individual performance against those duty statements, and taking positive action to improve and develop staff in appropriate ways. Significantly, these three stages equate with the characteristics of accountability stated earlier: ascription of duties, rendering of accounts, intervention by those to whom accounts are rendered.

Evaluation of groups or staff teams takes cognisance of the increasing importance of collaborative planning, teaching and administration in school life. In secondary schools the functioning group is likely to be the department or pastoral care unit, while in primary schools it may be the section or curriculum group. Responsibility for the performance of these units should be taken by their respective heads, who should be formally accountable to the senior school management, and to the principal in particular. Departmental or sectional policies, aims and objectives should be set against which performance can be examined.

Exactly the same three steps apply to the whole school. A school development plan provides the yardstick against which performance is examined, the school staff through the principal render their account to the school council and state ministry, each of whom may wish to react and intervene on the basis of the report. In finer detail the school development plan provides the school with a means of setting out clearly its strategies for achieving certain targets or outcomes, such as improved teaching–learning programs and better management. Part of the plan contains a review of the extent to which the school's achievements are measured against the objectives stated in the plan. These measures provide a basis for deciding what changes to make to improve outcomes further: modifications to objectives, priorities, teaching–learning strategies, management and resource allocation. In the context of the whole school operating in a school-based management system with its decision-making groups, accountability may be expressed as the school's ability to account for the extent to which it achieves the objectives stated in the school development plan (Western Australian Ministry of Education, 1988).

Key elements in these school processes and procedures in future are management skills in objectives-setting, the drawing up of duty statements, evaluation, rendering of both written and oral accounts, and the skills to make appropriate and effective responses and interventions. Without positive outcomes to accountability procedures, the whole concept is likely to be seen as negative and destructive by teachers.

Principles into Practice: The Way Ahead

There is no doubting the powerful forces pushing for greater accountability in Australian school systems. However, it is important that the systems of accountability currently being put in place reflect the concerns and interests of teachers, and are not simply measures to placate hard-headed bureaucrats in central ministries, politicians and electorates. Accountability systems should reflect well on teachers, departments and whole schools who are performing well. Equally, they should lead to positive outcomes and actions to address the problems of those who are not performing successfully. Intervention should therefore be selective and fine-tuned.

If accountability is to be a positive and powerful process in Australian government schooling, then the following principles need to be practised.

1. Much greater clarity of roles and responsibilities is needed; aims and objectives are required at individual, department and whole school levels.
2. More refined performance indicators are required to reflect more accurately on the quality of schooling and its processes, as well as on the quantitative, affective and product aspects of school outcomes; in short, school accountability should focus on improved teaching and quality of student learning.
3. Lines of accountability need to be clear and well understood by all participants in the school system.
4. Accountability relationships need to be reciprocal, especially between people at different hierarchical levels, whether within school, or between ministry, or regional/district office and school; they should be ongoing, negotiable and subject to review, rather than an annual event.
5. The purposes of accountability should be clearly set out, as should the rights of those engaged in accountability.

6 The school should be the prime focus for accountability, and the network of accountability channels and relationships should embrace the individual teacher and administrator as well as staff teams and whole schools; schools should incorporate accountability as well as evaluation into their development plans, administrative structures and management processes.
7 A network of accountability relationships operating in many directions is necessary to provide a system of checks and balances.
8 Generic management skills should be seen as the centrepiece for effective accountability, particularly at the school level; such skills and processes include staff appraisal and evaluation, clear, accurate, functional communication and reporting between all parts of the school and its environment, and the capacity to intervene selectively and positively to reward and enhance the professionalism of teachers and administrators.

The importance of creating a climate of trust and goodwill into which accountability can be introduced was aptly summed up by Stenhouse (1977): 'Accountability must be associated with feelings of responsibility: when people feel accountable they attempt conscientiously to improve their performance; when people feel unfairly called to account, they devise ways of beating the accountants without actually improving the balance sheet.' Herein perhaps lies the ultimate test of the success or failure of accountability in Australian government school systems. Will the accountability models adopted encourage the individual teacher to step out and take responsibility for his or her own performance and self-evaluation against the backdrop of moral accountability to students and parents, professional accountability to self and peers, and contractual accountability to employers (state ministry) and school council?

Introducing accountability systems will necessarily change the balance of power and the nature of relationships between participants in Australian school systems. However, since most school systems in Australia are undergoing periods of rapid and significant restructuring, the time for accountability seems to have arrived. As Levin (1974) concluded:

> A significant tightening of the accountability linkages in education is probably impossible without substantial changes in the governing processes and organization of the educational sector. Yet educators are fond of talking about accountability as a technical problem which does not require any major restructuring of institutions. Such a viewpoint may place the educator at centre stage in the accountability movement, but it is not likely to make

much of a difference in the overall functioning of the schools or society.

If accountability is to make a difference, it has to be recognized as a managerial and political process involving changes in relationships and patterns of influence (Dimmock, 1982). Structural changes in Australian government school systems, particularly the decentralizing and devolving of responsibilities to schools, together with the awakening need for more overt management at school level, hold promise for the introduction of a tighter system of accountability. As one American commentator stated, greater empowerment for schools will elicit professional commitment and organizational involvement, but is insufficient by itself to sustain school reform (Guthrie, 1986). Without effective 'feedback loops' schools will feel isolated and their standards may suffer. Greater autonomy for schools demands appropriate accountability for the good of all parties.

Predictably, Australian school systems will spend much of the 1990s fashioning and determining the types and forms of accountability system they regard as feasible and desirable. Emergent patterns and schemes will undoubtedly be a reflection of tensions already existing between the bureaucratic form of accountability associated with centralized ministry control and influence and the democratic model of accountability inspired by participatory decision-making at school and local community levels. It is to be hoped that key participants in accountability systems will pay due cognisance to the forces of bureaucracy and democracy. In arriving at a satisfactory and workable system of accountability, one way forward would be to try to achieve a balance between bureaucratic and democratic elements. This would entail dispensing with old, and creating new forms of bureaucratic accountability to the centre, while at the same time establishing new procedures to secure democratic accountability, especially to professional colleagues and local communities.

Greater emphasis than hitherto placed on procedures to secure democratic accountability, combined with appropriate monitoring and evaluation by central ministries, could meet the essential challenge of accountability in the 1990s. That would be to create accountability systems which facilitate growth, development and improvement in the way Australian schools are managed and organized, in the standards of teaching and, above all, in student learning and performance. Provided that elements of bureaucratic and democratic accountability are managed in coherent and sensitive ways, it is possible for both to be complementary and to provide a positive and pluralistic pattern of checks and balances. Tension between bureaucratic and democratic then becomes purposeful and productive.

References

BEARE, H. (1983) 'The Structural Reform Movement in Australian Education during the 1980s and Its Effect on Schools.' *Journal of Educational Administration* 21, 2, 149–68.

BECHER, T., ERAUT, M. and KNIGHT, J. (1981) *Policies for Educational Accountability*. London: Heinemann.

CHAPMAN, J. (1987) 'Decentralization, Devolution and the Administration of Schools.' *Education Research and Perspectives*, 14, 2, 62–75.

CALDWELL, B.J. and SPINKS, J.M. (1986) *Policy Making and Planning for School Effectiveness*. Hobart: Tasmanian Education Department.

CALDWELL, B.J. and SPINKS, J.M. (1988) *The Self-Managing School*. Lewes: Falmer Press.

DIMMOCK, C.A.J. (1982) 'The Micropolitical Dimension in School Evaluation and Accountability in England and Wales.' *Compare*, 12, 2, 167–81.

GOVERNMENT OF WESTERN AUSTRALIA (1986) *Managing Change in the Public Sector: A Statement of the Government's Position*. Parliamentary White Paper. Perth: Government of Western Australia, June.

GUTHRIE, J.W. (1986) 'School-based Management: The Next Needed Education Reform.' *Phi Delta Kappan*, 68, 4, 309.

HATTIE, J. (1988) 'The Quality of Education and Accountability.' Paper submitted at conference on School-Based Decision-Making, held at Woodend, Victoria, April 1988.

KOGAN, M. (1975) 'Institutional Autonomy and Public Accountability: Autonomy and Accountability in Educational Administration.' In M. HUGHES and J. RICHARD (Eds), *Proceedings of the Fourth Annual Conference of the British Educational Administration Society*.

KOGAN, M. (1986) *Education Accountability: An Analytic Overview*. London: Hutchinson.

LAWTON, D (1980) 'Responsible Partners.' *The Times Educational Supplement*, 7 March, p. 4.

LEVIN, H.M. (1974) 'A Conceptual Framework for Accountability in Education.' *School Review*, 82, May, 363–91.

PRING, R. (1978) 'Accountability.' In D. LAWTON et al. (1978) *Theory and Practice of Curriculum Studies*. London: Routledge and Kegan Paul.

SMART, D. (1988) 'Reversing Patterns of Control in Australia: Can Schools be Self-Governing?' *Education Research and Perspectives*, 15, 2, 16–24.

SOCKETT, H. (1976) 'Teacher Accountability', *Proceedings of the Philosophy of Education Society of Great Britain*, 10, July.

STENHOUSE, L. (1977) 'A Proposed Experiment in Accountability.' *The Times Educational Supplement*, 13 May.

WATSON, K.P. (1978) 'Accountability in English Education.' *Educational Administration: Journal of the British Educational Administration Society*, 6, 2, 9–22.

WESTERN AUSTRALIAN MINISTRY OF EDUCATION (1986) *Better Schools in Western Australia: A Programme for Improvement*. Perth: WA Ministry of Education.

WESTERN AUSTRALIAN MINISTRY OF EDUCATION (1988) *School Development Plans and School-Based Decision-Making Groups*. Discussion Document. Perth: WA Ministry of Education, October.

Chapter 10

Financial Issues in the Tension between Democracy and Bureaucracy

Ross Harrold

Curriculum and resource provisioning policies for state government schools have historically been made at ministerial and head office level, then implemented in schools via regulations and directives. These mandates have been transmitted and monitored through the bureaucracy. In recent decades, however, there has been some tendency to limit the number and scope of these mandates and to make more frequent use of policy guidelines, which allow school personnel more discretion in how they respond. These are typically supplemented by financial support and information (including in-service programs) to encourage and prepare schools to behave of their own accord in ways consistent with policy goals.

In terms of policy implementation, the 'hard' policy instruments of regulations and directives which demand compliance have been 'softened' by the use of guidelines which allow discretionary responses. These have often been employed in conjunction with other 'softer' policy instruments, such as finance, designed to induce school decision-makers to respond consistently with policy intentions. Softer instruments give more opportunities for community and staff participation in adapting policy responses to local situations.

The potential power of the softer instrument of finance to transform the delivery of government education is not often recognized, because the attention of state policy-makers has been on harder policy instruments. The first section of this chapter briefly considers how a switch from the funding of institutions to the funding of clients could radically change the balance between bureaucracy and democracy in Australian education. If finance has this potential for change, why has it been used so little by states to date? The second section suggests some answers. This leads to the main part of the chapter which reviews where and why policy-makers have devolved more financial decision-making to the school — first at the state and second at the Commonwealth level. It is argued that the main motive of state administrators devolving financial control has not been to encourage more democratic decision-making but to improve administrative efficiency. At the federal level the Commonwealth has used financial instruments far more deliberately and more effectively. State policy-makers could well reflect on some of the more effective Schools Commission programs for lessons about the prospects for using grants as instruments to encourage constructive community involvement in schools. The chapter concludes, however, that senior state administrators have displayed a marked resistance to forego their power and to allow the diversity implicit in the wide use of such softer instruments of policy.

Radical Financial Arrangements

Finance issues are frequently taken for granted and even seen as irrelevant by personnel in schools. This is understandable, since under the current methods of resourcing schools in most states the sums of money flowing through the bureaucratic systems to the schools are relatively trivial. Yet a few fundamental changes to the method of funding schools could materially transform the relations between democracy and bureaucracy in Australian schooling.

Let us examine how these changes might happen. In Australia the finance needed to purchase resources for schools comes from consolidated revenue funds. This is the central reservoir into which taxation and other public revenues flow and from which the recurrent outlays of most public services are financed. Consolidated revenue funds are 'voted' to education and other functional ministries via the annual budget process. The money is then placed at the disposal of ministries to implement the policies on which the government was elected.

There is no logical reason why a government must use the voted funds to supply the services through its own hierarchical, bureaucratic functional systems. It could dismantle much of its central and regional organization which uses the voted funds to hire and buy resources which are then supplied (with instructions and directions) to schools. Instead, it could channel its funds directly to the schools to enable school communities to purchase their own teachers and other materials and services they need. It could go further and channel the funds directly to parents of school-age children who could use them to purchase the teaching services of independently organized schools. This is generally known as the voucher system of funding.

Financial Issues in the Tension between Democracy and Bureaucracy

Both the proposals to fund schools directly and to fund parents are, or could be, under serious consideration by governments. The first is the nub of the provisions in the UK Education Reform Act; this enables schools to 'opt out' of their local educational authorities and to become 'grant maintained'. In New Zealand all schools are to become 'grant maintained' according to current developments in education administration reform (Taskforce to Review Educational Administration, 1988; Lange, 1988). Under current arrangements the principals and boards of trustees of New Zealand government primary and secondary schools can exercise discretion over only 10 per cent of their total expenditures. Under the proposed reforms this is to be lifted to 95 per cent. 'All funding will come to institutions as a bulk grant' (Lange, 1988, para. 1.3) The government will require that the board of trustees, with the principal and staff of each school, first prepare a charter of objectives within overall national guidelines. This charter will be the basis of an accountability contract with the school's local community. When the charter is accepted by the minister, the school will receive an annual bulk funding grant with which it will be expected to cover virtually all its expenses — from salaries for all staff (including principal and teachers) to the purchase and maintenance of equipment.

While an undertaking to study the voucher scheme of financing schools was on the platform of the Liberal/Country Party in the 1975 Commonwealth elections, the party quietly dropped the idea once it was elected. The scheme has reappeared in muted form in the current Liberal Party's 'Growth Plan for Higher Education'. The plan proposes that 80 per cent of Commonwealth recurrent funds be in the current form of grants to states for higher education institutions. The remaining 20 per cent of recurrent grants for undergraduate and postgraduate courses would, however, be available to institutions through their attraction of holders of Higher Education Scholarships (HES). These scholarships would enable the holders to meet their full tuition costs at either public or private higher education institutions. The more HES holders an institution attracts, the greater its recurrent income.

Nevertheless, the idea of using vouchers as an alternative to public provision of social services continues to provoke political debate. In July 1988, for example, the Minister for Finance, Senator Peter Walsh, proposed (unsuccessfully) to Federal Cabinet that future child-care funding in Australia be based on a voucher system. Currently subsidies are paid only to publicly provided child-care centres, which are used by parents, some of whom could well pay more than they do. The vouchers would have been provided only to the deserving parents, who could use them to pay for child-care in either public or private care centres.

Democracy and Bureaucracy

Overseas the Alum Rock School District near San José in California undertook a worthwhile experiment with educational vouchers between 1974 and 1979 (Cohen and Farrar, 1977; McGuire, 1979). In the United Kingdom the Thatcher government's Education Reform Act introduces local financial management and grant maintained schools. Many believe that if these reforms are successful and if the Conservative Party is returned to office at the next elections, vouchers could well become the basis of school funding in that country in the mid-1990s.

Arrangements which allowed wide discretion to school personnel in the use of finance and made the personnel primarily accountable to their local communities would be radical in the Australian context. Nevertheless, there are proposals in some systems to move towards 'self-determining' schools which are less bound by, and accountable to, their system hierarchies.

Sources of State Government Centralism

There seem to be four main causes of current departmental reluctance to allow more freedom for school communities to adapt curriculum offerings to local needs and to deploy and to raise resources: history, taxation, the law and fiscal accountability.

In Chapter 1 of this volume Hedley Beare describes how the pioneer settlements in Australia depended on the colonial capitals for the provision of public services. It is important here that colonial public services grew from their bureaucratic bases in capital cities. The major sources of power remain in the capital city-based bureaucracies, even though, since the Second World War, much has been made of moves to regionalize departments.

A high priority has always been given to equality of provision in this public sector growth. Colonial and state governments made considerable fiscal efforts to ensure that the services provided to their country constituents matched as closely as possible those received by city dwellers. While this was generally admirable, the stress on equality had organizational consequences. The recruitment and employment of teachers, for example, have traditionally been made by head offices, which have directed or persuaded them to teach in particular schools. More generally, central administrative mandates have reflected a concern to ensure a demonstrable equality of curricular offering and resource usage and an intolerance of diversity which would be construed as a source of inequality among schools. As M.C. Vile (1977: 5) has observed, 'The greater the recognition of equality, the greater must be the centralization of power and authority and its concomitant bureaucracy, to ensure and administer that equality.' Despite the devolutionary rhetoric of Scott (Management Review: NSW Education Portfolio, 1989) and of other recent reports on the reorganization of schooling, the ultimate power of the centre in state education has never been seriously challenged. This is partly because government schools have been almost completely dependent on central provisioning and have never had access to significant alternative sources of revenue. In countries such as Canada, the USA and the UK municipal property taxes have given schools some local independence from complete control by higher levels of government, even though this independence has been eroded in recent years.

Even more basic than control over resources is the final legal responsibility, and therefore authority, which state ministers have for their schools. The reserve power over education given to state governments by the Commonwealth of Australia Act 1900 has not to date been delegated to local government authorities. If the referendum of September 1988 had recognized local government as a tier of government in its own right, it is conceivable that local governments could eventually have become more involved in the support and control of government schools. If so, it could in the longer term have given a means for local authorities to have assumed more responsibility for, and control of, schools within their jurisdictions.

The fourth source of state centralism, accountability, is common to the themes of equality, revenue sources and legal authority. The current political preoccupation with small, lean government has increased pressures on state governments to demonstrate the efficacy of the use of public funds. Corporate management and program budgeting are both part of a larger strategy for politicians to have more direct involvement and control over the performance of their departments. The political rhetoric might be to encourage schools to be more accountable to their local communities. The reality is, however, that if a democratically made school board decision is found by some to be offensive, recourse to the minister through the local member can start a bureaucratic process which makes life a little more difficult for school administrators.

In short, the conditions for the devolution of significant decision-making powers to state schools have been, and are, currently unpropitious. Nor is there much chance of persuading state education ministers and their advisers to soften the policy instruments they use. Nevertheless, there are interesting moves to devolve financial power to schools. Ironically, the moves seem to have been made more out of a concern with administrative efficiency than with encouraging local participation in decision-making.

State Government Financial Devolution

In the early post-war years the head offices of education departments typically acquired the recurrent resources needed by their systems, then disbursed them to schools on requisition or according to formulae. Since about the mid-1950s action has been taken in all systems to replace these practices with procedures which give more purchasing discretion to local schools. The nature and pace of this evolutionary change have varied among systems, but the general sequence appears to be as summarized in Figure 10.1. The figure comprises two triangles of equal area, joined by a 'policy membrane' along their hypotenuse. The hatched area in the left triangle represents the total direct recurrent outlays of a system on its schools. The labels along the left-hand side of the figure are the categories of these expenditures, the height of each roughly representing its relative financial importance.

Figure 10.1 represents schematically the apparent policy sequence followed by government systems in devolving to schools discretion over the use of available funds. In a situation where the system bureaucracy made all significant purchasing decisions about the nature and quantities of educational inputs, the policy membrane would be impermeable and all the 'contents', representing total direct school outlays, would be in the left triangle. This could be taken to typify the situation in most states a generation or so ago, when virtually all items (including teachers) were 'on issue' from system head offices.

As systems grew in size and complexity during the 1960s and 1970s, the centralized state bureaucracies came under increasing criticism for their inflexibility and delays in responding to supply requests. Educational policy-makers responded by increasing the permeability at the bottom of the policy membrane. That is, they began to allow at least some purchasing power to flow directly to schools in the form of grants. This enabled schools to make some of their own decisions about what, and sometimes where, they would buy the materials they wanted.

One of the earliest examples of this devolution was subsidies to assist schools to purchase education-related items such as musical instruments, record players, tape recorders, TVs and videos, sporting equipment and sometimes library materials. These subsidies had the additional advantages of cutting the budgetary burden of central expenditures and of encouraging local parents' and citizens' fund-raising efforts. On the other hand, it was charged that the parents' and citizens' groups in more affluent areas were able to raise more money more easily than in poorer areas, thus attracting more subsidies. This ran counter to the strong

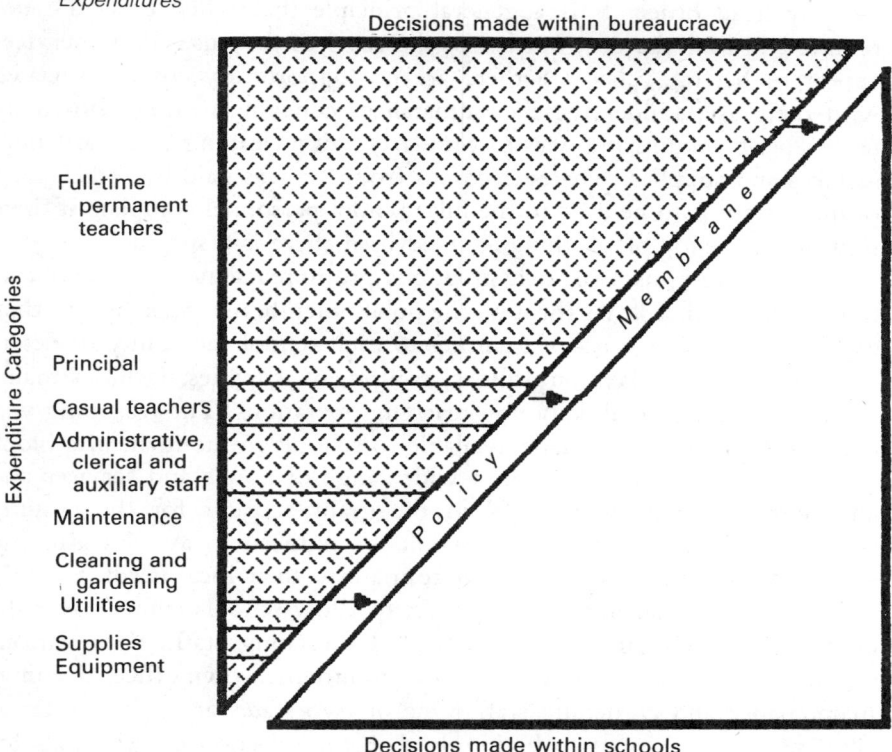

Financial Issues in the Tension between Democracy and Bureaucracy

Figure 10.1 Location of Decision-making with Respect to Direct Recurrent School Expenditures

Decisions made within bureaucracy

Expenditure Categories:
- Full-time permanent teachers
- Principal
- Casual teachers
- Administrative, clerical and auxiliary staff
- Maintenance
- Cleaning and gardening
- Utilities
- Supplies
- Equipment

Membrane / Policy

Decisions made within schools

concern of administrators with equality in the distribution of finances among schools.

There was a time when all stationery, ink and other consumable supplies were on annual issue from central stores. There was, however, obvious wastage in a system which rarely could exactly match supplies to the needs of individual schools. Concern to reduce this wastage led to some systems establishing notional credits with stores branch, against which schools could order their own annually requisitioned items. This has developed into some states giving their schools a financial grant which can be used to purchase supplies from either central stores (thus benefiting from bulk purchasing) or private suppliers. Exploratory efforts have been made by the ACT Schools Authority to have its own stores warehouse compete with private suppliers on a full cost recovery basis. It is believed that antagonistic reactions by commercial interests have led to the current shelving of the initiative, but there are hopes that the idea might eventually come to fruition.

Wasteful use is also likely when electricity, fuel and water bills are paid by head office. It is a general principle that when users are not required to bear the cost burden of the services they use, those services appear to be 'free', because there are no 'opportunity costs' associated with their use. Under these circumstances concern is rarely shown by users about minimizing waste. Similarly with cleaning and gardening services and supplies: whatever comes from, or was paid by, other parts of the system is to be used to the hilt. School personnel complain if there is an insufficiency of anything, but never if there is a surplus.

Critical responses to such situations prompted senior administrators to consider further flows through the policy membrane. Specifically, they experimented with ways of granting to each school the ability to determine their own outlays on utilities, equipment, supplies, facilities maintenance and on general daily non-teaching operations. The reasoning was that if the money were made available to schools in the form of a block grant which could be spent on a wide range of goods and services and any unspent funds be retained in the grant account for the ensuing financial year, school personnel would be induced to avoid waste and utilize the saved funds in ways appropriate to their local needs.

The major challenge is, of course, to allow schools control over the employment of their staff — particularly teaching staff. With various caveats, some states allow school boards to hire their own office, cleaning, maintenance and gardening staff. One or two states are going as far as allowing school boards to be involved in the selection of principals for their schools. No state has yet bitten the bullet (as New Zealand is proposing to do) of allowing school boards to select their own teaching staff (Lange, 1988, para. 1.1.20). The ACT Schools Authority has given a little more discretion to schools by instituting a points system which allows individual schools to make 'trades' between the employment of teaching and other professional staff.

Among the first states to experiment with such a grant scheme were South Australia (McDonald, 1980) and Victoria (Pederson, 1978). In the latter state the School Grants Scheme began in July 1973. The grant to each school was calculated on the basis of current enrolment, size of school buildings, size of school site and distance from Melbourne. Documentation accompanying the grant itemized its various components, but this itemization was meant to guide rather than constrain. Grant payments to each school were made initially into each school's Grant Account which, after the Education (Schools Councils) Act of 1975, was controlled by its council. The procedure enhanced the authority of these participative bodies.

After preparation of its budget for the ensuing year a school council would transfer a sum of money to an Extraneous Account for school administration, materials, requisites and library books. Payments from this account were controlled by the principal, although he or she was accountable for its use to the school council. Council was directly responsible for expenditures related to buildings and grounds maintenance and improvements.

Victoria's Schools Grant program was an early attempt to improve the efficiency of administration transferring discretion over financial decision-making from the departmental hierarchy to the schools. It also had the secondary benefit of introducing more participatory democracy into the school system — a valuable point in promoting the program to parent groups. Its apparent success provided encouragement for further decentralization within that state and for similar experiments in other states. For example, the Western Australian Ministry of Education in 1986 published its *Better Schools* report. It proposes a cash School Grant to 'self-determining' schools. The grant is intended to meet school outlays on:

> purchases of professional development services, including teacher relief, teacher travel and accommodation for teacher in-service courses;
>
> payment of school staff salaries for specialist or ancillary support such as instrumental teachers, swimming teachers, teacher aides and coordinators for special programs;
>
> purchase and production of resource materials, equipment and textbooks;
>
> furniture acquisition;
>
> building maintenance;
>
> equipment and instrument maintenance;
>
> utility charges (including telephone accounts);
>
> salaries of casual and relief staff.

The report is vague about who should control the school grant. It proposes, however, that oversight of school fund expenditures and the use of school resources and facilities should be carried out by a formal decision-making group representative of community and staff and allowing appropriate participation by students.

A more recent development is program budgeting, which directs budget allocations to the service of specific programs of activities in pursuit of stated educational goals (Brown, 1983: 41–3). Most state governments are implementing the mechanism in their functional departments, but in only a few education systems is program budgeting being taken down to the individual school level. In Victoria program budgeting has been introduced at the school level in conjunction with the School Improvement Plan, which utilizes Caldwell and Spinks' (1986) collaborative school management procedures as a basis for school decision-making. Beare (1986: 5–6) has reservations about the instrumentalism encouraged by program budgeting, but both schemes appear to be working successfully as vehicles to integrate school level program planning with resource allocation and in involving members of the local community in planning school improvements.

The devolution of financial decision-making to schools is placing additional demands on school staff. Few have had formal training in accountancy, budgeting or financial administration, yet they are expected to report on their financial stewardship to auditors and to businessmen on their school councils. Some assistance has been afforded through executive development in-service programs and various manuals and financial guides produced by system offices. The most important assistance is, however, the provision of additional bursarial staff to all schools — an expensive policy which the ACT Schools Authority has implemented in Canberra schools, despite times of budget recession.

Commonwealth Financial Instruments

The clearest demonstration of both the possibilities and the difficulties of using finance to influence the balance between bureaucracy and democracy in educational institutions can be seen in the operation of Commonwealth programs for schools. The simple reason why the Commonwealth relies on the softer instrument of financial grants to pursue its policy goals is that it cannot use harder ones, at least in the states. As pointed out earlier, the constitution does not give the federal government the legal power to use mandates, rules or regulations to impose its will on state educational institutions. The most it can do is attach 'conditions' to the grants it makes. As The Honourable Kim Beazely (senior) said when he was Commonwealth Minister for Education (*The Australian*, 3 May 1975): '[The Commonwealth's] vital role in financing education tends to make people believe that it has authority in education. Outside the Australian Capital Territory and the Northern Territory, it has no authority whatsoever.'

During its existence from 1974 till 1986 the Commonwealth Schools Commission (CSC) had considerable influence, if not authority, in promoting the process of devolution in state schools. This influence was exerted through special purpose programs, with relatively little outlay of funds. In 1985, before the consolidation of some programs into general recurrent grants, the expenditures on special or specific programs were $160 million and a further $46.3 million for joint government/non-government school programs (CSC, 1985: Appendix 6, 193). Compared with general government final consumption expenditures on schools of $5768 million in 1985/86 (Australian Bureau of Statistics, 1987: 8) these were trifling amounts.

One illustration of the approach of a special purpose program is given by Jean Blackburn (1983) who describes the Schools Commission's Disadvantaged Schools Program (DSP). The program ran on a budget of $21 million a year — only 3 per cent of all federal assistance to schools. The Commission wanted the funds to improve the learning circumstances of those from disadvantaged backgrounds without singling out particular pupils. It therefore made grants to whole schools. The Commission also wanted to encourage individual communities to design their own ways to improve the learning circumstances in their schools. It therefore paid grants only in response to project proposals submitted by representative committees of eligible school communities. There was a minimum of stipulations accompanying these grants; emphasis was placed on in-service preparation of project leaders and on the dissemination of information about successful projects. In short, the program used its grants to enlist and support local initiative and commitment to improving learning in disadvantaged schools.

It is difficult to separate the impact of particular funding programs from the influence of general social trends towards devolution and democracy in state school systems. Nevertheless, few would dispute the self-congratulatory claims made in the following extract from one of the last reports published by the Commonwealth Schools Commission (CSC, 1985: para. 1.4, 2):

> The school level activity and developmental work generated by Specific Purpose Programs, on a national scale, is impressive. In schools receiving specific purpose funding, groups of teachers and parents write submissions, develop educational programs, conduct inservice activities, prepare materials, document progress and take part in educational debate about goals and purposes of education in their community. A high proportion of this work is done after hours. Official and unofficial networks have been established for exchange across schools, systems and States. Within systems, support structures have been developed through

consultancy services and resource centres. This work taken over a ten year span has had significant system-wide effects in meeting the needs of students and establishing effective organisational structures and programs. It has made a major contribution to the professional development of teachers and has strengthened the capacity of parents to become effectively involved. Specific Purpose Programs in many schools provide the only discretionary funding available to support educational innovation and special projects. It is clear that by providing specific funds in this way, the Commonwealth helps to generate voluntary educational activity far beyond the formal requirements of each program. For this reason, Specific Purpose Programs represent outstanding value in terms of Commonwealth investment in education.

Various factors have contributed to the impact of Commonwealth special purpose programs. First, though the amount of funds allocated to these programs has not been large, they have operated 'at the margin', that is, they have provided additional discretionary resources above basic systemic allocations. These have given school personnel a little more freedom and encouragement to be innovative. Second, the programs have had a limited number of well articulated goals, which have made the programs both more credible and more easily evaluated. Third, the administrative procedures for grant disbursement have encouraged professionals and lay people together to clarify local needs and to develop feasible school-based projects to meet those needs. Finally, the conditions attached to the awarded grants have generally been non-prescriptive and, although formal audit statements are always required, some flexibility has been allowed in the way funds have been employed. In short, the CSC programs cleverly used the incentive effects of financial instruments, supported by administrative and informational techniques, to induce voluntary behaviour in the direction intended by the Commonwealth policy-makers. The 'light-house effect' of these programs has almost assuredly assisted the general movement toward democratization of school decision-making.

Not all CSC programs have been either successful or enduring. Program operations have been affected by the necessity to channel funds through state treasuries, and federal budgetary uncertainties have made state governments reluctant to allow their schools to become too committed to Commonwealth grants initiatives for fear that they might be required to continue funding programs from which the Commonwealth had withdrawn. In the late 1970s and in the 1980s, moreover, the

Financial Issues in the Tension between Democracy and Bureaucracy

functioning of the CSC was adversely affected by political manoeuvring and increasingly acrimonious debate among Commission members, particularly over state aid to non-state schools (Harrold, 1985).

The history of the general recurrent resources program for government schools provides an interesting example of a less effective grants program which policy-makers have modified in an attempt to increase its effectiveness. In its original form this was a relatively large program, absorbing approximately 25 per cent of all grants allocated on the recommendation of the CSC between 1974 and 1986 (Karmel, 1985: 12, Table 2.4). The initial program goals were simply to provide additional finance, on the basis of need, to help meet the general running costs of schools. The Commission hoped also that states would give part of these grants as cash disbursements to schools for discretionary purposes (CSC, 1975: 144, para. 13.34). But since they were unrestricted block grants and compliance to program goals could not be enforced, only Tasmania and one or two other states administered the grants in the spirit of the Commonwealth's intentions. Most added the grants to their general recurrent departmental funds, and reported their implied use within audit requirements. There is evidence, for example, that in the mid-1970s most states used the funds to try to minimize emergent teacher oversupply problems (Harrold, 1987). In 1981 the federal Minister for Education, Mr W. Fife, publicly accused the New South Wales government of 'abusing the flexibility allowed in Commonwealth educational financing by transferring about $30 million of school funds into other projects over the last five years' (*The Australian*, 11 September 1981, 4).

Commonwealth policy-maker frustration with the ineffectiveness of general recurrent grants as a financial instrument led to a change of approach in 1985. Under the new policy of 'resource agreements' the Commonwealth shifted from simply expressing the goals it hoped recipients would pursue, to seeking, as a prerequisite of funding, a commitment by each recipient to use additional grant funds for mutually negotiated objectives. The agreements included acceptance of the use of specific educational indicators to monitor progress toward these objectives (Karmel, 1985: Ch. 13). A broadly similar approach has been taken in the White Paper on Higher Education (Dawkins, 1988), which states that any institution wishing to enjoy the funding benefits of the 'unified national system' must apply for the privilege and, in applying, undertake to accept a series of conditions stipulated by the Commonwealth.

The introduction of the resource agreements approach represents a classic case of 'hardening' the grant instrument by incorporating closer targeting and accountability conditions, in an effort to increase the instrument's effectiveness but still respect the freedom of the recipient to choose not to accept the grant.

Reflections

A value premise of this chapter is that school communities should be given more opportunities and incentives to respond to local needs within state policy guidelines. It has been argued that finance can be used as a softer instrument to pursue such a value (McKinnon and Hancock, 1979). To date it has been rarely used by central policy-makers and their bureaucratic advisers, however, because they have preferred to implement their policy objectives with mandates, rules and regulations, administered through bureaucratic channels. These harder instruments have been simpler and quicker to use, and the required uniform responses have made it easier to demonstrate the system-wide equality of provision.

The chapter has suggested that central bureaucracies have nevertheless shown interest in the use of finance as a policy instrument through the devolution of financial discretion to school level. It has been argued that even though the effect of financial devolution has been consistent with reducing bureaucratic controls over school decision-making, bureaucrats' moves toward devolution appear to have been motivated by considerations of efficiency rather than democracy. These experiences provide a challenge to the conclusion drawn by Selleck (1985) in his historical review of proposals to reorganize the Victorian Department of Education. He points out that the main intention of the reorganization was to improve the effectiveness and economy of the department by transferring power and authority from the central office to regions and schools. He concludes that 'increased administrative efficiency has never been the precursor to community involvement: it is an alternative to it' (Selleck, 1985: 118). In terms of the theme of this book, action to improve bureaucratic efficiency has never contributed to school autonomy and democratic decision-making.

While Selleck's claim probably holds in terms of major organizational restructuring, the experiences related in this chapter suggest that his conclusion does not necessarily hold in the case of financial devolution to schools. Concern to avoid waste from inappropriate resource provisioning has helped motivate state educational policy-makers to replace the central disbursal of teaching supplies and the central payment of utilities and cleaning services with block financial grants to schools. While these actions have been intended to improve administrative efficiency, they have been consistent with increased community involvement in local schools. This is because financial devolution has given schools more power of choice over the type and mix of resources obtained as well as the way they are used. Further, to the extent that the direct grants have been paid into school council accounts, they have given non-professionals a more democratic involvement in school decision-making.

The significance of this devolution should not be overplayed, for the relative magnitudes of the sums devolved are not large. In 1986/87, for example, only 7.23 per cent of total appropriations and income available to the ACT Schools Authority were available for disbursement by schools themselves (ACT Schools Authority, 1987: Appendix 9). Of this, 1.14 per cent was obtained from fund-raising and voluntary contributions. Real progress will be made when school boards are given control over the hiring of their own teachers, as is proposed in New Zealand. Nevertheless, the responsibilities given by this financial devolution have supported the role of school councils and provided a useful basis for extending their role more fully into the schools' curricular decision-making.

The use of finance to implement policy has been developed most fully by the Commonwealth government, simply because it lacks the constitutional authority to employ mandates to induce changes in state educational systems. Its experience has shown that a well-designed grants program can be surprisingly effective, even without large financial commitments. The success of grants programs depends very much on how well they are targeted to a recognized but unmet community need, and how well disbursement arrangements are designed to provide motivated people with the incentives to act in ways desired by the granting authorities.

One could argue that authorities cannot afford the luxury of experimentation with financial instruments at the present time of recessionary budgets and unfavourable political climates for education. One could, on the other hand, argue that the development of financial instruments of policy implementation becomes the more important at this time. Far more fundamental than the issue of resource limitations is the question of the legitimacy of government schools and their responsiveness to local community needs. One response to these matters is to loosen the grip of the central administration and to place greater reliance on the judgment of those who represent, and who serve, local and regional communities. Moreover, the prime direction of accountability must be to the communities rather than to the system bureaucracy. Yet in this less bureaucratized organizational arrangement there still need to be incentives for school communities voluntarily to move in directions set by central policy-makers. The use of financial instruments is one means to achieve this.

References

ACT SCHOOLS AUTHORITY (1987) *Annual Report 1986/7*. Canberra: ACT Schools Authority.
AUSTRALIAN BUREAU OF STATISTICS (1987) *Expenditure on Education, Australia, 1985/6*. Catalogue No. 5510.0. Canberra: Australian Bureau of Statistics.
BEARE, H. (1986) *Shared Meanings about Education: The Economic Paradigm Considered*. Buntine Oration. Melbourne: Australian College of Education.
BLACKBURN, J. (1983) 'Title I and the Australian Disadvantaged Schools Program.' In G. HANCOCK, M. KIRST and D.L. GROSSMAN (Eds), *Contemporary Issues in Educational Policy: Perspectives from Australia and USA*. Canberra: Schools Authority and Curriculum Development Centre.
BROWN, I. (1983) 'Financial Control and Government Schooling.' *Choice and Diversity in Government Schooling*. Discussion Paper No. 4. Adelaide: Schools Commission.
CALDWELL, B.J. and SPINKS, J.M. (1986) *Policy-making and Planning for School Effectiveness*. Hobart: Tasmanian Education Department.
COHEN, D. and FARRER, E. (1977) 'Power to Parents? The Story of Educational Vouchers.' *Public Interest*, 48, 72–97.
COMMONWEALTH SCHOOLS COMMISSION (1985) *Quality and Equality: Commonwealth Specific Purpose Programs in Australian Schools*. Canberra: Commonwealth Schools Commission.
DAWKINS, HON. J.S. (1988) *Higher Education: A Policy Statement*. Canberra: Australian Government Publishing Service.
HARROLD, R.I. (1985) *The Quirks of QERC: An Investigation into the Establishment of the Quality of Education Review Committee*. Occasional Paper No. 7. Melbourne: Australian College of Education.
HARROLD, R.I. (1987) *Budgetary Responses of Australian State Governments to a Commonwealth Schools Grants Program, 1973 to 1977*. Unpublished PhD thesis. Armidale: University of New England.
INTERIM COMMITTEE FOR THE AUSTRALIAN SCHOOLS COMMISSION (1973) *Schools in Australia* (Karmel Report). (Chairman: Prof. P.H. Karmel). Canberra: Australian Government Publishing Service.
KARMEL, P. (Chair) (1985) *Quality of Education in Australia: Report of the Review Committee*. Canberra: Australian Government Publishing Service.
LANGE, RT HON. D. (1988) *Tomorrow's Schools: The Reform of Education Administration in New Zealand*. Wellington: New Zealand Government Printer.
MCDONALD, J. (1980) 'Ways of Funding Education.' In G. O'CALLAGHAN (Ed.), *Alternative Ways of Organizing Education*. Melbourne: Australian Council for Educational Research.
MCGUIRE, C.K. (1979) *Educational Vouchers*. Working Paper No. 23. Denver, Colo.: Education Commission of the States.
MCKINNON, K.R. and HANCOCK, G. (1979) 'Australia.' In ORGANIZATION FOR

ECONOMIC COOPERATION AND DEVELOPMENT, *Educational Financing and Policy for Primary Schools.* Country Reports, Vol. 1, 7–56.

MANAGEMENT REVIEW: NSW EDUCATION PORTFOLIO (1989) *School Renewal: A Strategy to Revitalize Schools within the New South Wales Education System* (Scott Report). Milsons Point, NSW: Management Review, NSW Education Portfolio.

PEDERSEN, B. (Leader) (1978) *The History of School Resource Allocation, 1960–1978.* School Resource Allocation and Management Project, Study B. Melbourne: Education Department of Victoria, Planning Services Branch.

SCHOOLS COMMISSION (1975) *Report for the Triennium, 1976–8.* Canberra: Schools Commission.

SELLECK, R.J.W. (1985) 'The Restructuring: Some Historical Reflections.' In M. FRAZER, J. DUNSTAN and P. CREED (Eds), *Perspectives on Organizational Change: Lessons from Education.* Melbourne: Longman Cheshire.

TASKFORCE TO REVIEW EDUCATIONAL ADMINISTRATION (1988) *Administering for Excellence: Effective Administration in Education* (Picot Report). Wellington: NZ Government Printer.

VILE, M.C. (1977) 'Federal Theory and the New Federalism.' In D. JAENSCH (Ed.), *The Politics of the New Federalism.* Adelaide: Australian Political Studies Association, 1–14.

WESTERN AUSTRALIAN MINISTRY OF EDUCATION (1986) *Better Schools in Western Australia: A Programme of Improvement.* Perth: WA Ministry of Education.

Chapter 11

Tensions in System-wide Management

George Berkeley

The management of state education systems represents a major share of management enterprises within the public sector. Capital and recurrent expenditure on education uses between a quarter and a third of government spending in the states. Education systems are major employers of public servants, particularly teachers, but also of very significant numbers of clerical and ancillary staff. Indirectly, the operations of school systems provide employment for large numbers of the building trades, in transport, in printing and publishing houses, in food and catering and in clothing and sports goods industries. Education is very big business and consequently its management has an impact on a broad sector of public and private economies.

Because of education's pre-eminent position, moves for change and reform in the public sector, whether they be for more accountability, for improved efficiency or effectiveness or simply for reducing expenditure, frequently target the education systems. Such moves often receive added impetus because education, by its very nature, generates demands for more and more of its services. In times of static or declining fiscal resources available to governments the provision of additional services can only be made at the expense of other social services or by improving efficiency in the delivery of existing services or, as is increasingly suggested, by the generation of income through entrepreneurial activities within the system.

Against such a climate there has been created a pressure for education systems to subject their management processes and administrative organizations to critical review. This need is exacerbated by the pressures of social, political and economic change operating within the environment within which education systems have to function. Systems increasingly have to ensure that they have the capacity to be adaptive and flexible as circumstances change and the demands of their clients alter. Further, in a democratic society in which the level of education of the populace is continually rising it follows that increasing numbers of that population will not only question decisions affecting them but demand a say in those decisions. Models of management sufficient for the nineteenth and the greater part of the twentieth century will clearly not suffice as we approach the close of the present century and the dawning of a new millenium. The existing structures were founded on bureaucratic, hierarchical, centralist principles which assumed much simpler, more stable environments than those that have evolved rapidly in recent times.

This chapter looks at the management structures and processes that have existed and exist today across Australian education systems, at the pressures for change and at the tensions resulting from such pressures. It also looks at the various patterns of management resulting from the current and continuing rash of reassessments and reviews of education in this country.

The Background to Present Management Structures

Historically and traditionally, state education systems in Australia have been managed by large, centralized and generally authoritarian bureaucracies. These origins have been traced by Hedley Beare (see Chapter 1) and are not the concern of this chapter, except that a proper consideration of management today, and over the last thirty years, can only occur in the context of understanding previous patterns of administration. As Cath Blakers (1982) maintains:

> the centralization of education, with time and size, inevitably produced rigidity of thinking, adherence to established practices and resistance to change ... discouraged community involvement ... encouraged a defensiveness and a fear to challenge within schools and departments.

Nevertheless, in any discussion of change and reform which tends to concentrate on faults and omissions, it needs to be remembered and acknowledged that state Departments of Education (or Public Instruction) from the 1970s to the last quarter of this century did manage successfully to provide education services to some millions of Australian children in our cities and across the wide spaces of our sparsely settled country. This contribution of administrators and teachers in the first century of public education should not be, nor appear to be, sold short.

As education departments across Australia faced the challenges of post-war growth resulting from baby booms, migration and changing retention patterns, their centralized management structures, for the most part, consisted of a permanent head (a Director or Director-General) responsible to a minister for education and operating under an omnibus Education Act or a number of acts with responsibility, generally, for the whole gamut of education from pre-school to university. Though the structure varied with the size of the system, the permanent heads were generally assisted by Deputy or Assistant Directors-General, or both, and by Divisional Directors. The latter, for the most part, controlled divisions within the departments with specific responsibility for sectors of schooling (e.g. primary, secondary, technical, special). Inspectors of schools provided the links between central and local management. The systems were essentially concerned with the management of schools and colleges operating under centrally determined policies and regulations.

Factors Necessitating Change

By the mid-1960s, as post-war growth became a significant factor in management, most states had introduced some administrative decentralization, generally in the form of geographic regions. In general these regions had few devolved powers and operated more as local branch offices of the central administration. We shall return to a more detailed discussion of the development of regions later. As well as setting up regions, most systems from the 1960s onwards created specialist or functional divisions or branches within their head office structures. These functional divisions varied from state to state, but generally included units devoted to personnel, curriculum and planning or research functions. Their evolution was a recognition of the growing complexity in managing the educational enterprise and of the need for specialist, as well as generalist, advice for chief administrators.

By the 1970s the structure of most education departments resembled the form shown in Figure 11.1. These administrative structures were hierarchical and centrally-oriented and, for a variety of reasons, unsuited to coping with the changing requirements of education systems faced with growth and then decline, altered social and political conditions, varying supply and demand situations and the problems of managing personnel not prepared to accept older views of employer–employee relations. The last quarter of a century has witnessed a range of attempts to vary these structures better to meet new challenges.

In examining the present management of state education systems and

Democracy and Bureaucracy

Figure 11.1   Typical Structure of Department of Education

Minister for Education

Advisory) Boards
Statutory)

Director-General of Education

Deputy Assistant/Directors-General

Divisional/Functional Directors

Regional/Area Directors

Schools

the tensions that arise because of the operations of large bureaucracies involved with communities, it is proposed to look at:

the nature of the management of education systems;

the pressures on that management resulting from changing social, economic and political conditions;

the response to those pressures, particularly in terms of administrative changes and reorganizations.

The Scope of Educational Management

A typical state Department of Education is engaged in managing an extremely large operation. For example, the state of Queensland, which in size occupies a middle position in the states, in 1988 employed in its school system 25,260 teachers, approximately 2500 administrative staff and 14,000 ancillary staff. Its administrative headquarters are housed in a modern twenty-two storey building with offices in several other city and suburban locations. There are twelve regional centres, each housed in modern office accommodation and employing professional and administrative staff ranging in numbers from eighteen in the smallest region to thirty-three in the largest.

The system delivers education services to and through some 1320

Tensions in System-wide Management

school locations as well as to a range of specialist centres such as those for distance education. In doing so, it caters for some 418,200 pupils and students. This picture is repeated in varying degrees in each of the states and territories.

The scale of operations of state education systems would be much larger were it not for the tendency in recent years for the scope of the responsibility of the permanent head of the Department of Education to be considerably lessened. Initially responsibility for university and higher education moved to statutory authorities or boards; more recently responsibility for technical and further education (TAFE) has in most cases moved to separate departments usually associated with employment and training. Shears (1984) outlined nine changes that took place in Victoria between 1965 and 1982, each of which he claimed was a splintering of the power and area of control of the Director-General in that state. These changes were:

> the establishment of the Victorian Institute of Colleges in 1965;
>
> the establishment of the Advisory Committee on Tertiary Education in 1968;
>
> the establishment of the State College of Victoria in 1972;
>
> the establishment of the Victorian Post-Secondary Education Commission in 1978;
>
> the inclusion in the Standing Committee of the Australian Education Council of officers other than the Directors-General of Education;
>
> the establishment in 1979 of the Victorian Institute of Secondary Education;
>
> the establishment of the TAFE Board and the separation of TAFE colleges from the Education Department in 1981;
>
> changes to the Education Act in 1981 which reduced the power of the Director-General;
>
> the establishment of the State Board of Education in 1982 as another avenue of advice to the Minister.

In varying degrees a similar reduction in the scope of the authority of the chief executive has occurred in most states. Given the growth that has taken place in school education, particularly with increased retention in secondary education and with the extension of facilities for special and pre-school education, such reduction has been necessary for management efficiency reasons if not for educational reasons. The change has, however, created a possible source of tension in that it has meant that the responsible minister now has more than one source of advice on education and these sets of advice may be in conflict, particularly in areas of mutual interest such as post-compulsory education.

A further change in the structures in which educational management has existed has been in the development of ministries of education. The original model of a Minister with a small personal staff assisted in the execution of his duties by a large Department operating under a Permanent Head as the agent and chief adviser of the Minister has been considerably changed in a number of states. The increasingly high profile adopted by a number of ministers as the politicization of educational decision-making has increased has led to, or been a result of, the growth in size and function of the ministry in a number of states. At times it has been difficult to distinguish the operations of the Minister from those normally handled by his Permanent Head. New South Wales in the 1970s significantly expanded the operation of the Ministry; in recent years structural changes in Victoria, South Australia and Western Australia have resulted either in the disappearance of the Department of Education, as such, or in a considerable modification of its functions.

Whether such changes may represent attempts to modify what Weber saw as 'the overpowering impact of the bureaucracy' is open to question. Certainly the direction of the earlier Victorian reforms would seem to have had such motivation with the Minister himself at least initially acting as Chair of the major decision-making and management group (Victorian White Paper, 1980). The growth of ministries and the changing role of ministers also saw the advent of ministerial advisers who, for the most part, were political appointments and not permanent members of the public service. The role of the Director-General as the chief adviser to the Minister was further modified and, indeed, in some cases subverted by such appointments.

The Press for Management Reform

At the centre of any discussion on the management of any large organization will be the issue of wherein lies the decision-making power. The rapid growth in enrolments in Australian state education systems in general led to more or less haphazard growth in the systems' management structures, a continuation of fairly rigid bureaucratic mechanisms, which frequently reinforced the tendency towards centralized control, and a large number of decision points considerably removed from the particular areas affected by those decisions.

These hierarchical structures tended both to lengthen and to slow the decision-making process. If, as was frequently the case, decisions within the area of educational management were also made by other departments, e.g. Public Service Boards or Commissions or Public Works Departments, the decision-making and action processes were further lengthened and complicated. Departments were also, for the most part, slow to harness technology to assist in tasks of data processing and information accessing so necessary for informed decision-making.

The tensions and frustrations created by these inadequate management structures caused the need for reform. Before this press for reform is examined, some of the characteristics of management likely to operate in a large education system should be considered.

Management essentially means making decisions about the conduct of the enterprise. New decisions are required when conditions and circumstances change, or when it has been judged that they are about to change. The first step in such decision-making involves an analysis of existing and changing factors. Such analysis requires, not only clear thinking, but access to all the appropriate information that governs existing and changing circumstances. The problem is thus mapped and options for its solution are hypothesized. Problem-solving occurs when a decision is made about which option is to be chosen, having had regard to all its intended and unintended implications and outcomes.

However, given the size of Departments of Education and the spread of their operations, it is difficult to judge whether decisions made at the centre are appropriate for all those who will be affected by such decisions. For this reason one of the major directions of reform has been towards either decentralization of decision-making or the devolution of decision-making powers to smaller units of the system, or to some mix of both. The premise, or at least the rhetoric, has been that an effective administration system should be as simple or flat as possible, and that decisions should be made as close as they can be to the area to be affected.

It is proposed next to examine in some detail aspects of the changes that have taken place in Australian/state systems in recent years. However, before doing so it needs to be pointed out that reforms to the management of public sector education did not occur in isolation. They are part of the movement to reform in the whole of the public sector. Indeed, in some states moves towards review and reform of Education Department administrations were a direct result of overall reviews of management of the public service. Such reviews reflected the calls for greater efficiency and effectiveness as resources diminished. Education as a major user of public monies has been in the forefront of such presses for reform. In order that its increasing demands could be met from static or even reduced (in real terms) resources, it was seen as necessary that it improve its efficiency and productivity.

In Victoria the report, *Corporate Planning in Victorian Government: Concepts and Techniques* (Victorian Government, 1984), pointed to the increasing pressure on government agencies to adopt a more rational, comprehensive approach to management; in advocating reform of management practices, it stressed the importance of corporate planning for departments. In South Australia the *Review of Public Service Management* (Government of South Australia, 1984) claimed that performance in the public service was limited significantly by excessive rigidities and controls, reducing its ability to respond readily to changing community demands. One recommended change was to give managers of departments both the responsibility and the authority to manage departmental operations within major policies and guidelines set by the government.

Somewhat similar findings were presented in Queensland (Savage, 1987), where a public sector review had among its terms of reference:

ensuring a more efficient, responsive and responsible public service;

streamlining of administrative processes; and

providing Permanent Heads with increased responsibility for and flexibility in the management of their departments.

In Western Australia the impetus for organizational change in the Education Department can be directly related to the recommendation of the Functional Review Committee in its report, *Managing Change in the Public Sector* (1986), which sought an administrative style of:

responsiveness and adaptability to the needs of the community;

flexibility in the use of resources to meet these goals; and

accountability to the government and the community for the standard of servicing and funding.

These public sector reviews often set a climate in which reviews of administration of education could take place. Their prevailing philosophy encouraged the removal of bureaucratic rigidities and increases in the flexibility and responsiveness to changing community and social needs. They also pointed in the direction of simpler and leaner central administrations. Given the size of the operations for which state education systems were responsible, leaner central administrations could only be framed if decentralization and devolution of power and authority from that central office were allowed to take place.

The fact that reviews of organization within Education Departments may have had their origins outside those departments could well have been a source of tension to senior officers. This, in turn, may have meant, as has been intimated in the Victorian reforms (Lacy, 1985) that some senior officers worked against the implementation or progress of these reforms.

Decentralization and Devolution

In the light of the issues discussed above it was little wonder that, as post-Second World War growth exacerbated the problems of management, education administrators sought to decentralize their operations. Overseas critics such as Kandel (1938), Butts (1955) and Jackson (1961) had caused administrators to reflect on their charges of undue centralization. Jackson went so far as to claim:

> In the two largest States there are clear indications that retention of the present system of inflexible central control, with little or no delegation of responsibility and authority, will inevitably bring the whole administrative machinery grinding to a full stop.

The lack of a strong system of local government and no tradition in this country of involvement by the third tier of government in the governance of education prevented any real consideration of decentralization by delegation to local councils. The result was a move to decentralization by the establishment of regions with limited control over education in their areas. The first regions were established in New South Wales in 1948 and in Queensland in 1949. Initially, these regions operated more in the nature of post offices or agents of the central system than as new loci for management decisions, but in more recent years the continuing delegation of more authority from central office has resulted in assigning responsibility closer to the area of operation.

Nevertheless, it is important to discuss whether such decentralization really involves the devolution of power and authority from the central to the regional office. Walker (1973) stated that in New South Wales, for example, the process of decentralization had been dubbed by some of its critics as 'recentralization'. Bassett (1970) referred to the regions in New South Wales and Queensland as microcosms of the systems as a whole, with centralized administration being retained. If one examines the decision-making structure that existed in state departments through the 1950s to the mid-1970s, a fair conclusion would be that most decision-making occurred at the central office, while that which occurred in the regions and schools was more of the order of interpreting and implementing already determined policy and associated rules and regulations. Walker (1973) maintained that real decentralization resulted from the devolution of governance rather than merely of administration.

Despite further delegation of administrative responsibility to regions in most Australian states through the 1970s, there was public and professional criticism that too much power and authority remained at the centre. Conversely, too little real delegation had occurred at the school or operational level, either for the professionals (school staff) or for the lay community (parents and citizens).

A characteristic of the regional/central model that has operated in a number of states, particularly but not only when the central administration has consisted mainly of school divisions, has been the confusion of roles and responsibilities between divisional directors with state-wide responsibilities in given areas and regional directors with overall responsibility for education services and delivery in a defined geographical area. This diffusion of roles created tensions and territorial disputes between regional and divisional directors. It could be argued that its resolution was one of the reasons departments, in their restructuring, moved away from sectoral division.

The establishment of a new education authority in the Australian Capital Territory in 1973, following more than a decade of public pressure for separation from the New South Wales system, provided the first example in Australia of a public education system with a measure of local control and direct citizen and teacher involvement in its governance. The administration of schools in the ACT differed from that of the state systems in that:

> its central governing body was a statutory authority with an appointed Chair and members representative of the Authority, the local legislature (initially), the profession, the community and parents;
>
> each school had a School Board consisting of Authority, school staff, parent and student (in high schools and colleges) representatives with functions in respect of school policy and management.

The ACT system was seen as a pace-setter and possible model by many, although others argued that the circumstances and conditions of the national territory were so different from those in the states that its translation to the state scene was not appropriate. This is not to say that the collaborative model of the ACT was not without its operating problems. Berkeley and Kenway (1987) comment that the management and conduct of a schooling system that espouses participation and consultation in an open climate is fraught with some difficulty. The same reviewers commented on the complexity of managing a school system by participative involvement at different levels of authority and responsibility of government, professionals and community.

Despite the apparent difficulties inherent in devolving the management of education systems, there have been significant moves in a number of states to shift decision-making nearer the impact point. In Victoria, despite different political motivations following changes of government and changes in the designers of reform, there has remained a consistent move towards more control at the local area and at school levels. The restructured Office of Schools Administration in Victoria has, inter alia, the following objectives:

> to decentralize decision-making by the transfer of operational responsibilities to regions and schools;
>
> to give schools greater discretion in the use of their resources;
>
> to enhance the capacity of schools to determine their own educational programs within the framework provided by central policies and guidelines, available resources and industrial agreements;
>
> to create a simplified and decentralized administrative system; and
>
> to facilitate the involvement of parents, teachers and students in participative processes at the different levels of decision-making both directly and through decision-making groups.

The Western Australian document, *Better Schools in Western Australia* (1986), maintains that the efficiency and effectiveness of the system can be improved only if schools have sufficient control over the quality of education they provide, and that it is only at the level of the school that meaningful decisions about the educational needs of each student can be made. For this reason the process of devolution of responsibility to schools needs to be completed; individual schools, the paper asserts, must become the focus for the administration and delivery of education.

Similarly, in South Australia it is proposed that the basic operational unit of the public education system will be the school, and that the major purpose of the Education Department will be to support, serve and enhance that relationship. Proposals for change are aimed at further decentralizing operational decision-making. To cater for South Australia's geographical and demographic characteristics, they have adopted a modified regional structure with further relocation of resources and authority from the existing functional directorates.

In Queensland, while the major move has been towards the further devolution of authority to the now twelve regions, there have been moves to shift some of the responsibility for management and resource decisions to the schools themselves. As Matheson (1988) states:

> As system level functions change, regional level functions must undergo review. As stated in the Task Force Review of Organizational and Management Services 'the functions of Head Office should be pitched at levels which encompass policy formulation, overall planning and negotiations for resources. Regional officers should be mainly concerned with matters such as tactical planning, implementation and supervision. Institutions should focus their attention on day to day operations required to implement effective educational programs'.

New South Wales has been the last state to look at its management structures. A report — *Schools Renewal: A Strategy to Revitalize Schools within the New South Wales State Education System* (Scott Report) — was published in June 1989. The review found there was a clear need to change dramatically the system of educational administration on the grounds that the traditional centralized system is no longer appropriate for today's schooling needs. It calls for significant devolution of authority and reform in staffing policies and practices (Management Review: NSW Education Portfolio, 1989).

Unlike reforms in some other states, the New South Wales report recommends the maintenance of the Department but with a new name — the Department of School Education — to distinguish it from the Department of Technical and Further Education. Both departments are to report to the one Minister — the Minister for Education and Youth Affairs.

In arguing for a decentralized, school-centred approach to educational administration, the review concluded that the principle of applying uniform state-wide practices does not work because:

> it causes much of the decision-making to be embedded at the centre, away from the point of teaching and learning;
>
> it allocates resources in accordance with rigid formulae rather than on a basis of need; and
>
> it seriously impairs each school's ability to respond to the requirements of its students.

Tensions in System-wide Management

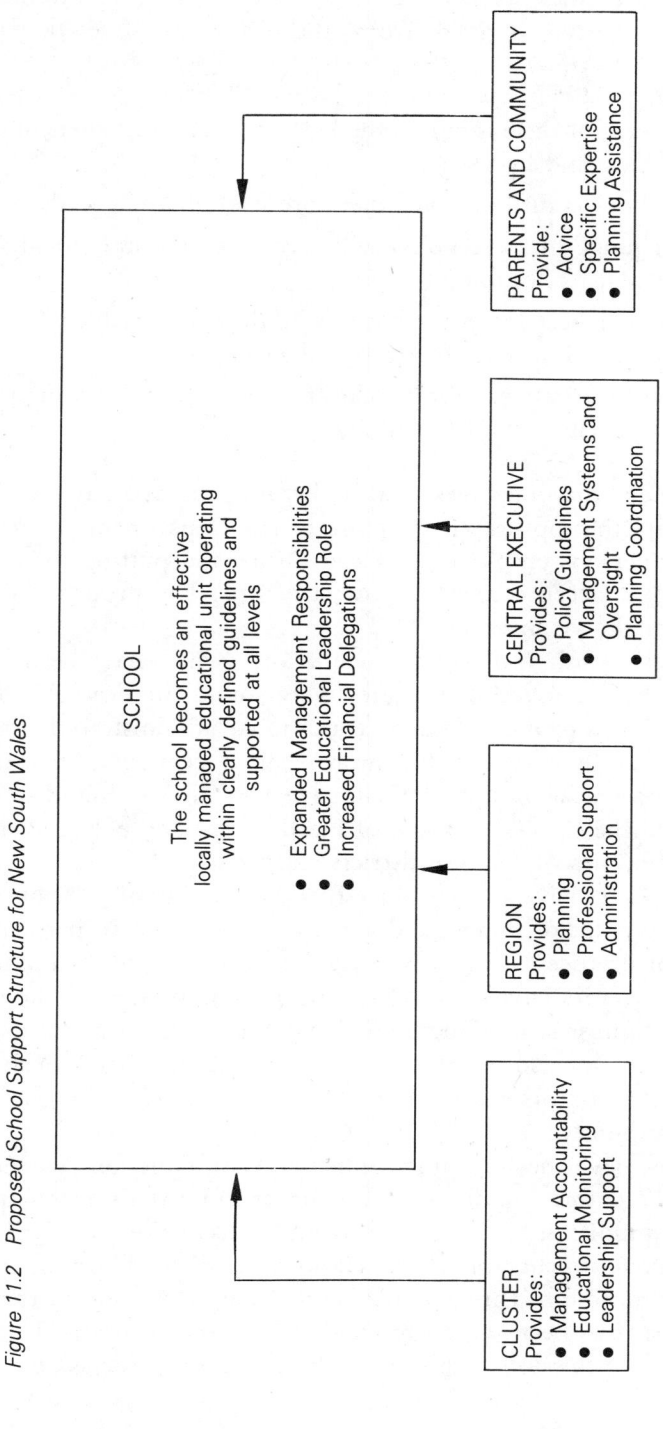

Figure 11.2 Proposed School Support Structure for New South Wales

```
                    ┌─────────────────────────────────────────┐
                    │                                         │
                    │                                         │
                    │               SCHOOL                    │
                    │                                         │
                    │    The school becomes an effective      │
                    │    locally managed educational unit     │
                    │    operating within clearly defined     │
                    │    guidelines and supported at all      │
                    │    levels                               │
                    │                                         │
                    │    • Expanded Management Responsibilities│
                    │    • Greater Educational Leadership Role │
                    │    • Increased Financial Delegations    │
                    │                                         │
                    └─────────────────────────────────────────┘
        ▲                ▲                ▲                ▲
        │                │                │                │
  ┌──────────┐    ┌──────────┐    ┌──────────────┐   ┌──────────────┐
  │ CLUSTER  │    │ REGION   │    │   CENTRAL    │   │  PARENTS AND │
  │Provides: │    │Provides: │    │  EXECUTIVE   │   │  COMMUNITY   │
  │• Management│  │• Planning│    │Provides:     │   │Provide:      │
  │  Accountability│• Professional│• Policy      │   │• Advice      │
  │• Educational│ │  Support │    │  Guidelines  │   │• Specific    │
  │  Monitoring│  │• Administration│• Management │   │  Expertise   │
  │• Leadership│  │          │    │  Systems and │   │• Planning    │
  │  Support  │   │          │    │  Oversight   │   │  Assistance  │
  │           │   │          │    │• Planning    │   │              │
  │           │   │          │    │  Coordination│   │              │
  └──────────┘    └──────────┘    └──────────────┘   └──────────────┘
```

Source: Management Review: NSW Education Portfolio (1989), p. 9. (Reproduced with permission from Office of Management Review, NSW Education Portfolio.)

To overcome these deficiencies, the Scott Report recommended a strategy for change derived from the following five fundamental premises:

> the school, not the system, is the key organizational element providing teaching and learning;
>
> every school is different and therefore has different needs;
>
> the best judge of these needs will usually be the individual school's teachers and its community;
>
> schools will best meet their needs if they are enabled to manage themselves in line with general guidelines; and
>
> the role of the system, if it is to be effective, must focus on providing support to schools and their leaders.

To achieve the objectives of this rhetoric, the Scott Report recommends ending the top–down structure of the Department, reducing the numbers of persons employed in Head Office and putting the school at the centre of a decentralized support structure. The proposed structure has the form shown in Figure 11.2.

The New South Wales recommendations, which have been accepted in principle by its government, effectively sound the death knell to the centralized, bureaucratic forms of educational administration that have been operating in Australia for more than a century. All states and territories have now modified their structures in varying degrees. All have reduced the operational role of Head Office and enlarged the roles and responsibilities of regions/districts and/or schools.

Such changes have as their objectives the moving of decision-making nearer to the point of impact and greater involvement of participants in the educational process. In that way teachers, parents and community and local administrators have been, or are being, empowered at the expense of central administrators. Theoretically at least, and in practice at best, this should remove some of the tensions that have previously arisen between administrators and teachers and between teachers, administrators and the community.

There is, nevertheless, some conflict and contradiction evident in this change in the nature of educational management. At the very time that education administration is moving from the centre to the field, politicians and governments of all persuasions seem to be seeking tighter control and more direct involvement in the administration of their portfolios. There has been a general reaction to the growth of statutory boards and commissions with their ability to make decisions at arms length from governments and ministers. At the same time there are strong moves towards national decision-making with respect to curriculum, reporting and assessment. Funding, particularly that provided by the Commonwealth, can only be along specified lines. A future tension may be caused by determining what is to be centrally decided and what is to be locally decided. The solution may be found in the notion of central office personnel as corporate managers and regional and institutional personnel as operational managers.

The Concept of Corporate Management

Hedley Beare (1988) believes that if educational management is to meet the changed demands of the post-industrial era, then a restructuring, incorporating the best practices from commerce and industry while retaining the uniqueness of education, is necessary. Corporate management, Beare argues, is applied to complex institutions, bodies corporate with many limbs. Such complex insitutions will survive beyond bureaucracies because they can be simultaneously tightly controlled yet free-wheeling, locally autonomous yet centrally cohesive, using the benefits of big size but operating like small businesses.

State systems, in various ways and to different degrees, are moving towards corporate management. Victoria's White Paper (1980) proposed a corporate management group comprising the Minister, the Assistant Minister, the Director-General, the Deputy Director-General and the four Executive Directors as its major policy and managing body. Bates (1985) argues this particular model 'spelled an effective end to a long-sustained tradition of ... the separation of political and administrative functions enshrined in the Westminster tradition.' However, political implications aside, it was the notion of a small group of senior personnel making the policy decisions. Graham Allen (1985), Victoria's first Chief Education Officer under its restructuring, saw corporate management as implying

> the application of management principles and techniques of the harsh and unforgiving world of large business corporations to the gentler and more cerebral environment of schools, TAFE Colleges and institutions of higher education ... and ... as a more comprehensive and coordinated approach to planning across all education sectors; or the removal of barriers between sectors which inhibit flexibility in the matching of resources to sectors; or improvement in the capacity of the education system to anticipate

and respond to changes in the economic, technological and social environment in which it operates.

If corporate management can achieve all these things, then surely we should hasten its implementation in our systems.

This change to a business management model highlights a fact to which Beare draws attention: education departments are not 'schools writ large', and school level administration and head office administration are different and demand different levels of skill and training.

The move towards a corporate management model which has occurred in most states has emphasized the planning and policy functions of the central or head office of state systems and has involved shifts of both the delivery and management of educational services to either the regional or the institutional level. Whether the particular system publicly espouses a corporate management model or not, there have been significant shifts in power, authority and responsibility. One consequence has been a marked change in the nature of the role of the Permanent Head of the Department, whether he be called a Director-General or a Chief Executive Officer.

The Changing Role of Directors-General

Mention has already been made of the reduction in the scale of operations of Education Departments and consequently in the locus of control of Directors-General. The move towards corporate management models and the press for business-derived measures of effectiveness, efficiency and productivity are also reflected in title changes of senior education officers. These changes have been from the militaristic titles of 'Director-General' and 'Director' to business-aligned terms such as 'Chief Executive Officer' and 'Manager'. These title changes, as well as emphasizing the management roles of the chief education administrators, perhaps also reflect some disillusionment with the management effectiveness of professional educators. As well, the changes emphasize growing government concern that public education systems were, and had been for a long time, using up the major portion of government funds.

Anne Susskind in an article in the *Sydney Morning Herald* (28 January 1988) commented:

> Judging by some recent appointments, Governments are obviously not satisfied with the way professional educators are managing education. The old school educators — bureaucrats who have

come up often through the teaching ranks and are steeped in educational philosophy, jargon and idealism — are inexorably being replaced at Federal and State levels by people chosen for management and budgeting skills.

Those responsible for the management of such large enterprises as Education Departments need to have business skills appropriate to such tasks, but it should also be recognized that education is more than a business. The conduct of schools is concerned with the development of children, and it is essential that at least a good proportion of those administering the system have experience, and understanding, of the educational process and of schools, teachers and children.

A further pointer to changing roles for Directors-General is suggested by Badcock (1987), writing of the Victorian situation: 'Both [Liberal and Labor Ministers] viewed public servants as more respectable than teachers; both elevated laymen, to the denigration of professional educationists, both made educational objectives subservient to administrative structures.'

Mention has already been made of how some ministers of education have assumed much more up-front roles in policy development and administration to the detriment of the role of Permanent Head. Harman *et al.* (1987) point out that this has occurred more when ministers have been teachers and have their own ideas about policy.

The Impact of Commonwealth Intervention

In their struggles to cope with growth during the 1960s the Directors-General of Education, working through their ministers and the Australian Education Council, produced compelling evidence in documents entitled *A Statement of Needs* that there was need for a massive injection of funds to upgrade state schools to an acceptable standard. At first assistance came in the form of capital grants for laboratories and libraries. With the advent of the Whitlam government and the Commonwealth Schools Commission in 1975, recurrent and capital funding amounting to up to 8 per cent of state funding was provided to augment general programs and for specific purposes, especially programs concerned with alleviating disadvantage. However, this additional resourcing came at a cost to management.

The preparation of submissions to acquire such funds, the administration of programs based on the funds and accounting of expenditure added considerably to the administrative load of the central offices of state systems, often, at least in the minds of state administrators, a load inordinately higher than should have been required by that proportion of total funding. State systems in varying degrees established sections, branches or divisions with the express purpose of dealing with the administration required in connection with Commonwealth funding for schools and, where it fell within their area of responsibility, for technical and further education.

Directors-General were also involved in regular and frequent meetings with Commonwealth officers, not only on funding and accountability for such funding, but often in either ideological arguments governing or determining the direction of funding or arguments over the extent of Commonwealth control once funding had been allocated. The issues of centralism versus state rights, of Commonwealth or national goals, of constitutional and local responsibility for delivery of educational services and of priorities for action assumed increasing importance on the agendas of Conferences of Directors-General. This restriction on Directors-Generals and their senior staff to have complete decision-making authority over expenditure under their control created tensions and further eroded the range of powers of the office. As well, despite the importance of this supplementary funding, senior officers often felt that it took up an undue proportion of their time and energies and led to neglect of equally important local issues.

Commonwealth involvement in, and influence over, education has continued to grow, with consequent management implications in state systems. The agenda of Australian Education Council meetings and the meetings of its Standing Committee are today largely concerned with issues of Commonwealth–state relations and dual or shared responsibilities. The modern chief executive is consequently much more involved in these national issues than were his counterparts of a few decades ago. It is, perhaps, just as well that senior executives at the central office level have been able to shed many of their operational responsibilities through decentralization or devolution.

Conclusion

It is sometime alleged that if Rip Van Winkle had been a teacher and had dozed in his classroom for those fifty years, his readjustment to his environment on awakening would not have been too dramatic — so ephemeral have been the changes to the teaching–learning situation. Can the same be alleged for management of education? This chapter has outlined considerable change that has been effected in the corridors of power of Education Departments. It needs to be determined whether the rhetoric of reform has been translated into actuality.

New policies decree the devolution of power and authority to regions and/or schools, in many instances with community participation. For the most part these reforms have been designed with limited consultation with those affected by the changes. The top–down rather than the collegial, democratic, consultative model has been used. In some instances there is evidence that recipients of the redistributed power do not actively welcome their new responsibilities, at least in existing circumstances. Principals and parents may object to additional duties if they claim resources or training are inadequate to the new tasks. Others argue that the reasons for change may be more a shift of responsibility for resources as governments seek ways to contain expenditure rather than a real attempt to relocate decision-making.

Teachers' unions are in the main conservative bodies who are wary of change, particularly if it alters their bargaining relationship with employers. Their own organizations are essentially centralized and bureaucratic, and discussion and confrontation are simpler with a central group than with dispersed authority. For this reason they may only pay lip-service to democratic reforms which should, on the surface, give their members more say in their operations. Structural reforms invariably create new tensions between employers and employees.

Reference has already been made to the change in status and power of senior officers that has resulted from management change. Unfortunately, the way in which those changes have come into effect in a number of states has meant more than just change for many officers — it has meant the end of their careers. The human effects of structural change can be devastating when they are handled as insensitively as they have been in some states in Australia in recent times.

This book examines the tensions that exist or have existed in state education systems governed by bureaucratic administrations operating in a democratic society. As teachers have become better prepared and more professional, there have been the inevitable tensions arising from the distribution of power and authority. As parents and the community have become more aware of their rights and have raised their expectations of what 'free, secular and compulsory' state education should do for their children, administrations have had problems in adjusting to these altering relationships. As students have stayed longer and longer at school, they too have sought different relationships with teachers and administrators from those operating in more autocratic times.

In recent years changes to management arrangements have been attempts to adjust to those new imperatives and to 'free up' the systems, to reduce tensions, increase their responsiveness and flexibility while making them effective, efficient and accountable. Governments' attempts to revitalize education's contribution to the economy add new tensions. The task of the remaining years of this century, both for management and for the widening range of participants in the schooling process, will be to settle down to new, more democratic, arrangements while avoiding further traumatic system upheavals.

References

ALLEN, G.J. (1988) 'Corporate Management in Education: The Victorian Case.' In AUSTRALIAN COUNCIL FOR EDUCATIONAL ADMINISTRATION, *Australian Contributions to Educational Management: Some Commentaries by Chief Executives*. Australian Council for Educational Administration, Monograph Series No. 4. Perth: Western Australian Government Printer.
AUSTRALIAN COUNCIL FOR EDUCATIONAL ADMINISTRATION (1988) *Australian Contributions to Educational Management: Some Commentaries by Chief Executives*, Australian Council for Educational Administration, Monograph Series No. 4. Perth: Western Australian Government Printer.
AUSTRALIAN EDUCATION COUNCIL (1971) *A Statement of Needs*. Sydney: Australian Education Council.
BADCOCK, A.M. (1987) 'Downgrading the Professionals in the Victorian Education Department.' *ACES Review*, November, 6–9.
BASSETT, G W. (1970) 'Bureaucracy and Centralization.' Paper presented to the International Visitation Program, Sydney.
BATES, R.J. (1985) 'The Socio-Political Context of Administrative Change.' In M. FRAZER et al. (Eds), *Perspectives on Organizational Change*. Melbourne: Longman Cheshire.
BEARE, H. (1988) 'School and System Management in Post-Industrial Conditions: The Rationale behind Corporate Management Structures in Education.' *Unicorn*, 14, 4, 248–55.
BERKELEY, G. and KENWAY, N. (1987) *A Management Review of the ACT Schools Authority*, Report to the ACT Schools Authority. Canberra: ACT Schools Authority.
BLAKERS, C. (1982) 'If Wishes Were Horses.' Discussion paper prepared for The Challenge of Change. Canberra: ACT Schools Authority.
BUTTS, R.F. (1955) *Assumptions Underlying Australian Education*. Melbourne: Australian Council for Educational Research.
FRAZER, M., DUNSTAN, J. and CREED, P. (Eds) (1985) *Perspectives on Organizational Change: Lessons from Education*. Melbourne: Longman Cheshire.
GOVERNMENT OF SOUTH AUSTRALIA (1984) *Review of Public Service Management: Initial Report*. Adelaide: Government Printer, March.
GOVERNMENT OF WESTERN AUSTRALIA (1986) *Managing Change in the Public Sector: A Statement of the Government's Position*. A Parliamentary White Paper presented by the Hon. Brian Burke MLA, Premier of Western Australia. Perth: Government Printer, June.

HARMAN, G., WIRT, F.M. and BEARE, H. (1987) 'Changing Roles of Education Chief Executives at the State Level in Educational Policy in Australia and America.' In W.L. BOYD and D. SMART (Eds), *Educational Policy in Australia and America: Comparative Perspectives.* Lewes: Falmer Press.

HUNT, A.J. and LACY, N. (1980) *White Paper on Strategies and Structures for Education in Victorian Government Schools.* Melbourne: Government Printer.

JACKSON, R.W.B. (1961) *Emergent Needs in Australian Education.* Toronto: University of Toronto, Department of Education Research.

KANDEL, I.L. (1938) *Types of Administration.* Melbourne: Australian Council for Educational Research.

LACY, N. (1985) 'Implementing Change.' In M. Frazer et al. (Eds), *Perspectives on Organizational Change.* Melbourne: Longman Cheshire.

MANAGEMENT REVIEW: NSW EDUCATION PORTFOLIO (1989) *Schools Renewal: A Strategy to Revitalize Schools within the NSW State Education System* (Scott Report). Milsons Point, NSW: Management Review, NSW Portfolio.

MATHESON, I. (1988) 'The Regionalization of Education: The Queensland Case.' In AUSTRALIAN COUNCIL FOR EDUCATIONAL ADMINISTRATION, *Australian Contributions to Educational Management.* Perth: Western Australian Government Printer.

MINISTRY OF EDUCATION (SCHOOLS DIVISION), VICTORIA (1987) *The Structure and Organization of the Schools Division.* Melbourne: Ministry of Education, December.

SAVAGE, E. (Chairman) (1987) *Public Sector Review.* Report of the Public Sector Review Committee, Queensland. Brisbane: Public Sector Review Committee, July.

SHEARS, L.W. (1984) *Administrative Structures in Education: A Report to the Minister for Education in Victoria.* Melbourne: Office of the Coordinator-General of Education.

SUSSKIND, A. (1988) in *Sydney Morning Herald*, 28 January.

VICTORIAN GOVERNMENT (1980) *White Paper on Strategies and Structures for Education in Victorian Government Schools.* Melbourne: Government Printer.

VICTORIAN GOVERNMENT, DEPARTMENT OF MANAGEMENT AND BUDGET (1984) *Corporate Planning in Victorian Government: Concepts and Techniques.* Melbourne: Government Printer.

WALKER, W.G. (1973) 'Administrative Structures: Centralization or Decentralization.' In G.S. HARMAN and C. SELBY-SMITH (Eds), *Designing a New Education Authority.* Canberra: Australian National University.

WESTERN AUSTRALIAN MINISTRY OF EDUCATION (1986) *Better Schools in Western Australia: A Programme for Improvement.* Perth: WA Ministry of Education.

Chapter 12

Reforming Bureaucracy: An Attempt to Develop Responsive Educational Governance

Fazal Rizvi and Lawrence Angus

In modern societies it is difficult to imagine a future without bureaucracy. While criticisms of bureaucracy are ubiquitous, and often justified, few of its critics are prepared to argue that we can do without it entirely. If we are to continue to hold a commitment to mass schooling, funded by the public purse, then some organizing principles for the coordination of activities and resource distribution, and a structure to enforce those principles, would appear to be necessary. If permanent functions are to be carried out in a predictable fashion, informed by a concern for equity, then it is difficult to see how some form of bureaucracy can be avoided. Indeed, as Bernheim (1985: 52) has argued, 'stable roles seem obviously important, and continuous monitoring of operations is very much preferable to sporadic responses in operations.' If problems which arise in educational governance are to be tackled rationally and effectively, then careful planning and a coordinated implementation of solutions are clearly preferable to ad hoc attempts to deal with issues. Without bureaucracy, there would appear to be not only uncertainty but also an arbitrary exercise of power.

But the case against bureaucracy seems equally strong. Bureaucracies are not always efficient; sometimes they interfere with the capacity to accomplish objectives. As Blau and Mayer (1987: 139) suggest, 'excessive rigidity in the application of rules and regulations leads to the incapacity of bureaucracies to change in response to external shifts and to the organizational growth in excess of what might be expected on the basis of task demands.' Bureaucracies are highly inflexible: they inhibit innovation and are characterized by bias and inertia. Common to most critiques of bureaucracy (Fischer and Siriaani, 1984: 5) is the concern that bureaucracies serve the interests of the élite in our community and thus perpetuate and perhaps even accentuate social class differences, and that their very structure inhibits them from being responsive to the needs of the community that they often profess to serve. As Weber (1968) had recognized, bureaucracy was a social force with power and values of its own, which existed in a constant conflict with democratic aspirations.

Herein lies the dilemma of bureaucracy and democracy. Its abolition may result in irrationality, inefficiency and the arbitrary exercise of power; but with its retention we would continue to face the dangers of excessive control over the democratic values and relations that human beings so dearly cherish. As Jacoby (1979: 151), following Weber, has argued, although democracy suggests minimization of domination, it must be ambivalent towards bureaucracy, since the only way to ensure equality before the law and legal guarantees against arbitrariness is by means of formal, rational 'objectivity of the administration as contrasted with dependence on personal discretion and the grace of the old patrimonial system.' For Jacoby, the dilemma has to do with the survival of democratic forms, which cannot be achieved without some reliance on bureaucracy to ensure consistency of treatment.

The way out of this dilemma would seem to lie in our constant search for ways of reforming bureaucracy. What we require are organizational structures that retain some of the virtues of bureaucracy — precision, predictability, impartiality and efficiency — while at the same time acquiring a character that makes them more responsive not only to the demands of innovation and change but also to the democratically expressed wishes of the community. In this chapter we discuss an experiment in bureaucratic reform. The experiment, mounted by the Victorian Participation and Equity Program (PEP), rested on the assumption that genuine educational reform could not be achieved unless schools were supported by an organizational structure that was responsive to the needs of their communities. The architects of PEP sought to devise a form of administration that both encapsulated the Program's democratic aspirations and ensured efficiency and effectiveness in its operations. For the Program in Victoria, the practical resolution of the dilemma between bureaucracy and democracy was seen as a constant challenge to be met by all its participants. In attempting to resolve that challenge, the Program met with some success. However, we suggest that in the final analysis its success remained constrained by the demands of the broader bureaucratic structure of the Education Ministry within which it was located, the deeply seated bureaucratic cultural norms which informed the work of many of its participants, its acceptance of a pluralist model of decision-making, and factors beyond its control such as the premature cuts to its budget even before the Program had sufficient time to become established. However, the experiment that Victorian PEP represented did point to possibilities and lessons that we can ill afford to ignore.

'Reforming Bureaucracy'

The notion of 'reforming bureaucracy' is highly troublesome, and may be interpreted in a variety of ways. It could, for example, be viewed in an entirely technical way, referring to efforts required in improving its machinery, in order to render it more efficient and effective. In the language of structural-functionalism this could be said to involve attempts to reform the internal relations within bureaucracy so that it functions in a more coherent, speedy, less cumbersome and inflexible way; so that its various parts work towards the achievement of the same organizational objectives. For example, management agencies, such as Personnel Australia (PA), hired by the Liberal government of Victoria in the early 1980s to suggest ways of improving the state's educational bureaucracy, believed that the performance of the Education Department could be improved by a more tightly defined structure of roles and relationships, a better coordinated hierarchical accountability system and a clearer definition of the enterprise's goals (Personnel Australia, 1981). PA consultants saw reform in purely technical terms, devoting little attention to the examination of educational goals, which they saw as being independent of the issues of organizational efficiency and effectiveness.

Reforming bureaucracy in this technical sense may or may not involve making the internal decision-making structures of the bureaucracy more democratic. Attempts to make them more democratic constitute a second sense in which bureaucracy may be reformed. Recent experiments in industrial democracy have encouraged greater worker participation in the operations of organizations (Crouch and Heller, 1983). The purpose of such reform has been to induce greater motivation from the workers towards the realization of organizational goals. But the goals have not been negotiable; worker participation is generally restricted to procedural issues. A third sense in which it is possible to reform bureaucracy relates to attempts to make it more representative. The idea of 'representative bureaucracy' (Krislov, 1974) implies that ethnic, class and gender composition of the organization approximates that of society as a whole. In this way it is expected that the social background of the bureaucrats would affect the decisions and policies they make and communicate to the groups they represent. Here too efficiency remains the overriding goal, since the idea of a representative bureaucracy does not entail an alteration to the structure of organizational goals and bureaucratic operations. Experiments with this strategy have demonstrated that existing bureaucracies have a considerable capacity for co-opting members of disadvantaged groups within their own distinctive culture.

More fundamentally, the appeal of 'representative bureaucracy' may lie in the view that through such reform it is possible to make bureaucracy more accountable to the public. The development of new models of administrative responsibility, through which bureaucrats may be made more accountable not only to their superiors but also to elected officials and to the public at large, constitutes a fourth sense in which to interpret the notion of 'reforming bureaucracy'. Since Weber, various theorists have suggested ways in which bureaucracies can be brought under the greater scrutiny and control of elected politicians. The notion of administrative responsibility has referred to a requirement that officials both give reasons for the way they propose to implement political goals, and indicate that operations have been carried out along the lines of well specified processes. Thus governments in Australia have often appointed public accounts committees and ombudsmen to ensure that bureaucracies have acted efficiently, effectively and impartially.

While attempts to reform bureaucracies in the ways identified above have no doubt contributed in varying degrees to making them more efficient and fair, the extent to which these reforms have served to resolve the dilemma of bureaucracy and democracy remains a moot point. In our view these attempts are insufficient and inadequate because they remain trapped within the Weberian perspective of bureaucratic rationality (Rizvi, 1989). The traditional Weberian perspective on rationality sees bureaucracy as value-neutral and hierarchical. Weber's view of bureaucracy is notable for two important and related features: its celebration of organizational efficiency and its recognition of explicit tensions between bureaucracy and politics.

Bureaucracy and Organizational Efficiency

Max Weber, the theorist who is most closely associated with the formulation of the characteristics of bureaucracy as an ideal type, argued that organizational rationality of bureaucracy afforded it technical superiority over other forms of organization.

> The fully developed bureaucratic apparatus compares with other organisations exactly as does the machine with non-mechanical

modes of production. Precision, speed, unambiguity, knowledge of files, continuity, discretion, unity, strict subordination, reduction of friction and of material and personal costs — these are raised to the optimum point in the strictly bureaucratic organization. (1968: 973)

For Weber, the central feature of bureaucracy is a hierarchy of clearly defined roles and responsibilities. This means a formal structure in which relationships, in the interests of efficiency and rationality, are rather impersonal between the occupants of role positions. That is, relationships between people are role relationships rather than interpersonal; they are defined in terms of a hierarchy of role positions within a clearly specified division of labour and specialization of functions. Whatever tasks or interactions a person performs within the bureaucracy, therefore, these are always associated with the person's status and function in the hierarchy.

The formalization of such impersonal and hierarchical relationships results in the centralization of power at the apex of the hierarchy. Authority is vested in position rather than in persons, and responsibilities and roles are defined in formally prescribed rules and regulations governing the conduct of work, which becomes routinized in duty statements or performance objectives to be attained by administrators. There is an emphasis on performance indicators and standardized management procedures, which are universally applied to ensure predictable, specified outcomes. In the Weberian machine-like bureaucracy, coldly rational, efficient coordination and impersonality prevail: 'Bureaucracy develops the more perfectly the more it is "dehumanized", the more completely it succeeds in eliminating from official business love, hatred, and all purely personal, irrational, and emotional elements which escape calculation' (Weber, 1968: 975). Such impersonality is thought to be particularly important because it means that the essential bureaucratic concerns of efficiency and fairness are not compromised by considerations of personal values and preferences. The ideal bureaucracy is value-neutral. Moreover, bureaucratic administration is thought to be content-free. That is, it is assumed that issues that are related to the area to be administered, say education, can be separated from the actual administration of education, which should be conducted in a rational and value-free manner by trained administrators whose skills could equally well be applied to other areas of administration in the same expert, impersonal manner.

The impersonal relationships within an ideal bureaucracy extend also to relations between officials and people outside the bureaucracy. Officials are expected to relate to members of the public in an impersonal manner that betrays no hint of personal values and attitudes. In this way bureaucracy can be impartial and without favouritism in its treatment of citizens or petitioners. The cost, however, is that such a bureaucracy makes responsiveness to the particular, sometimes unique needs of individuals difficult to achieve. Moreover, to achieve the ideal of impartiality or even-handedness, the discourse of ideal bureaucracy is one-directional. Bureaucratic discourse flows along the 'chain of command' so that it privileges the words of more senior officials. It also privileges the language of officials over the language of the public — because what officials say is bound by bureaucracy's own rules and regulations. Such discourse is couched in terms which give directions to people rather than engaging them in open dialogue.

Because of this impersonal, directive, one-directional dialogue, the public must deal with the ideal bureaucracy on its own terms. That is, members of the public must learn to adjust to the language, priorities and rules of bureaucratic structure if their concerns are to be dealt with by the bureaucracy. The public must be submissive to bureaucracy and adapt as best they can to the distinctive norms and culture of bureaucracy. The sense of alienation that is felt by many people, including many who work within bureaucracies, in dealing with bureaucracy, often results from their inability to deal with the unique requirements of bureaucratic communication.

The Distinction between Bureaucracy and Politics

The full significance of the emphasis on impersonality and value-neutrality in the ideal bureaucracy is brought home in Weber's distinction between the role of bureaucrat and that of politician:

> According to his proper vocation, the genuine official ... will not engage in politics. Rather, he should engage in impartial 'administration'.... The honour of the civil servant is vested in his ability to execute conscientiously the order of the superior authorities, exactly as if the order agreed with his own conviction.... The honour of the political leader, of the leading statesman, however, lies precisely in an exclusive *personal* responsibility for what he does, a responsibility he cannot and must not reject or transfer. (Weber, 1970: 95)

Although not optimistic about the ultimate influence of bureaucracy on democratic society, it was Weber's hope that what he foresaw as the burgeoning of bureaucracy would be somewhat balanced by the separate and quite distinct development of parliamentary processes. However powerful the bureaucratic administration, it could maintain both legitimacy and efficiency by its ability impartially to serve whichever political masters were elected by means of the appropriate political processes. Throughout all, the bureaucracy would remain remote from any struggles for power that are the province of the politicians. Bureaucrats stick to the neutral application of a rational legal structure of rules, professional expertise in handling administrative problems, a hierarchy of office and impartiality in dealing with particular cases. For Weber, these features of bureaucracy epitomized the notion of rationality (Bates, 1985). Nevertheless, Weber was keenly aware that the modern bureaucracy posed a major threat to the project of democracy: 'The great question is what we can set against this mechanization to preserve a section of humanity through ... the complete ascendancy of the bureaucratic ideal of life' (Weber in Thompson, 1983).

Despite his concerns about the tensions between democracy and bureaucracy, Weber's conception of the ideal bureaucracy, whose functions are clearly separated from the political sphere, has generally been accepted as appropriate by writers on politics and public administration (e.g. Wilson, 1953). Indeed, as one writer recently summarized the prevailing view:

> With few exceptions, there is common agreement transcending differences in political ideology, culture, and style, that bureaucracy should be basically instrumental in its operation — that it should serve as agent and not as master.... All agree that the state bureaucracy should be responsible to the political leadership, however intimately it may be brought into the processes of decision making by the will of the political elite. (Healy, 1984: 407–8)

The apparent distinction between bureaucracy and politics is particularly useful for governments and those who are generally well served by predominant interests. Particular issues in many cases can be effectively depoliticized and removed from the public sphere by being defined as matters of administrative management and determination rather than as matters of public debate and concern (Bates, 1985; Wilenski, 1979). This is largely because the maintenance of the dichotomy between politics and administration sustains a simply procedural view of administrative tasks and administrative legitimacy. The public interest is thought to be represented by elected politicians who are owed a duty of service by the bureaucracy. For instance, the election of Victorian and federal Labor governments in the early 1980s was accompanied by the expectation that the bureaucracy would implement new policies in a neutral manner. This was based on the assumption that the bureaucracy should not attempt to represent the public in policy considerations, but exists merely to implement the policy decisions made by elected representatives.

The dichotomy between the development and implementation of policies is the central plank of Woodrow Wilson's influential treatise on administration. As he strongly and clearly stated: '... administration lies outside the proper sphere of *politics*. Administrative questions are not political questions. Although politics sets the tasks for administration, it should not be suffered to manipulate its offices' (1953: 72). According to Wilson and later writers of the so-called 'science of administration' school (Finer, 1941; Hyneman 1950), politics, through appropriate legislative procedures, made decisions and established ends, while administration, through a permanent and impartial bureaucracy, ensured neutral and efficient means to those ends.

'Responsive' Bureaucracy in a Weak Democracy

Within the framework of contemporary democratic theory, the Weberian concept of neutral bureaucracy, clearly separated from and subordinate to the realm of politics, is consistent with only a very weak notion of responsiveness. The bureaucracy owes responsibility to the public indirectly, to be achieved through the responsiveness of officials to the elected representatives of the people. The major problem with this notion of responsiveness, however, is that it is associated with an extremely limited notion of democracy which relies entirely on formal representation. This notion is often referred to as 'overhead democracy' (Saltzstein, 1985) or 'weak democracy' (Barber, 1984), with its associated 'tool' view of the bureaucracy (McNeil, 1978: 67).

As a number of critics have pointed out, this notion offers an extremely benign view of politics in which the political sphere is seen to be occupied appropriately by professional politicians and expert officials (Wood, 1984; Pateman, 1970). Critics also point out that such professionalization of politics facilitates the dominance of the political arena by those who are best placed to protect and extend their own interests — that is, by 'white, middle-class, middle-aged men' (Hambleton, 1988: 142). Moreover, the nature of participation that is afforded by representative democracy is passive and minimal, with the expectation that citizens cast their vote in formal elections but then leave matters to those who should know best. As Hambleton explains, 'this form fits very well with the paternalistic "leave it to us" approach' (1988: 142) that characterizes managerialist government and bureaucracy.

This rather simplistic view of political process is made a little more complex, but not seriously challenged, by pluralist versions of democracy (e.g. Dahl, 1956). These generally assume that some degree of responsiveness is owed by the bureaucracy not only to the elected government but also to groups that have won sufficient support within the electorate. In the process of political bargaining and compromise, the interests of such groups will be advanced if they have managed to attain their own niches within the bureaucracy. An example in Australia of a powerful interest group having formal influence in the bureaucracy is that of the Returned Servicemen's League, to which the Department of Veterans' Affairs is particularly responsive. An example of more limited bureaucratic responsiveness to groups is the influence that was achieved in Victoria by the so-called 'five organizations' — teacher union and parent groups — upon the Ministry of Education, especially in the years of the Fordham Ministry immediately following the victory of the Labor government in 1982 (Deakin Institute for Studies in Education, 1984).

Carried to its extreme, this notion of romantic pluralism, as Salaman and Wamsley point out, holds that, if agencies of the bureaucracy are responsive to groups, then political outcomes in harmony with the public interest can be achieved because 'if each agency so responds, the result will be a richly competitive public pluralism' (1975: 153). The problems with this view are similar to those that beset the notion of 'representative bureaucracy'. That is, it is difficult, if not impossible, to determine to which claims made by which particular groups the bureaucracy most owes responsiveness. Moreover, given the nature of pluralistic competition, responsiveness to one group is extremely likely to preclude responsiveness to some other group (Saltzstein, 1985). Again, the groups most likely to 'win' responsiveness from the bureaucracy within such competition are unlikely to include the socially disadvantaged.

What seems evident is that only a very weak notion of democracy can be accommodated within the logic of Weberian bureaucratic rationality. If more complex, stronger (Barber, 1984) notions of democracy are desired, then key assumptions of bureaucratic rationality have to be rejected. In particular, the distinction between means and ends, politics and administration, cannot be sustained. Nor can the ideas of unidirectional discourse, informality of relationships between bureaucracy and the public, value-neutrality of functions and hierarchical power structure be retained in the form that Weberian bureaucratic rationality demands.

Theories of participative rather than merely representative democracy suggest that we reject Schumpeter's notion of politics as an 'institutional arrangement for arriving at political decisions in which individuals acquire the power to decide by means of a competitive struggle for the people's vote' (1943: 269). They require that political and administrative decision-making alike should not be the realm only of elected leaders but should involve a degree of citizen participation (Pateman, 1970; Wood, 1984). Castells, for instance, argues that to build such a participatory environment, 'we need a new instrument of political management — an institutional device that closely connects the state and civil society through local self-government, administrative decentralization, and citizen participation' (1983: 14). These requirements demand a new, more complex view of bureaucratic responsiveness, one which is capable of accommodating participatory democratic aspirations without sacrificing the virtues traditionally associated with bureaucracies.

It is our belief that such a view of bureaucratic responsiveness is unlikely to emerge from abstract theorizing. We reject the notion of generalized, universally applicable models of administrative structures and processes. The dilemma between democracy and bureaucracy is a practical one, located in specific contexts and informed by unique historical features relevant to those contexts. However, while it may not be possible to resolve the dilemma in an a priori way, it is instructive to examine practical experiments that have been attempted to develop the kind of instruments of bureaucratic responsiveness which Castells discusses.

One such experiment is represented by the Victorian Participation and Equity Program, conducted from 1984 to 1987. In what follows we describe the Program's reform strategy and discuss the ways in which it fell short of its initial ideal of devising a genuinely democratic form of administration. The data upon which our discussion of PEP is based were collected by one of us during an extensive overview evaluation of the Victorian Program between 1985 and 1987. The evaluation was informed by qualitative principles and covered the entire range of Program activities from the politics of its conception to its administration and implementation in schools. The findings of the evaluation, and a discussion of its methodology, can be found in Rizvi and Kemmis (1987).

Participation and Equity Program

The Participation and Equity Program (PEP) was a program of educational reform initiated by the Australian government in 1983, in a context of high unemployment and social alienation among youth, and (by OECD standards) comparatively low retention rates in upper secondary schooling. Some concomitant educational concerns for the national government, therefore, were to encourage curriculum change, to seek changes to the organization of secondary schooling and through these measures to promote equity.

National in scope, the Participation and Equity Program in the schools sector worked under the aegis of the Commonwealth Schools Commission and was administered in each state by a joint State–Commonwealth Committee. These committees were responsible for implementing the Program according to Commonwealth guidelines and reported to a National PEP Committee, as well as to state ministers responsible for education. The responsibilities of these committees included developing specific guidelines in the light of local needs and circumstances, engaging the necessary personnel for the development and organization of the Program, identifying target schools, monitoring and evaluating outcomes and providing system level support to effect system-wide reform. There was considerable scope for the states to develop the Program in their own unique ways.

In Victoria PEP complemented the recently published *Ministerial Papers*, which emphasized the ideas of democratic governance, community participation and responsive bureaucracy. The Victorian architects of the Program stressed the need to *practise* the Program's democratic aspiration, thus setting themselves the challenge of developing a structure that tackled the traditional dilemma of bureaucracy and democracy.

The Participation and Equity Program in Victoria eschewed centre–periphery conceptions of educational change, rejecting its rationalist assumptions. Most particularly, it rejected the notion that reform can be administered through strategies constructed from universal, logical and efficient procedures. It also rejected the idea that means and ends can be easily separated. Consistent with its own educational values of participation and equity, the Program adopted an approach to reform and a theory of change that recognized the importance of school-based development and decision-making. Arguing that the processes of education must be informed by the values of participation and equity, the designers of the Program construed the process of reform as an *educational* process, committing themselves to adopt these values as central principles around which to structure the Program's administration. The Program's rhetoric emphasized the importance of forms of discourse, activities and structures that encapsulated PEP's democratic aspirations, and thus provided models for the operation of the Program at school and classroom levels.

'Participation' and 'equity', as they came to be interpreted in the

Program, were part of a constellation of ideas about social democracy and justice which Labor governments, both at Commonwealth and Victorian levels, had traditionally celebrated. In PEP this implied formal participatory structures that sought to enable broadly-based decision-making at all levels. From the very beginning PEP in Victoria rejected the classical image of administration as value-neutral, and stressed that unless it was open about its moral and political goals, the Program could not expect to generate enthusiasm in schools for its central objectives.

The designers of PEP in Victoria had recognized that achieving democratic practices in an institution as centralized and bureaucratized as the Victorian Education Ministry would not be easy. They were familiar with a tradition of administrative writing that had demonstrated the tension between democracy and bureaucracy. They had recognized that educational governance could not be democratized unless questions about the nature and form of bureaucracy in a democratic system were also attended to. Many of the characteristics we normally associate with bureaucracy — hierarchical accountability, reliance on technical expertise, impersonal relationships, unidirectional communication — stand sharply opposed to the ideals of democratic community, including reciprocal and many-sided relationships, equality and individuality. These last were the values that PEP documents stressed repeatedly.

Yet designers of the Program had also determined that PEP was to be a 'mainstreamed' program. That is, it would operate through the existing bureaucratic structure of the Education Ministry, rather than stand apart from it as was the case with earlier Commonwealth programs like the Transition Education Program. Their hope was to establish democratic innovations that would serve to provide models for other sections of the bureaucracy seeking, and indeed mandated by the *Ministerial Papers*, to become 'responsive'.

No single reform strategy was thought to be appropriate. The Program designers thought it best to work in a variety of ways in challenging traditional modes of administration, which were increasingly seen as hostile to participative educational relationships in classrooms and schools. The PEP emphasis was on democratic relationships in the organization of education and on devising new structures that were more responsive to the needs of local school communities. The critical and the constructive elements of the strategy were to complement each other. In this regard, while we do not have space to detail fully the design of the Participation and Equity Program (see Rizvi and Kemmis, 1987), it is important for our arguments to draw attention to some of its broad features which explicitly challenged aspects of conventional bureaucratic structure and authority.

For instance, traditional hierarchical relationships within schools and between schools, regions and central office were challenged by the Program's deliberate emphasis upon collaborative, participative, school-based decision-making. This emphasis also ran counter to bureaucratic expectations of centralized control. In the same vein the participative emphasis challenged the division of labour and differentiation of functions that have become traditionally associated with the administration of schools and school systems. Indeed, the Program explicitly encouraged the crossing of traditional boundaries between specialized functions of, for instance, principals and teachers, and teachers and parents. Moreover, the impersonal, one-directional discourse and emphasis on formally prescribed rules that are associated with bureaucracy were to be challenged by an emphasis on informal dialogue between interested parties, and on the notion of responsive bureaucracy. Finally, the bureaucratic notion of neutral, content-free administration was directly challenged by the Program's commitment to a set of politically defined goals — participation and equity — which teachers, administrators and school communities were expected to practise as personal values.

In such ways the Program hoped to foster values, forms of social relationship and interpersonal activities which together could be characterized as 'responsive'. It envisaged a new form of organization in education and educational administration (variously described in terms of 'collaborative, participative decision-making' and 'the responsive bureaucracy'), described and justified in a new discourse (a discourse based on democratic political theory) and enacted in new practices (in terms of both the activities of people in schools and the activities of system administrators — practices which encouraged rather than inhibited collaborative decision-making and the sharing of responsibility).

Despite its considerable efforts, however, the Program was bedevilled by a contradiction between its democratic aspirations and rhetoric and the bureaucratic practice characteristic of its day-to-day operations. Put another way, the promise of its new rhetoric of responsiveness was not redeemed in new forms of activities and practices. Despite its collaborative rhetoric, the Program's practices and forms of organization remained highly bureaucratized. Indeed, as the Program developed, contradictions between the Program's discourse and its practice and organization became more evident. PEP was increasingly suffused with, colonized by and coopted into the very bureaucratic values and practices it aimed to resist. Rather than registering a resistance to bureaucracy in Victorian education, it became an extension of that bureaucracy.

The tensions which led to the incorporation of PEP into the education bureaucracy can be demonstrated by an examination of several aspects of the Program: the efforts to 'mainstream' the Program's operations within the wider Victorian education system; the operation of the Program's committees; the nature and scope of the work of the Program's exchange and its diminished capacity to support school-based activities; and the effects of 'the cuts' — the rescheduling of the Program's funding and its bureaucratizing effect.

The Mainstreaming of PEP

The term 'mainstreaming' was used to refer to the idea that the objectives of the Program — participation and equity — informed all practices in all schools and in the system generally. The 'mainstreaming' strategy was chosen because locating PEP within the system, it was thought, would lend authority to its policy and prescriptions, and lessen the likelihood that it could easily be dismissed as peripheral. Thus PEP's Secretariat and its central office were located within the Special Programs Branch of the Education Ministry with lines of accountability to its Director. Similarly, Regional PEP Consultants were members of the staff of regional offices of the Ministry, accountable to the senior officers in their regions.

Although it was argued that the mainstreaming strategy would confer system-wide authority on the officers and objectives of PEP, their location within these bureaucratic hierarchies might actually have served to isolate them. Their roles could be understood by analogy with the roles of functionaries in other sections, branches and divisions of the Ministry. They were considered by many to be 'specialists' employed to serve particular administrative functions in relation to the implementation of 'the Program'. Despite the fact that PEP's objectives were supported by the authority of recently published *Ministerial Papers*, and despite the endorsement of PEP's principles by the senior officers of the Ministry, officers of the Program related to other officers in the Ministry through routine hierarchical channels. A junior officer in PEP could only communicate with senior officers of other sections of the Ministry through her or his own equivalent senior officer. Thus bureaucratic practices were maintained, undermining the collaborative rhetoric.

The Program gradually lost its capacity to challenge other parts of the Ministry. The routine business of the bureaucracy — answering 'Ministerials', responding to demands for evidence of Program achievements from Canberra, dealing with an increasing tide of correspondence with schools and regions and the like — took precedence over promoting administrative reforms.

The difficulty of the strategy of mainstreaming was that it offered limited resources while aiming to provoke substantial changes in whole systems. After all, the whole system had previously operated in established ways which showed no particular respect for the aims of participation and equity. Such a system was resistant to change simply by virtue of its traditions and size. For the policy of mainstreaming to work, it would have required a measure of authority, time and resources commensurate with its task.

The notion of 'mainstreaming' also had important implications for the relationship between the Program's central office and its Secretariat. The Program in Victoria was established with a Secretariat responsible for providing executive support for the Program's committees and with a central office staff responsible for the operational implementation of the Program. The Secretariat and central office were accountable to the Special Programs Branch of the Ministry of Education.

Given the administrative 'mainstreaming' philosophy adopted by the Program, its central administration was structured on established principles of staffing, seniority, salaries and procedures in the Victorian education system and public service. Yet many officials working in the program viewed themselves as 'activists'. They were thus located at the very intersection of bureaucracy and democracy; as a consequence they experienced several kinds of role conflict between their personal values and commitments, their roles as officers bound to implement the government's policies in the Program, their formal roles as officers of the Ministry and in many cases their role as members of representative organizations.

Allegiances formed between like-minded people (and frequently developed 'outside' the Program in representative organizations) increasingly coincided with the internal divisions within the central office. The initial image of the Program's central office was probably that it would be a 'hot-house' of Program ideas, modelling collaborative, participative decision-making through democratic staff meetings, and modelling the idea of the 'responsive bureaucracy' in its relations with schools and regions. Two years into the Program the reality was different. Collaborative, participative decision-making in staff meetings was increasingly being pre-empted by information-giving sessions, and was decreasingly possible given the interpersonal tensions precipitated in the structuring, staffing, restructuring and reorganization of the program.

PEP's Committee Structure and Operations

Although the Program's committee structure was established in an effort to enact the objective of participation in decision-making, what eventually emerged was a structure that embodied mechanisms of representation that were overwhelmingly framed and constrained by the bureaucratic demands of the Program. To the extent that the Program's representative committees themselves worked in bureaucratic ways, PEP administration in Victoria became an extension of the existing bureaucracy of the Victorian Ministry of Education.

During the first year of PEP in Victoria program officials found themselves confronted with a great dilemma. On the one hand, there was a need to create a large-scale, complex program in a short period of time; on the other hand, they were aware of the Program's commitment to the widest possible consultation. The dilemma was resolved through the creation of an enormously large and complex system of representative committees. The need to demonstrate participation at all levels, however, was often made at the cost of accepting simplistic notions of representation. In an accelerating spiral, the creation of more committees effectively forced more decisions 'underground', which led in some instances to the need to create further committees.

Members of the many and varied committees found that the consultative processes that had been institutionalized under PEP involved decision-making in contexts that were often established, agreed, fixed and determinate. Some members complained that 'important decisions had already been taken elsewhere' and became the agendas of meetings that were so packed they could not devote sufficient time to individual items. The chairpersons of most of the Program committees were members of the Ministry of Education who often directed the discussion proceedings. The content, time scales and procedures for much of the work of representative committees were, moreover, established not by the committees themselves, but by the Program bureaucrats, both at state and Commonwealth levels. At other times these committees were required to approve various administrative 'decisions' put to them by the Program's central office. The agendas were so constructed as to provide individual members with little opportunity to raise substantive issues of educational concern.

Most committees of the Program were made up of representatives from the nominated organizations of teachers and parents, officials of the Program administration and nominees of other divisions of the Ministry. There was also provision, seldom taken up, for student membership on the committees. At most meetings the members who were Ministry employees and those who were organizational representatives were roughly equal. However, in sub-committees, where important decisions on such issues as the budget were discussed, Program officials invariably outnumbered others attending. In any case many organizational representatives deferred to the official who they assumed to have had a broader understanding of the Program.

Moreover, there can be little doubt that the committee structure of the Victorian PEP was designed as an interest group model of politics, in which representatives were advocates of the self-interests of their own constituencies. To fulfil these self-interests, some groups found it convenient to make informal alliances with particular members of the Program's central office, with their approaches to decision-making becoming increasingly indistinguishable from those bureaucratic forms which PEP sought to oppose. Their co-option into the culture of bureaucracy meant that the Program in Victoria became devoid of oppositional voices.

The PEP Exchange

The initial design of the Victorian Program embodied an explicit and deliberate tension between bureaucracy and democracy. On the one hand, the design provided for a Secretariat which established PEP's bureaucratic lines of accountability to the Special Programs Branch and to the PEP committee structure. On the other hand, the design included an 'Exchange' whose purpose was to coordinate and share the learnings of the Program, linking developmental work at school and college levels with the work of regional consultants and field officers, and with the work of other elements of the Program's structure. The Exchange was to be a locus for communication in the Program and for the integration of functions which had, in the work of other programs, been bureaucratically separated from one another: functions of consultancy, evaluation, in-service education and publication. In the overall design of Victorian PEP the Secretariat was to provide the (necessarily bureaucratic) enabling links required for the Program to exist, and the Exchange was to provide a means of fostering pan-programmatic collaboration and participation, especially by providing a locus for intercommunication between the Program's parts.

At the time of the formation of the Program this was regarded by many as a sophisticated design. It met the requirements of bureaucratic accountability and at the same time seemed able to nurture and protect a certain independence and collaborative autonomy for the Program. It offered the prospect of resolving the tension between two different images of the Program: PEP as an 'implementation program' (implementing the policies of the Program through an administration which supported certain types of system level and school level initiatives) and as a 'learning program' (exploring new ideas and approaches and sharing learnings across the system, between schools, and between schools and the system as a whole). As it turned out, the struggle to sustain these opposed images of the Program within a single design was an unequal one, and the history of the Exchange may be read as evidence of the increasing dominance of the 'implementation program' view.

Because of pressures to get the Program 'up and running' quickly, staffing the Exchange became a lower priority than staffing the other areas of the central office organization. Other areas had clearly defined developmental tasks and required central staff to get the work going. The Exchange was seen as more responsive to school-based developments, so it seemed less urgent to get its staff in post.

Exchange staff were at first temporarily and then permanently transferred to other central administration tasks. The 'transfers' further limited the capacity of the Exchange to operate independently and to respond to schools and regions in keeping with the image of the 'learning program'. This correspondingly strengthened the capacity of the central administration to operate bureaucratically and to respond to Commonwealth and state demands for the information necessary at first to defend, and later to manage, the Program as an 'implementation program'.

The Exchange lost ground in the contests which erupted when rumours that the Program would be terminated began circulating. When the resulting Commonwealth demands for early evaluation information arrived, and once cuts to the Program's budget were announced, there were debates about how the Program should be reorganized more efficiently. These events had a major impact on the development of the Exchange, both in terms of staffing and in terms of its proposed style of functioning. The crisis required a coordinated response from the Program's central administration, and it was during and soon after this period that positions allocated to the Exchange began to be transferred to other areas of central administration — in service of the bureaucratic demands made on the Program by the Commonwealth and the Victorian Secretariat, which was responsible for organizing Victoria's response to the Commonwealth's demands. Like staff in other areas of the central administration, Exchange staff were required to generate the data needed to defend the Program and were thus brought more closely into the bureaucratic operations of the Program. Despite its relative independence (perhaps because of it), the Exchange was not immune to the centralizing and bureaucratizing effects of the crisis; it was just one more part of the Program, needing to be 'rationalized' and reorganized to take account of the new situation. The way the cuts were implemented — by a bureaucratic process — demonstrated the strength of the hold of bureaucratic approaches to problem-solving on the operations of the Program and the relative fragility of the 'anti-bureaucratic', collaborative, participative modes of operation represented by the Exchange.

The image of the Program embodied in the Exchange — that of 'the learning program' — increasingly came under attack. The Exchange suffered increasingly in terms of staffing, funding, operations and style of work. Designed to be located at the very intersection of the tension between bureaucratic and democratic views of the Program, the Exchange demonstrates how the bureaucracy of the Program could control the progressive reorganizations of its work in ways which extended and elaborated its bureaucratic character and modes of operation, at the expense of its more democratic arrangements.

The Threat of Cuts to the Program's Budget

The climate of 'cuts' — both when they were rumoured and after they were announced — served to bind staff to the Program as a bureaucracy. Since the Program's funding and structure, even its very existence, were at stake, some in the central office began to develop a notion of loyalty to the Program. This meant not criticizing the Program in public. Several members of the central office staff were rebuked by their colleagues for taking openly critical stances on such ideas as parent participation or collaborative decision-making. Increasingly, it seems, central office staff were being normalized to the Program — expected to behave as Program 'officials'. Especially after the cuts the structure of the Program was more clearly defined. What had been won and lost in the process (and who had won and lost) was more clearly defined. By late 1985 the informal structure of relationships in the Program was more closely aligned with the formal structure.

The cuts operated to bureaucratize the Program in another way as well. When the possibility of the Program being cut altogether was rumoured, central staff were called upon to produce early evidence of its success. This generated a coordinated effort in which central staff were obliged to work more from central office, requesting, collecting and collating data from regions and schools. They were less able to work in the face-to-face consultative and developmental roles that many of them had enjoyed; they were increasingly bound to their desks, to paperwork, to their telephones, and to the directions of the senior staff who were coordinating the 'accountability' exercise. The cuts thus redefined the work of central staff. These shifts produced a tighter, more coordinated, more closely controlled bureaucracy within the Program, and actually extended the size and bureaucratic character of the Program.

With hindsight, one wonders whether the Program might not have been significantly more effective in devising approaches if there had been less panic about the impending cuts — if, in the early days, the state officials of the Program had been less concerned about their perception that the Commonwealth needed more data to protect the Program and less preoccupied with providing information which could be used to defend it; that is, if there had simply been more circumspection about responses to the attacks on the Program apparently emanating from the Commonwealth Department of Finance.

There can be no doubt that the turmoil created by the cuts made the Program less efficient. While it fought to defend itself, it could not get on with its appointed tasks. More significantly for the Program's principles, however, the cuts undermined its exploratory, responsive and democratic mode of operation, binding the Program more securely into a bureaucratic mode of operation. The doubts raised about its aims when it was challenged created a climate of uncertainty and a bureaucratic pattern of response from which it was unable to recover. Though the Program was designed to provide opportunities through which a range of people involved in Victorian education could develop remedies for the perceived bureaucratic ills of the Victorian education system — and though its history demonstrates moments and areas of significant achievement in classrooms, in schools and in the system as a whole — at the system level, it gradually succumbed to the illness itself.

Conclusion

The attempted democratic reform of bureaucracy came up against prevailing theories of organizational action which have assumed, explicitly or implicitly, that norms of formal rationality must prevail (Thompson, 1967). The wide acceptance of such traditional views of bureaucracy is well illustrated in the work of Meyer and Rowan (1977), who argue that organizational structures and processes do not necessarily derive from technical work requirements, as traditional bureaucratic theory would suggest, but from institutional and normative pressures within organization membership and clientele. These are such, however, as to force organizations to adopt the formal features of bureaucratic structure, at least in terms of myth and ceremony, in order to gain acceptance and legitimacy from the general public and from other organizations.

The dominance of entrenched expectations regarding bureaucracy,

Bahro (1978) argues, amounts to a bureaucratic ideology which he characterizes as 'Bureaucratic Centralist Authoritarianism', a concept with the following features:

> (a) the existence of a bureaucracy as the dominant organizational form of political and economic apparatus in a social formation; (b) concentration and centralization of power and authority into organizations; (c) the participation of the major portion of the working population in bureaucratic organizations in a form that produces subalternity (i.e. subordination and dependence); and finally (d) an evaluative/belief orientation toward existing bureaucratic structural arrangements as generally efficient, proper and, if not inevitable, at least highly resistant to intervention and transformation. (Johnston, 1985: 336)

Because of such entrenched understandings, the nature of power relationships between those who are seen to manage a service such as education and those who are seen to deliver and receive it is not necessarily challenged by administrative reforms and restructuring of the bureaucracy (Angus and Rizvi, 1989).

The emergence of adversarial activity that one might expect from wider and more vigorous participation in areas such as education is impeded, Johnston (1985: 337) argues, because individuals have long been encouraged 'to adopt a position of dependence relative to organizations and to refrain from assuming personal or collective responsibility in responding to social problems.' The sense of dependency relates to the instrumental and impersonal social relations that are a feature of bureaucratic organization. With a society geared to bureaucratic social relations, 'the organization of the central office can appear professional, efficient and effective in the eyes of the community' (Johnston, 1985: 340). This form of social pressure, we believe, was very influential in the steady bureaucratization of the PEP as the ideological structure of bureaucratic organization pervaded its operations, particularly during a period of uncertainty, despite the rhetoric of democratic reform.

The persistence, indeed reassertion, of bureaucratic relationships within the PEP and the Victorian Ministry of Education (Angus and Rizvi, 1989) illustrates important points about the nature of power:

> The judgement of power is not only synchronic, but diachronic; it is not simply a matter of the momentary relation at present, but how that relation (a) stands against previous relations involving those (or other) persons and (b) affects potential future relations

involving them (or others). Hence the second point: Judgements of power refer to a historical background ... (and the) ... perpetuation of a pattern of relations. (Burbules, 1986: 98)

The bureaucratization of PEP, therefore, can be seen to be partly a response to a perceived need for greater efficiency which led to more rigid and formal structures, and also to a general entrenched acceptance of bureaucratic relationships as being appropriate for educational administration.

None of the above should be taken to indicate that the PEP experience in Victoria was a complete failure. It was a noble experiment in reforming democracy. The principles of participatory rather than hierarchical decision-making, decentralized responsibility for locally negotiated outcomes, and collective, cooperative approaches to particular problems remain particularly strong in many local, school level situations where participants' autonomy was enhanced and has since been defended.

Perhaps the greatest potential for reform within PEP was the early realization that existing social, political and organizational constraints upon educational governance should not be accepted as givens. A responsive system that encouraged genuine, equitable participation of students, teachers and citizens would need to challenge and reappraise all such constraints. The overall pattern of inequity would then be challenged by an educational bureaucracy committed to total responsiveness to the broad public interest. The gradual bureaucratization of PEP, however, signalled that the dichotomy between politics and administration is still strong.

Despite the attempted reforms, we can expect many educational administrators to continue to regard value-laden issues such as equity and participation as ones to be decided by elected officials to whom they should rightly defer for policy directions. Such an approach sees bureaucratic responsiveness to elected officials as important, but minimizes citizen participation. That is no bad thing, however, for those who value the sort of 'efficiency' that is associated with the automatic implementation by the bureaucracy of policy determined within government. Such bureaucratic values have become so implicit in our consciousness that, despite our best efforts, we find it difficult to resist being incorporated into the dominant modes of administrative thought and practice. This case study supports Thompson's (1983) contention that we have yet to devise democratic ways of organizing social life that might have a greater chance of controlling bureaucratic power in the modern state. The Weberian prophecy, it seems, remains unchallenged by the experience of PEP in Victoria.

References

ANGUS, L. and RIZVI, F. (1989) 'Power and the Politics of Participation.' *Journal of Educational Administration and Foundations*, 4, 1, 6–23.
BAHRO, R. (1978) *The Alternative in Eastern Europe*. London: New Left Books.
BARBER, B. (1984) *Strong Democracy: Participatory Politics in a New Age*. Berkeley, Calif.: University of California Press.
BATES, R. (1985) *Public Administration and the Crisis of the State*. Geelong: Deakin University Press.
BERNHEIM, J. (1985) *Is Democracy Possible?: The Alternatives to Electoral Politics*. Cambridge: Polity Press.
BLAU, P. and MAYER, D. (1987) *Bureaucracy in Modern Society*. 3rd ed. New York: Random House.
BURBULES, N. (1986) 'A Theory of Power in Education.' *Educational Theory*, 36, 2, 95–114.
CASTELLS, M. (1983) 'Crisis, Planning and the Quality of Life: Managing the New Historical Relationship between Space and Society.' *Environment and Planning D — Society and Space*, 1, 3–21.
CROUCH, C. and HELLER, F. (Eds) (1983) *International Yearbook of Organizational Democracy*. Chichester: John Wiley and Sons.
DAHL, R. (1956) *A Preface to Democratic Theory*. Chicago, Ill.: University of Chicago Press.
DEAKIN INSTITUTE FOR STUDIES IN EDUCATION (1984) *Restructuring Victorian Federation: Current Issues*. Geelong: DISE.
FINER, H. (1941) 'Administrative Responsibility in Democratic Government.' *Public Administration Review*, 1, 4, 335–50.
FISCHER, F. and SIRIAANI, J. (Eds) (1984) *Critical Studies in Organization and Bureaucracy*. Philadelphia, Penn.: Temple University Press.
HAMBLETON, R. (1988) 'Consumerism, Decentralization and Local Democracy.' *Public Administration*, 66, 125–47.
HEALY, F. (1984) *Public Administration: A Comparative Perspective*. New York: Marcel Dekker.
HYNEMAN, C. (1950) *Bureaucracy in a Democracy*. New York: Harper and Row.
JACOBY, H. (1973) *The Bureaucratization of the World*. Berkeley, Calif.: University of California Press.
JOHNSTON, B. (1985) 'Organizational Structure and Ideology in Schooling.' *Educational Theory*, 35, 4, 333–43.
KRISLOV, S. (1974) *Representative Bureaucracy*. Englewood Cliffs, N.J.: Prentice-Hall.
MCNEIL, K. (1978) 'Understanding Organizational Power: Building on the Weberian Legacy.' *Administrative Science Quarterly*, 23, 1, 65–89.
MEYER, J. and ROWAN, B. (1977) 'Institutional Organizations: Formal Structure as Myth and Ceremony.' *American Journal of Sociology*, 83, 2, 340–63.
PATEMAN, C. (1970) *Participation and Democratic Theory*. Cambridge: Cambridge University Press.
PERSONNEL AUSTRALIA (1981) *The Victorian Department of Education: The Rationale and Definition of the Proposed Organisation Structure*. Melbourne: Department of Education.
RIZVI, F. (1989) 'Bureaucratic Rationality and the Promise of Democratic School-

ing.' In W. CARR (Ed.), *Quality in Teaching*. Basingstoke: Falmer Press, 55–78.
RIZVI, F. and KEMMIS, S. (1987) *Dilemmas of Reform: The Participation and Equity Program in Victorian Schools*. Geelong: Deakin Institute for Studies in Education.
SALAMAN, L. and WAMSLEY, G. (1975) 'The Federal Bureaucracy: Responsive to Whom?' In L. RIESELBACH (Ed.), *People vs. Government*. Bloomington, Ind.: Indiana University Press.
SALTZSTEIN, G. (1985) 'Conceptualizing Bureaucratic Responsiveness.' *Administration and Society* 17, 3, 283–306.
SCHUMPETER, J. (1943) *Capitalism, Socialism and Democracy*. London: George Allen and Unwin.
SIMON, H. (1957) *Administrative Behaviour*. 2nd ed. New York: Free Press.
THOMPSON, J. (1967) *Organizations in Action*. New York: McGraw-Hill.
THOMPSON, J. (1983) 'Bureaucracy and Democracy.' In G. DUNCAN (Ed.), *Democratic Theory and Practice*. Cambridge: Cambridge University Press.
WEBER, M. (1968) *Economy and Society*. 2 vols. New York: Bedminster Press.
WEBER, M. (1970) *From Max Weber*. Ed. by H. GERTH and C. MILLS. London: Routledge and Kegan Paul.
WILENSKI, P. (1979) 'Political Problems of Administrative Responsibility and Reform.' *Australian Journal of Public Administration*, 38, 4, 347–60.
WILSON, W. (1953) 'The Study of Public Administration.' In D. WALDO (Ed.), *Issues and Ideas in Public Administration*. Westport, Conn.: Greenwood Press.
WOOD, G. (1984) 'Schooling in a Democracy: Transformation or Reproduction?' *Educational Theory*, 34, 3, 219–34.

Notes on Contributors

Lawrence Angus is Senior Lecturer in Education at Monash University, where he has worked since 1986. Prior to that he taught in state and private schools in South Australia, Victoria and England before joining the Social and Administrative Studies Group at Deakin University in 1983. Dr Angus has a major interest in critical approaches to educational administration and has, since 1983, conducted research into educational restructuring in Victoria, Australia.

Hedley Beare has been Professor of Education at the University of Melbourne since 1981. After serving as one of the first Regional Directors of Education in South Australia (1971), he helped to set up and then headed the two most recently established public school systems in Australia, those of the Northern Territory (1972–1975) and the Australian Capital Territory (1975–1980). Recent works include *Creating an Excellent School: Some New Management Techniques*, *The Curriculum for the 1990s* and *Shared Meanings about Education: The Economic Paradigm Considered*.

George Berkeley retired from the position of Director-General of Education in Queensland at the end of 1986 after forty years' service in that Department as a member of its Directorate since 1971. He is currently Deputy Chair of the Schools Council of the National Board of Employment, Education and Training and chairs its Working Parties on Teacher Quality and Career Education. He is a Fellow of the Australian College of Education, a member of its Council and Chair of its Publications Committee. His publications include papers in the areas of educational planning and finance, mathematics teaching, curriculum and children's reading. He is a Member of the Order of Australia.

Notes on Contributors

Garth Boomer is currently Associate Director-General of Education (Curriculum) with the South Australian Education Department. He began his career as a secondary teacher of English, mathematics and Latin. After specializing as consultant and inspector in English and drama, he was Director of Wattle Park Teachers Centre from 1980 to 1984. In 1984 he took up the post of Director of the Curriculum Development Centre, Canberra, and in 1985 he was appointed Chairman of the Commonwealth Schools Commission. He returned to his present post in South Australia in 1988. He is author of a range of textbooks and books on education, including *Changing Education* and *Metaphors and Meanings*. He is past president of the Australian Association for the Teaching of English and past chair of the International Federation for the Teaching of English.

William Lowe Boyd is Professor of Education in the College of Education at Pennsylvania State University, USA. He specializes in educational policy and politics and has recently served as president of the Politics of Education Association. He was a Visiting Fulbright Scholar to Australia in 1984 and serves on the Steering Committee of the US–Australia Education Policy Project. He also serves on the editorial board of the *International Encyclopedia of Education*, and is co-editor of the following recent books: *Educational Policy in Australia and America*, *The Politics of Excellence and Choice in Education*, *Willard Waller on Education and the Schools* and *Private Schools and Public Policy: International Perspectives*.

Judith D. Chapman is Director of the School Decision Making and Management Centre within the Faculty of Education, Monash University. After a teaching career in Australia and Europe she undertook postgraduate studies in the United States of America. Since her return to Australia she has directed major projects on behalf of national and international agencies. Her most recent works include *School Effectiveness and Educational Resource Management* and *Decentralization and School Improvement* on behalf of OECD; *Institutional Management* and *Micro-level Planning and Management in Asia and the Pacific* on behalf of UNESCO; and *The Australian School Principal* on behalf of the Australian Commonwealth Government. She is editor of *School-based Decision-making and Management* and *Improving the Quality of Australian Schools*, and is a Fellow of the Australian College of Education and the Australian Council of Educational Administration.

Lyndsay Connors is Chairperson of the Schools Council, one of the four Councils of the National Board of Employment, Education and Training. Between 1983 and 1987 she was a full-time member of the

Commonwealth Schools Commission and, in that capacity, Chair of the Curriculum Development Council. She was previously a parent member of the ACT Schools Authority, Information Officer for the Australian Council of State Schools Organisations and a freelance writer on education and social issues generally.

Christine Deer was appointed Professor of Education at the University of Technology, Sydney in 1989 after having been Associate Professor in Education and Director of the Teacher Education Program at Macquarie University. Her teaching and research interests include curriculum studies, particularly curriculum implementation and change, and teacher education.

Clive Dimmock lectured in educational management and organized training programs for school principals for ten years at University College, Cardiff, before moving to the University of Western Australia, where he now runs a specialist master's degree program in educational management. He has published articles on performance management and appraisal, evaluation, in-service education and managing for school effectiveness.

Jeffrey F. Dunstan is Deputy Chief General Manager of the Office of Schools Administration, Ministry of Education, Victoria. During a career spanning forty years in Victorian education he has been eminent as a teacher, teachers' college lecturer, inspector of schools, regional director of education, executive director of schools, deputy chief general manager and, for significant periods, acting chief general manager. He completed his PhD in educational administration at the University of Wisconsin–Madison, and has been heavily involved in the restructuring of education in Victoria. He was co-editor of *Perspectives on Organisational Change: Lessons from Education*. Dr Dunstan has led many significant ministerial reviews during the 1980s. He is the Minister's nominee on the Council of the University of Melbourne, a Fellow of the Australian College of Education and a contributor to professional educational activities.

Grant Harman is Professor of Educational Administration at the University of New England. He holds higher degrees from the University of New England (MA Hons in history) and from the Australian National University (PhD in political science). His main research interests are in the politics of education, higher education policy and institutional management.

Notes on Contributors

Ross Harrold is an economist who is Senior Lecturer in the Department of Administrative and Higher Education Studies at the University of New England. His current interest is in the internal economics of educational institutions. He spent 1989 on secondment to the Department of Education in the Australian Capital Territory, with the task of devising means by which information on curriculum arrangements and resource deployment can be made available to decision-makers at school and system levels.

John Hattie is Professor of Education at the University of Western Australia and has published articles and books on measurement, self-concept, management and cognition.

Brian V. Hill is Professor of Education at Murdoch University in Western Australia and was founding dean of its School of Education. Initially a high school teacher, he obtained his BA and BEd at the University of Western Australia, an MA from Sydney and a PhD from the University of Illinois. He is author of several books, including *Called to Teach: Education and the Endangered Individual*, *Faith at the Blackboard*, *Choosing the Right School* and *That They May Learn*.

David McRae taught for eleven years in secondary schools and at Melbourne State College, and then worked for the Victorian Secondary Teachers Association as its curriculum officer, later becoming a consultant to the Victorian Minister for Education. During this period he was a member of the Victorian Ministry's Structures Project Team. Since then he has worked as a freelance consultant to a wide range of government departments and agencies. He has participated in the development of the new Victorian Certificate of Education; he has written widely on education and for a time presented Radio National's *Education Now*. His most recent published work is *Getting It Right: Schools Serving Disadvantaged Communities* for the Schools Council of the National Board of Employment, Education and Training.

James F. McMorrow is former First Assistant Secretary, Commonwealth Schools Commission. He was previously Executive Secretary of the National Catholic Education Commission. His experience includes teaching in government and non-government schools and, at the tertiary level, in Papua New Guinea and a period as Assistant Secretary of the Queensland Teachers' Union.

Notes on Contributors

Fazal Rizvi is Senior Lecturer in Education at Deakin University in Victoria. He completed his PhD in philosophy of education from Kings College, University of London. He was a major author of *Dilemmas of Reform: An Overview Evaluation of the Participation and Equity Program in Victorian Schools*. His major research interests include theories of democracy and problems of democratic reform in education; multiculturalism as an educational policy; and ethics and educational administration.

Index

accountability
  administrators and, 164, 166–7
  bureaucratic model of, 6, 165–7, 172
  characteristics of, 168–70
  and decentralization, 172
  definitions of, 158–9
  democratic model of, 6, 165–7, 172
  in education, 2–3, 6, 81–2, 101–2, 155–73, 179, 189
  evaluation and, 168–70
  and financial issues, 179, 189
  management in, 168–70
  models of, 6, 165–7, 172
  parents and, 161–2, 165
  prerequisites for, 168–71
  pressures for, 155–7
  principals and, 160, 161–2, 163–5, 166, 169
  principles of, 170–1
  and process-oriented approach, 167
  and product-oriented approach, 167
  and responsibility, 171, 189
  school councils and, 162, 164
  schools and, 164, 168–70
  'strong' form of, 159, 161
  teachers and, 2–3, 158–63, 164–6, 168–9, 171–2
  types of, 159
  'weak' form of, 159
ACT
  see Australian Capital Territory
ACT Schools Authority
  see also Australian Capital Territory
  abolition of, 91–2
  additional bursarial staff in schools in, 184
  aims of, 91–2
  and assessment, 147
  and community participation, 69, 90, 91–2, 93, 202
  educational funding in, 181, 182, 184, 189
  establishment of, 68, 77, 90, 91–2
  parents and, 91, 92, 93
  and purchase of supplies, 181
  and staff appointments, 182
  teachers and, 91, 92
administration
  see also educational administration
  and cultural factors, 42
  definition of, 41
  and politics, 222
administrators
  and accountability, 164, 166–7
Advisory Committee on Tertiary Education, 197
advisory educational services, 51
alienation
  of students, 50
  of teachers, 52
Allen, G., 207–8
Alum Rock School District [California, USA]
  educational vouchers in, 178
Andrews, C., 45
Anglican Church
  see Church of England

245

Index

Angus, L.
  see Rizvi and Angus
Aristotle, 59
assessment, 147, 149, 151–2
  and curriculum, 147
  and employment, 149
Assumptions Underlying Australian Education, 46, 65
Austin, A.G., 44
Australia
  accountability in education in, 165–72
  binary post-school system in, 19–20
  and British education system, 65–6
  bureaucracy in, 67–8
  bureaucracy and education in, see bureaucracy
  centralization in education in (1870s–1939), 10–12
  decentralization of education in, 1–2, 3–4, 9–24, 156, 158–65, 182–3, 167, 199, 200–7
  democracy in, 59–62, 65–8; see also democracy
  devolution and education in, see devolution
  economic change in, 10–12
  education and local community in, see community participation
  educational funding in, 7, 175–91, 209
  egalitarianism and education in, 5
  federal government and post-school sector in, 18, 19–20
  federal government and taxation in, 18
  free, compulsory and secular education in, 10, 14, 211
  government intervention in, 17–20, 128–9, 138–42, 144–7, 150–2, 184–9, 209–10; see also Australia, states and education in
  higher education in, 19–20
  history of education in, 1, 3–4, 9–24, 43–55, 57, 64–8, 76–7, 131–42, 194
  and independence from Britain, 12
  national curriculum policy in, 140
  need for reconstruction in, 128
  pluralism of society in, 80–1
  politics of education in, 4–5, 57–74
  population change in, 20–2
  public sector reform in, 6, 155–7, 199–200
  school-based governance in, 15–17, 25
  social change in, 21
  states and education in, 10–12, 17–18, 75–7, 89, 142, 178–9, 180–4, 199–201, 209–10
  technical education in, 11
  and US education system, 65–6
  and Vietnam War, 48, 49
Australian Capital Territory (ACT)
  see also ACT Schools Authority
  curriculum in, 138
  educational management in, 202
  educational reform in, 68–9, 70, 77, 91, 202
  and independence from NSW Department of Education, 68–9, 202
  Parents' and Citizens' Associations in, 68–9, 71
  retention rates in, 135
Australian Council of State Schools Organizations, 83
Australian Education Council (AEC), 6, 20, 87, 138–9, 197, 209, 210
  Standing Committee of, 197, 210
Australian National University, 147
Australian Universities Commission, 19

Bailey, M., 149–50
Baumgart, N., 149
  see also Braithwaite and Baumgart
Beare, H., 3, 9–24, 91, 178, 194, 207, 208
Beattie, N., 16–17
Beazely, The Hon. Kim, 184
Beazley Report, 16, 47
Becher, T., Eraut, M. and Knight, J., 159
Beetham, D., 63–4
Berkeley, G., 7, 193–213
Better Schools in Western Australia, 17, 156–7, 183, 203

Index

Blackburn, Jean, 185
  see also Blackburn Report
Blackburn Report, 146
Blakers, Cath, 194
Board, P., 45
Boomer, G., 5–6, 115–30
Boyd, W.L., 4, 25–40
Boyer, E., 28
Braithwaite, R. and Baumgart, N., 136
Britain
  educational funding in, 177, 178, 179
  grant maintained schools in, 177, 178
  local financial management in, 178
  national curriculum in, 28
  school-based governance in, 16
  voucher system in, 178
bureaucracy
  as administrative procedures, 221–2
  advantages of, 215, 216, 218–19
  and Australian education, 62–4 (and passim)
  and 'Bureaucratic Centralist Authoritarianism', 235
  case study of reform of, 216–17, 224–36
  and change, 127
  characteristics of, 9–10, 62–4, 123–4, 218–20
  and communication, 220, 223
  concerns of, 57–73
  conservatism of, 127–8
  as contested, 5–6
  definitions of, 9–10, 62–3, 123
  and democratic classrooms, 6, 123–30
  and democratic control, 7
  and dependence, 235
  disadvantages of, 215–16
  and efficiency, 63–4, 218–20, 236
  and explicitness, 123, 124–5
  as hierarchical, 218–20, 223
  ideal, 124–6
  as impartial, 219–22
  and inertia, 124, 126–8
  and interest groups, 223
  and negotiation, 123, 125
  and participative democracy, 224
  and pluralist democracy, 223
  and policy implementation, 127–8
  and political will, 123–4
  and politics, 220–2
  and power, 235–6
  and questioning, 123, 125–6
  and reflection, 123, 126
  reform of, 215–34
    and accountability, 218
    and administrative responsibility, 218
    and bureaucratic rationality, 218–20
    and democratic decision-making, 217
    and representativeness, 217–18
    technical sense of, 217
  as representative, 217–18
  as responsive, 222–4
  as value-neutral, 218–23
Bush, G. [President, USA], 28
business
  see also companies
  and education, 109–12, 207–8
Business Roundtable, 28
Butts, R. Freeman, 11, 46, 65, 66, 67

Caldwell, B., 28
Caldwell, B.J. and Spinks, J.M., 184
Callahan, R., 12
Campbell Primary School (ACT), 69
Canada
  educational funding in, 179
Canberra Times, The, 69, 71
Carnegie Forum, 27, 33
Carrick Report, 138, 143–4, 145
Catholic Church
  change in, 21
  and education, 20, 43, 94
Catholic Education Commission, 142–3
centralization
  see education, and centralization
Certificate of Secondary Education [proposed], 148
Chapman, J.D. and Dunstan, J.F., 1–7
child-care centres
  and voucher system, 177

247

Index

China [People's Republic of]
  centralization of education in, 160–1
Church of England, 21
classrooms
  bureaucracy and, 5–6, 123–30
  democracy in, 5–6, 115–30
  explicitness in, 118–19
  features of ideal democratic, 118–23
  negotiation in, 119–20
  questioning in, 120–1
  reflection in, 121–2
Coleman Report [USA], 15
Common and Agreed National Goals for Schooling in Australia, 138
Commonwealth of Australia Act (1900), 179
Commonwealth Reconstruction Training Scheme (CRTS), 18
Commonwealth Scholarships, 14, 18
Commonwealth Tertiary Education Commission (CTEC), 19–20
community
  see also community involvement; community participation
  definition of, 75–6
community involvement
  see also community participation
  definition of, 76
  and education, 52–3, 54
community participation
  see also community involvement; parents
  bureaucrats and, 82, 84–5
  and community-school links, 78, 79
  and curriculum, 87–8
  definition of, 76
  and democratic reformism, 77–8
  and devolution, 92–7
  in education, 5, 16–17, 52–3, 54, 68–72, 75–98, 157, 202–3
  and education for democracy, 78, 80
  and educational accountability, 78, 81
  and educational diversity, 78, 80–1
  educational implications of, 78–82
  and goals for education, 67, 86–7
  and home-school relationships, 78, 79
  ideological base of, 94
  implications of, 94–7
  media and, 82, 85–6
  parents and, 82–3
  and participatory structures, 89–94
  and perceptions of education, 94–5
  and resources, 89
  political implications of, 82–6
  politicians and, 82, 85
  and school boards, 92–4
  and school as learning community, 78, 79–80
  and social reformism, 77–8
  and staffing, 88–9
  teachers and, 82, 83–4
Community School District No. 4 [New York City], 35
companies
  see also business
  and excellence, 30, 31, 108–11
  and 'loose-tight' properties', 30, 31, 112–13
Conferences of Directors-General, 210
Connors, L. and McMorrow, J., 5, 75–98
corporate management, 207–8
Corporate Planning in Victorian Government, 200
CSC [Commonwealth Schools Commission]
  see Schools Commission
curriculum
  academic, 133, 136–8, 143, 145
  and assessment, 147–50, 151–2
  and centralization, 6, 131–54
  change in, 150–2
  Commonwealth government and, 139
  and community participation, 87–8
  control over, 6, 131–54
  core, 147, 151
  and credentials, 147–50
  and decentralization, 6, 131–54
  definitions of, 131, 132
  and educational outcomes, 134
  and examinations, 147–50
  fragmentation of, 121–2
  and government intervention, 139–42, 144–7, 150–2
  'hidden', 42, 160

Index

implementation of change in, 150–2
key areas defined in reports on, 147, 148
and knowledge, 134, 147–50
media and, 142
ministerial influence over, 141–2
national policy on, 140
negotiation of, 119–20, 121–2
in New South Wales, 142–5
and retention rates, 134–8
and school-based development, 6, 87–8, 131, 132, 139–40, 151–2
and social change, 138
and societal goals of education, 139
and standards, 157
states and, 139, 142–5
technical, 133–4
unit approach to, 50, 55 n10, 157, 160
vocational, 133–4
Curriculum Development Centre (CDC), 147
Currie, Sir George, 69
see also Currie Report
Currie Report, 20, 69
Curtin, J. (Prime Minister), 12

Davies, A.F., 67
Dawkins, J. (Minister for Employment, Education and Training), 19–20, 36 n2, 140, 141–2, 147, 151, 187
decentralization
see education, and decentralization
Deer, C., 6, 131–54
democracy
in ancient world, 9, 59
and Australian education, 4–5, 59–62 (and *passim*)
and the classroom, 5–6, 115–30
concerns of, 57–73
conditions for, 61–2
and control, 129
definitions of, 9–10, 59–60, 100, 115
ends of, 61
failure of, 107–8
key issues regarding, 60–2
limits of, 61

and means, 61
nature of, 9–10
as participatory, 79, 99, 100, 224
and power, 129–30
as representative, 72, 99, 100, 222–3
and responsibility to rule, 60–1
and responsive bureaucracy, 222–4
rewards in, 129
and social justice, 115–16
and social responsibility, 115–16
theory concerning, 59–60
'weak' form of, 222–4
Department of Education
typical structure of, 195–6
Department of Education [NSW], 91, 145
Department of Education [Victoria], 188
Department of Education [Western Australia]
Functional Review Committee of, 200
Department for Education and Science, 20
Department of Education and Youth Affairs, 90
Department of Finance, 234
Department of School Education [NSW], 204
Department of Technical and Further Education [NSW], 204
Department of Veterans' Affairs, 223
devolution
see also education, and decentralization; education, and devolution
bureaucrats and, 84–5
and curriculum, 87–8, 96
definition of, 76
and education, 1–2, 16, 69–70, 75–98, 156–7, 199, 200–7, 211–12
and goals for education, 86, 96
ideological implications of, 94–6
media and, 82, 85–6
parents and, 82–3
and participatory structures, 89–94
politicians and, 82, 85
and resources, 89, 96

249

Index

and school boards, 92–3
and staffing, 88–9, 96
teachers and, 82, 83–4
Dimmock, C. and Hattie, J., 6, 155–73
Director-General of Education, 84, 124, 125, 197–8, 208–9, 210
and corporate management, 208–9
and educational funding, 210
role of, 197–8, 208–9
Disadvantaged Schools Program
see Schools Commission, Disadvantaged Schools Program of
Discussion Paper on the Curriculum in New South Wales Schools, 144
Dunstan, J.F.
see Chapman and Dunstan

East Sussex Accountability Project, 159
economy
as post-industrial, 11–12, 207
Edmonton Public School District [Alberta, Canada], 32
education
see also educational administration; educational funding; educational management; 'New Education'; school management
accountability in, 2–3, 6, 78, 81–2, 101–2, 155–73, 179, 189
and administrative influences, 41–2
and administrative values, 42, 44–5
aims of, 140
in Australia, see Australia
and autonomy and control, 27, 28–30, 33–5, 111–12
and bureaucracy/democracy tensions, 2, 4–5, 6–7, 43–4, 57–74, 123–30, 155–73, 175–91
and bureaucratic model, 10–12
and business, 109–12, 207–8
Catholic Church and, 20, 43, 94
and centralization, 5, 10–12, 25–36, 64–5, 72, 75–6, 86–7, 160–1, 178–9, 201
changing perceptions of, 94–5
and changing school population, 140–1

and child-centred approach, 80, 81
and community participation, 5, 16–17, 52–3, 54, 68–72, 75–98, 157, 202–3; see also community participation
and compulsion, 118–19, 158
and conservative values, 49–52
and consumer choice, 34–5, 36, 37 n5 and n6
consumer model of, 80, 81
contradictions in, 50–2
and control, 27, 28–30, 33–5
and corporate loyalty, 113
and corporate management model, 12
and cultural factors, 42, 43, 44, 47, 49–50
and curriculum, see curriculum
and decentralization, 1–2, 3–4, 9–24, 25–36, 156, 158–65, 167, 182–3, 199, 200–7
democracy and, see democracy
and democratization, 47
and devolution, 1–2, 16, 69–70, 75–98, 156–7, 199, 200–7, 211–12
and economic factors, 10–12, 18–19, 78, 81, 130
and economic rationalism, 17, 78
and education for democracy, 78, 80
and educational diversity, 78, 80–1
and effective schools, 28–30
efficiency in, 6, 155
and egalitarian ideology, 5, 130, 178–9
and elites, 70–1
and employment, 131, 135, 136, 142, 149
and entrepreneurship, 111
and ethnic background, 140–1
and excellence, 27
as free, compulsory and secular, 10, 14, 211
and funding, see educational funding
goals of, 86–7, 140–1, 143
and government intervention, 17–20, 128–9, 138–42, 144–7, 150–2, 184–9, 209–10
and 'guided democracy', 78

Index

and 'hard' policy instruments, 7, 175, 187–8
and home-school relationships, 78, 79
interest groups and, 4–5
international movements and reform in, 4, 26–7
legal responsibility for, 179
and management structures, 194–212
and managerialism, 33–5, 155–6
megatrends and, 10
ministerialization of, 128
and models of control, 35
and nationalization, 72
and new conservatism, 49, 50
objectives of, 67
organization of, 3–4, 9–24
outcomes of, 134
parents and, 5, 14–15, 22, 27, 33–5, 36, 37 n5 and n6, 75–98, 101–3
and participatory structures, 89–94
and paternalism, 10–11, 14, 75–6
performance in, 110
and political conservatism, 17, 49, 50
politics of, 4–5, 57–74
and population change, 20–2, 140–1
in post-industrial economy, 11–12
and power, 178–9
and professional autonomy, *see* teachers, and professionalism
and public sector reform, 199–200
and recentralization, 156, 201
and regions, 201–2
and religious groups, 43, 45–6
reorganization of public, 1–7, 9–24, 25–40
resources for, *see* educational funding
and restructuring, 4, 25–40
and school-based management, 14, 28, 30–3, 35–6, 36 n3 and n4, 158
school boards and, 15–17, 182
and school as learning community, 78, 79–80
simultaneous centralization and decentralization in, 25–36
and social justice, 129–30

and 'soft' policy instruments, 7, 175, 184–5, 188
and staffing, 88–9
states and, 10–12, 17–18, 75–7, 89, 142, 178–9, 180–4, 199–201, 209–10; *see also* entries for particular states
and strategic planning, 29–30
and system-wide management, 7, 193–213
teachers and, *see* teachers
and 'testing regime', 121–2
in United States of America, *see* United States of America
and value neutrality, 45, 52
and value vacuum, 48–9, 50–2, 53
and values, 4–5, 25–40, 41–56, 72–3, 96
Education Act (1866, NSW), 66
Education Act (1872, Victoria), 44
Education Act (1880, NSW), 66
Education Act (1973, South Australia), 77
Education Act (1981, Victoria), 197
Education Bill (1872, Victoria), 14
Education Commission (NSW), 14, 90
Education and the Cult of Efficiency, 12
Education Reform Acts [Britain], 16, 177, 178
Education (Schools Councils) Act (1975, Victoria), 77, 182
Education in South Australia, 77
education systems
international movements to reform, 4, 26–7
educational administration, 7, 30–3, 41–56, 57–74, 193–213
see also education; educational management
bureaucratic model of, 62–3, 71–2
charity school model of, 43
democratic model of, 52–4, 71–2
establishment-bureaucratic model of, 43–4
managerial model of, 49–52
models of, 44–6, 49–54
and value-neutrality, 4, 41–56
educational funding, 6–7, 89, 175–91, 209

251

Index

see also education
and administrative efficiency, 179
and bureaucracy/democracy tension, 7, 175–91
changes proposed in, 176–8
and Commonwealth government, 184–9
and conditions, 187–8
and devolution within states, 180–4
and families, 7
and local participation, 179, 183–4
and program budgeting, 183–4
and voucher system, 176, 177–8
educational management
see also education; educational administration; school management
and change, 5, 196, 197, 198–201, 202–6, 210–12, 217
characteristics of, 199
and corporate management, 207–8
and decentralization, 201–7
and decision-making power, 198–9
development of structures for, 194–6
and devolution, 201–7
premises of, 206
problems of, 202, 206–7
scope of, 196–8
and reform, 198–201
Elwood Primary School, 71
Eraut, M.
see Becher et al.
Eulau, H. and March, J.G., 58
Europe
parent participation and schools in, 16–17
Excellence and Equity New South Wales Curriculum Reform, 144, 151

Federation of Parents' and Citizens' Associations, 142–3
Fife, W. [Minister for Education], 187
financial devolution
see also educational funding
and administrative efficiency, 188
and local participation, 189
and school councils, 189
within states, 180–4

financial policy
and 'hard' instruments, 7, 175, 187–8
and 'soft' instruments, 7, 175, 184–5, 188
Fordham Ministry [Victoria], 223
France
centralization of education in, 160–1
Freidman, M., 60
Fullan, M., 150–1

gender
and retention rates, 136, 137
Germany
technician education in, 11
Gilding Report, 147
Goodman, E., 30
Gorbachev, 26
Greiner, N., 143
see also Greiner government
Greiner government, 143–4, 148, 149
'Growth Plan for Higher Education', 177

Harman, G., 4–5, 57–74
Harrold, R., 6–7, 175–91
Hattie, J.
see Dimmock and Hattie
Hayek, F., 60
HES
see Higher Education Scholarships
higher education
in Australia, 19–20
Higher Education Board, 20
Higher Education Scholarships (HES), 177
Higher School Certificate (HSC), 135, 143, 148
Hill, B.V., 4, 41–56
HSC
see Higher School Certificate
Hudson, Ainslie, 107
Hughes Report, 16
Hunt, A., 71

Independent Teachers' Association [NSW], 142–3
Innovations Program

252

see Schools Commission, Innovations Program of
Interim Committee for the Australian Schools Commission
see Schools Commission, Interim Committee for the

Jacoby, H., 216

Kandel, I.L., 11
Karmel Report, 16, 68, 69
Keeves Reports, 16
King [Governor], 43
Kirner, Joan, 83
Knight, J.
  see Becher *et al.*
knowledge
  and curriculum, 134, 147–50
  as multidimensional, 149–50
Kogan, M., 159, 161, 168

Levin, H.M., 171–2
Liberal/Country Party
  and voucher system of funding, 177
Lortie, D.C., 27, 35

McCrae, D., 5, 99–114
McMorrow, J.
  see Connors and McMorrow
Macpherson, C.B., 62
Macquarie [Governor], 43
Managing Change in the Public Sector, 155, 200
March, J.G.
  see Eulau and March
Marcuse, H., 45
Martin Report, 19, 20
media
  and community participation in education, 82, 85–6
Metherell, Dr [Minister for Education and Youth Affairs, NSW], 143
Michigan State Accountability System, 165
Migrant Education Program, 18
Minister of Education
  role of, 124, 125
Minister for Education and Youth Affairs [NSW], 143, 204

Ministerial Papers [Victoria], 16, 26, 225, 226, 228
ministries of education
  changes in, 198
  original model of, 198
Ministry of Education [Victoria], 146, 226, 228–9, 230, 235
  Schools Division of, 146
Ministry of Education [Western Australia], 156–7, 162, 183
Ministry Structures Project Team [Victoria], 92–3
Murray Report, 19

Naisbitt, J., 10
Nation Prepared, A, 27, 33
Nation at Risk, A, 27
National Board for Employment, Education and Training (NBEET), 20
National Fitness Council, 18
National Governors' Association, 27
National Roads and Motorists' Association (NRMA), 149
'New Education', 42
New South Wales
  assessment in, 148
  Basic Skills Tests in, 148
  characteristics of education system in, 68
  community participation and education in, 93
  consultation on curriculum in, 143–4
  curriculum in, 138, 141, 142–5, 146, 151
  decentralization in, 47, 204–6
  democratization of education in, 47
  Department of Education in, 68–9
  development of secondary education in, 45, 134–5
  devolution in, 204–6
  educational management in, 198, 201, 204–6
  educational reform in, 26, 47, 142–5, 201, 204–6
  establishment-bureaucratic model of education in, 44
  population of, 146

Index

recentralization in, 201
regions and educational management in, 201
retention rates in, 134–5, 143
teaching of religion in, 44
union opposition to school boards in, 16
New York City, 35
New Zealand
  educational funding in, 177
  teacher appointments in, 189
Northern Territory
  curriculum in, 147
  retention rates in, 135

Office of Schools Administration [Victoria], 203
Organization for Economic Cooperation and Development (OECD), 29–30

parents
  see also community participation
  and accountability, 161–2, 165
  and alliance with teachers, 84
  and bureaucratic responsiveness, 223
  and choice, 34–5, 36, 37 n5 and n6
  and civic activism, 82–3
  and community participation, 82–3
  and education, 5, 14–15, 22, 27, 33–5, 36, 37 n5 and n6, 75–98, 101–3
  and political activism, 82–3,
  and public schools, 5
  responsibilities of, 160
Parkes, H., 66
Participation and Equity Program (PEP), 100–4, 139, 216–17, 224–36
  achievements of, 236
  administrative structure of, 225, 228–33
  and bureaucracy, 216–17, 224–36
  and bureaucracy/democracy tensions, 226, 227–34
  bureaucratization of, 227–36
  central office of, 229
  context of, 224–5
  democratic aims of, 216, 225
  and equity, 225–7, 236
  and 'Exchange', 228, 231–33
  and funding, 228, 232, 233–4
  Guidelines for, 101–2
  as 'implementation program', 231–3
  as 'learning' program, 231–3
  and mainstreaming, 228–9
  and Ministry of Education, 226, 228–9, 230
  operation of committees of, 228, 229–31
  and participation, 225–7, 236
  problems of, 216–17
  and reform strategy, 226–34
  and responsiveness, 227, 229, 230–1, 234, 236
  and school-based decision-making, 225, 227
  Secretariat of, 229, 231
  values underlying, 225–7, 236
Partridge, P.H., 66
PEP
  see Participation and Equity Program
perestroika
  politics of, 26, 31, 33–5
Personnel Australia (PA), 217
Peters, T.J. and Waterman, R.H., 30, 108–9, 110–11, 113
Plato, 59
politics
  and administration, 222
  and bureaucracy, 220–2
  definition of, 58
  of education, 4–5, 57–74
Primary Purpose, The, 141
principal (school)
  and accountability, 160, 161–2, 163–4, 164–5, 166, 169
  roles of, 31, 48–9, 84, 88, 89, 103–4
  values of, 52
private schools
  and corporate management, 156
  establishment of, 43
  resources for, 53
  and secondary education, 45
  teachers and, 43, 52
Professional Development Program
  see Schools Commission, Professional Development Program of

program budgeting, 183–4
Public Instruction Act (1880, NSW), 44
public schools
  see education
public sector
  reform in, 6, 155–7, 199–201

Queensland
  assessment in, 147
  community participation and education in, 93
  decentralization in, 204
  educational management in, 196–7, 201, 204
  public sector reform in, 200
  regions and educational management in, 201
  retention rates in, 135

Regency Park Primary School, 71
regions
  in educational management, 201–2
Reich, C., 48, 49
religion
  teaching of, 44, 48
religious groups
  and education, 20, 43, 45–6, 94
Report of the Committee of Inquiry into Education in Western Australia, 147
Report of the Ministerial Working Party on the State Language Policy, 144
Reports and Records of Achievement for School Leavers, 149
retention rates
  and financial factors, 136
  gender and, 136, 137
  in schools, 134–8
Returned Servicemen's League, 223
Review of Public Service Management, 200
Rizvi, F. and Angus, L., 7, 215–38
Robertson Report, 47
Rousseau, J-J., 62
Russia [Union of Soviet Socialist Republics]
  centralization of education in, 160–1
Ryan, Susan, 83

school-based decision-making (SBDM), 14, 28, 30–3, 35–6, 36 n3 and n4, 158
  see also school management
  characteristics of, 31–2
  implementation of, 32–3
  justification for, 31–2
  and parents, 32–3
school boards, 15–17, 182
  see also school councils
School Certificate, 151
school councils
  see also school boards
  and accountability, 162, 164
School Grants Scheme [Victoria], 182–3
School Improvement Plan [Victoria], 184
school management, 5, 99–114
  see also educational management
  and accountability, 5, 101–2
  case study of decision-making in, 105–7
  collaborative, 184
  as democratic, 99–114
  flexibility in, 5, 110–11
  and leadership, 5, 103–4
  parents and, 101–3
  problems of democratic, 101–8
  requirements of, 113–14
  and speed and efficiency, 5, 105–8
  students and, 101–3
  teachers and, 101–3
schools
  see also education; school-based decision-making; school management
  accountability in, 164, 168–70
  and curriculum, see curriculum
  decision-making in, 101–8
  as effective, 28–33, 158
  and financial devolution, 180–4
  and funding, see educational funding
  leadership in, 5, 103–4
  and performance indicators, 158
  and public scrutiny, 157–8
  religious instruction in, 44, 48
  retention rates in, 134–8

255

Index

as self-managing, 156–7
and value charters, 4, 52–3, 54
Schools in Australia, 77–8, 79–82
Schools Commission, 14, 16, 20, 68, 69–70, 77–8, 79–82, 90, 92, 133, 136, 140–1, 176, 184–7, 209
  and community participation, 90, 92
  demise of, 90
  Disadvantaged Schools Program of, 78, 100, 139, 142, 185
    aims of, 185
    budget of, 185
  and general recurrent resources program, 187
    aims of, 187
    limitations of, 187
  Innovations Program of, 78, 139, 142
  Interim Committee for the, 77, 79–82, 86
  parents and, 90, 92
  Participation and Equity Program of, *see* Participation and Equity Program
  Professional Development Program of, 78
  role of, 90
  special programs of, 184–7
    achievements of, 185–7
    impact of, 186–7
  teachers and, 90, 92
Schools Renewal
  see Scott Report
Schools Year Twelve and Tertiary Entrance Certificate (STC), 145, 146
scientific management school
  beliefs of, 108–9
Scott Management Review
  see Scott Report
Scott Report, 26, 64, 145, 151, 179, 204–6
Secondary College Record [ACT], 147
Selleck, R.J.W., 188
Shopping Mall High School, The, 37 n6
Sieber, S., 112
Socrates, 59
South Australia
  community participation and education in, 102

consultation on curriculum in, 146
curriculum in, 146, 147
decentralization in, 203–4
educational management in, 198, 203–4
educational reform in, 16, 77, 146, 182, 203–4
population of, 146
public sector reform in, 200
retention rates in, 135
school-based governance in, 16
school grants scheme in, 182
Spinks, J.M.
  see Caldwell and Spinks
State Board of Education [Victoria], 14, 90, 197
State College of Victoria, 197
State Scholarships, 14
Statement of Needs in Australian Education, A, 20, 209
STC
  see Schools Year Twelve and Tertiary Entrance Certificate
Stephen, J.W., 14
students
  alienation of, 50
  and curriculum, 6
  and empowerment, 122, 134
  and intention to learn, 119–20
  and knowledge, 6, 134, 147–50
  and motivation, 119
  and question-asking, 120–1
  and reflection, 122
  and self-regulation, 120
  and tests, 121–2
Support Kit [Ministry of Education (Schools Division), Victoria], 146
Susskind, Anne, 208–9
Sweden
  centralization of education in, 160–1
Sydney Morning Herald, 142, 208–9
systems management, 7

TAFE
  see Technical and Further Education
Task Force Review of Organizational and Management Services, 204
Tasmania

Index

community participation and education in, 16, 93
school-based governance in, 16
Tate, F., 45
Taylor, F.W., 10
Taylor, N., 102
Taylor Report [Britain], 16
teachers
see also teachers' unions
and accountability, 2-3, 158-63, 164-6, 168-9, 171-2
alienation of, 52
and alliance with parents, 84
appointment of, 182
and autonomy, 112, 158
and award restructuring, 52, 56 n12
and bureaucracy, 13-14
and career prospects, 51-2, 53
and community participation, 82, 83-4
and cultural context, 116-17
and democracy, 116-18
and devolution in education, 82, 83-4
and educational bureaucracy, 77
and educational habits, 117
and educational reform, 70-1
and educational socialism, 119-20
and empowerment, 30
industrialization of, 54
and militancy, 13
and motivation, 112
and negotiated classrooms, 120, 121-2
politicization of, 54
and power, 5, 116-18
and professionalism, 13-14, 15, 27, 33-5, 36, 80, 157, 158
and questioning, 120-1
responsibilities of, 50-1
and rule-making, 117-18
and school-based curriculum development, 139-40
and school management, 101-3
status of, 13-14, 50-1, 111-12
and tests, 121-2
values of, 46-7, 119
Teachers' Federation [NSW], 142-3

teachers' unions
see also teachers
and bureaucratic responsiveness, 223
and devolution, 211
Technical and Further Education (TAFE), 19, 134
Technical and Further Education Board, 197
tertiary education
federal government and, 19-20
Thatcher government [Britain], 16, 178
Time for Results, 27
Transition Education Program, 226

United Kingdom
see Britain
United States of America
centralization and education in, 26, 160-1
competing values in education in, 4, 25-6
educational funding in, 179
educational reform in, 16, 27-36, 127
school-based governance in, 16
transmission model of teaching in, 127
'waves' of educational reform in, 27-8, 34
universities, 19-20
University Grants Committee [Britain], 19

value charters
for schools, 4, 52-3, 54
values
and administrative variables, 42
and cultural variables, 42
and educational variables, 42
values education, 54-5
Victoria
administrative values and education in, 44-5
bureaucracy and interest groups in, 223
community participation in education in, 69, 92, 102, 145

Index

corporate management in, 207–8
curriculum in, 145–6
decentralization and education in, 69, 70, 71, 182–3, 203
development of secondary education in, 45
devolution and education in, 69, 71, 92–3, 133, 203
educational management in, 197, 198, 200, 217
educational reform in, 16, 26, 31, 35, 36 n3, 68, 69, 70, 71, 77, 92–3, 100, 133, 145–6, 182–3, 203
Green Paper [on education] in, 71
Participation and Equity Program in, *see* Participation and Equity Program
population of, 146
program budgeting in, 184
public sector reform in, 200, 201
retention rates in, 135
role of school principal in, 103–4
school-based governance in, 16, 31, 36 n3, 68
School Grants Scheme in, 182–3
secular-bureaucratic model of education in, 44–5
value neutrality and education in, 53
Victorian Institute of Colleges, 197
Victorian Institute of Secondary Education, 197
Victorian Post Secondary Education Commission, 197
Vietnam War, 48, 49
voucher system, 176, 177–8

Walsh, P. [Minister for Finance], 177
Waterman, R.H.
  see Peters and Waterman

Weber, M., 10, 62, 63, 71, 72, 216, 218–23, 236
  and bureaucracy, 218–22
  and bureaucracy/politics distinction, 220–2
  and organizational efficiency, 218–20
  and rationality, 218, 221
Western Australia
  accountability in education in, 167
  change in public sector in, 155
  community participation and education in, 93
  curriculum in, 55 n10, 147, 151, 160
  democratization of education in, 47
  development of secondary education in, 45
  devolution in, 203
  educational management in, 198, 203
  educational reform in, 16, 17, 47, 93, 156–7, 183, 203
  public sector reform in, 200
  responsibility for subject choice in, 160
  school-based governance in, 16, 17
  school grant scheme in, 183
What Our Students Learn at School, 141
White Paper (1980, Victoria), 207
White Paper on Higher Education, 187
Whitlam government, 12, 15, 19, 20, 77, 142, 209
Wilkins, W., 43–4
Willmot, E., 91–2
Wilson, Woodrow, 222
Wyndham Report, 47, 135

Yes, Prime Minister, 41, 123
youth subculture, 48–9